TRANSPARENT DESIGNS

Michael G. Ketcham

TRANSPARENT DESIGNS

Reading, Performance, and Form
in the *Spectator* Papers

THE UNIVERSITY OF GEORGIA PRESS

Athens

© 1985 by the University of Georgia Press
Athens, Georgia 30602
All rights reserved

Designed by Kathi L. Dailey
Set in 11 on 13 Linotron Ehrhardt with Caslon 540 display

The painting on the title page is "Mr. Oldham and His Friends" by
Joseph Highmore. Courtesy of the Tate Gallery, London.

The paper in this book meets the guidelines for
permanence and durability of the Committee on
Production Guidelines for Book Longevity of the
Council on Library Resources.

Printed in the United States of America

89 88 87 86 85   5 4 3 2 1

Library of Congress Cataloging in Publication Data

Ketcham, Michael G.
Transparent designs.

Bibliography: p.
Includes index.
1. English essays—18th century—History and
criticism.   2. Spectator (London, 1711–14)
3. Addison, Joseph, 1672–1719—Criticism and
interpretation.   4. Steele, Richard, Sir, 1672–1729—
Criticism and interpretation.   I. Title.
PR925.K38 1985   824'.5'09   84-24046
ISBN 0-8203-0771-8 (alk. paper)

Portions of this book are based on the following previously published
articles by Michael G. Ketcham: "The Arts of Gesture: *The Spectator*
and Its Relationship to Physiognomy, Painting, and the Theater,"
Modern Language Quarterly, vol. 42, no. 1 (1981); and "Setting and
Self-Presentation in the Restoration and Early Eighteenth Century,"
Studies in English Literature, 1500–1900, vol. 23 (1983).

Contents

Preface

The *Spectator* is commonly acknowledged to be among the most successful, polished, and influential essay periodicals of the eighteenth century, yet there has not been an extended commentary on it. This book is an attempt to supply such a commentary.

Any serious reading of *The Spectator* would be impossible without Donald F. Bond's superb edition of *The Spectator*, in five volumes (Oxford: Oxford University Press, 1965). All of my quotations are from this edition. Quotations from *The Tatler* (1709–11) and from *The Free-Holder* (1715–16) are from the bound copies of the original sheets at the University of Texas Humanities Research Center, and quotations from *The Guardian* (1713) are from the first collected edition, two volumes (London, 1714).

For myself, I want to thank Ronald Paulson, whose skill has guided me through this book, and whose insights into eighteenth-century art and literature have often showed me potential directions in my own thought. I want to express my indebtedness to the late Earl Wasserman, who first taught me how to read eighteenth-century literature. And I want to thank the many colleagues—and friends—who have helped me with a long series of revisions.

Most of all, I want to thank my wife, Janice, whose sensitivity to cant has often prevented me from becoming mired in false paths, and whose patience has made this book possible.

Introduction

In his essay "Of Liberty" Abraham Cowley reaffirms the idea of the *beatus ille* which, through his models Horace and Montaigne, reaches back to a basic mythology of European culture. The ambitious man, Cowley says, has sold that "estate of Life [which] does best seat us in the possession of it": "I do not say, That he who sells his whole time, and his own will for one hundred thousand, is not a wiser Merchant than he who does it for one hundred pounds, but I will swear, they are both Merchants, and that he is happier than both, who can live contentedly without selling that estate to which he was born."[1] Some fifty years later, Swift, like any number of political propagandists, drew on this same conservative imagery in his *Examiner* 13: "Let any Man observe the Equipages in this Town; he shall find the greater Number of those who make a Figure, to be a Species of Men quite different from any that were ever known before the Revolution; . . . So that *Power*, which, according to the old Maxim, was used to follow *Land*, is now gone over to *Money*; and the Country Gentleman is in the Condition of a young Heir, out of whose Estate a Scrivener receives half the Rents for Interest, and hath a Mortgage on the Whole; and is therefore always ready to feed his Vices and Extravagancies while there is any Thing left."[2]

For both Cowley and Swift, the source of virtue lies in a traditional past, represented by the inherited self-sufficient estate. The world of the city or court is disordered and dissipating because, at best, its order is achieved only through manipulation or intrigue; at best, it is organized by a refined Hobbesian warfare, such as that we see in Restoration comedy. This imagery has further implications as well. First, the conservative imagery of the world of commerce does not refer only to money, although money is a useful symbol for the moral point Cowley wishes to make or for Swift's political one. Instead, it includes any type of social exchange that is not based on "true" wealth but only on tokens that can be falsified and whose value depends only on convention. The man who sells himself into this world of commerce sells himself into a world of conventional performances "whose value is in Custom and in Fancy." "He's guarded with Crowds, and shackled with Formalities. The half hat, the whole hat, the half smile, the whole smile, the nod, the embrace, the Positive parting with a little bow, the Comparative at the middle of the room, the Superlative at the door."[3] A range of social gestures takes on a grammar of its own, but the whole fabric of words, gestures, clothing, manners, and money is a false theater that dissipates the "natural" and "interior" self. The true self is defined not by exchange but by the estate and the inheritance. So, second, the conservative imagery of the estate suggests a whole concept of the self and its relationship to society. The self can be preserved in the securely bound realm of the estate, but it can only be lost in the multifarious encounters of the city with its profusion of signs and social symbols, mere tokens which turn all men into merchants.

One task of the urban literature of the eighteenth century was to give an imaginative order to this realm of exchange which Cowley assumed was chaotic and which Swift, more deliberately, used as an emblem of social disorder. That is, the task was to give it an imaginative order without resorting to the already prejudiced contrasts between country and city, land and money, preservation and dissipation, but without abandoning the notion of a stable interior self that the *beatus ille* tradition sought to preserve. One approach to this challenge was through journalism, an approach not surprising for two reasons. First, following the lines of political debate, journalists such as Defoe in the *Review* attempted to judge the legitimacy of trade, to describe its abuses, and to assess its legitimate limits in terms of people's behavior. Second, journalism inherently deals with the changing surfaces of social life, with public events and political rumor, with fashions, changes in taste, and recent successes in the arts.

Among the most influential of the early periodicals were a remarkable series of essay periodicals written by Joseph Addison and Richard Steele. Along with some lesser journals, these included *The Tatler* (1709–11), *The Spectator* (1711–12 and 1714), *The Guardian* (1713), Steele's *The Englishman* (1713–14 and 1715), and Addison's *The Free-*

Holder (1715–16). *The Tatler, The Spectator,* and *The Guardian* were social periodicals addressed to questions of manners, taste, and morality, and written through a succession of personae—Isaac Bickerstaff in *The Tatler,* Mr. Spectator, *The Guardian*'s Nestor Ironside. *The Englishman* and *The Free-Holder* were defenses of Whig policy and the Hanoverian succession. Common to all, however, is an attempt to describe a society based on reasonable benevolence. Steele and Addison practiced, as Addison came to recommend in *The Free-Holder,* a style which had "a Tendency rather to gain, than to irritate those who differ[ed] with [them] in their Sentiments," which would "incorporate [opponents] into their own Community, and make them happy in the same Government with themselves" (*Free-Holder* 19).

The most successful in achieving these ends, the most ambitious and cohesive of these periodicals was *The Spectator. The Spectator* avoided the political issues which had become part of most periodical rhetoric and focused instead on a variety of subjects in manners, learning, and the arts, and on peoples' various forms of self-presentation, in order to reveal a more fundamental basis for social order. In doing this, *The Spectator* retained much of the established imagery of retirement, and it retained much of the imagery that describes the false self. But it made a significant departure from the conservative rhetoric of Cowley by giving a unified picture of the intricate fabric of signs and surfaces which makes up our experience of urban life. An abuse of public signs may mean a dissipation of the private self, but *The Spectator* implicitly argues, too, that these processes of exchange are the basis for social order and that a stable and benevolent community can be created, sustained, and communicated in the profusion of signs that makes up social life.

This shift in rhetoric is one reason for this reading of *The Spectator:* the essays reflect assumptions about the structures of social life which in turn reveal changing images of social man in the early eighteenth century. A second reason is to be found in the form of the essays themselves and in their rhetorical relationship with their readers. To begin with, the *Spectator* essays were a phenomenal publishing success. Appearing six days each week, from March 1, 1711, to December 6, 1712, for a total of 555 issues, the original papers were printed in runs of three to four thousand in the austere format of most contemporary newspapers, in double columns on both sides of a single folio half-sheet. Each sheet contained one essay, of about twenty-five hundred words, with advertisements and announcements printed at the end. The original sheets were available at the publishers and at booksellers; they could be found lying on the common tables of most coffeehouses; people could order the papers delivered by subscription. At the end of each month, the papers were collected into portfolios, and before the end of *The Spectator*'s first year, subscriptions were issued for a gilt library edition in two volumes and for a "very neat pocket Edition." Encouraged by the success of the first series, Addison began a second series of *Spectators* which ran for eighty issues between June and December 1714. The two series came to a total of eight volumes and went through eleven editions by 1729. By the 1760s Hugh Blair could assume that *The Spectator* was "in the hands of every one."[4]

The Spectator's popularity resulted from a carefully sustained program. Addison and Steele each wrote or edited 251 of the papers in the original series, and they had two occasional collaborators, Eustace Budgell (29 issues) and John Hughes (7 issues). Several papers or parts of papers were submitted by one-time contributors, and scores of letters from anonymous correspondents were incorporated into the essays. This variety of contributors was held together by the fictional editorship of Mr. Spectator, who moves freely among the public assemblies of London, where he has resolved to learn something from everything he sees. The membership of his club—including Sir Roger de Coverley (the Tory squire), Sir Andrew Freeport (the City merchant), Captain Sentry, the Templar, Will Honeycomb (an aging ladies' man), and the Clergyman—is emblematic of Mr. Spectator's willingness to consider all phases of social life. He writes essays about himself, his papers, and their readers, about the members of his club, about popular amusements, fashions, and customs of all types, about marriage and the family, about the proper behavior for men and women, about religion, poetry, drama, esthetics, and learning. The styles of the papers include formal discourse, character sketches, dramatized scenes, satire, conversational colloquialism, allegory, apologue, and romance.[5]

These papers, Addison says in a famous capsule description of his program, were designed "to enliven Morality with Wit, and to temper Wit with Morality" (No. 10). They were "calculated to diffuse good Sense through the Bulk of a People" (No. 124), and the complication of wit and morality is a confessed trickery by which this diffusion succeeds: "As they neither of them know what I proceed upon, the sprightly Reader, who takes up my Paper in order to be diverted, very often finds himself engaged unawares in a serious and profitable Course of Thinking; as on the contrary the Thoughtful Man, who perhaps may hope to find something Solid, and full of deep Reflection, is very often insensibly betrayed into a Fit of Mirth" (No. 179).

Mr. Spectator's attention to the details of behavior, in particular, helps give a form to urban life. *The Spectator* is a kind of writing to the moment since Mr. Spectator's attention to the world is marked by instants of perception. Within these instants he exhibits two types of response which become increasingly important in the eighteenth century: he responds with immediate sympathy and with critical judgment, and his psychology combines sentiment with skepticism about the impostures of social languages. This combination of responses gives Mr. Spectator his tolerant irony, and it shapes *The Spectator*'s concept of society, one marked by sympathetic respect for the commonplaces of daily life, by recognition of the family as a center of human affection, and by tolerance of eccentricity.

In these various ways, *The Spectator*'s conventions of social representation illustrate how words, gestures, clothing, looks and glances, manners, familiar letters, painting, or theatrical performances work as forms of communication. The *Spectator* essayists, however, create these conventions in order to establish rather than question an idea of social order. They do not test conventions or test language in order to examine their inadequacies or hidden potentials. Instead, they create conventions which will, in turn, create a self-confirming system of values. We do not find incisive thinking in *The Spectator* nor ironic undermining of expectations, but we find a social structure being created out of a literary structure.

Within these conventions a reader soon recognizes differences between Steele's essays and Addison's. Addison's are the more controlled. He does write what he calls "essays," random collections of observations or commonplaces, but most frequently his papers are held together by fluid transitions where a word or idea from one paragraph is taken up as the topic of the next. His Saturday papers and other "methodized" essays explicitly divide their subjects into subtopics in the manner of Tillotson's sermons, as in No. 185, on zeal. At

the same time Addison is more willing to accept, with caution, the
values of the world, so that his work often moves forward through a
series of judicious qualifications ("But however unreasonable and absurd this Passion for Admiration may appear in such a Creature as
Man, it is not wholly to be discouraged, since it often produces very
good Effects" [No. 73]).

Steele's essays, on the other hand, are "agglutinative," as Steele
accumulates observations that bear on a single central contrast, as in
No. 6, which begins: "I know no Evil under the Sun so great as the
Abuse of the Understanding, and yet there is no one Vice more common. It has diffus'd it self through both Sexes and all Qualities of
Mankind; and there is hardly that Person to be found, who is not
more concern'd for the Reputation of Wit and Sense, than Honesty
and Virtue. But this unhappy Affectation of being Wise rather than
Honest, Witty rather than Good-natur'd, is the Source of most of the
ill Habits of Life." The body of the essay restates repeatedly the substance of these sentences with new phrasings and new examples ("I
am of Opinion, to polish our Understandings and neglect our Manners is of all things the most inexcusable"; "when Modesty ceases to
be the chief Ornament of one Sex, and Integrity of the other, Society
is upon a wrong Basis, and we shall be ever after without Rules to
guide our Judgment"; "any Man who thinks can easily see, that the
Affectation of being gay and in fashion has very near eaten up our
good Sense and our Religion"). Because the papers lack a prepared
framework, we have two contrary impressions of Steele's prose: that it
oppressively repeats a rigid set of dualisms, and that it pulls away, at
the same time, from any central idea.

Addison's syntax, too, is more controlled, and more abstract since
he relies more than Steele on copulas and other attenuated verb
forms. Jan Lannering[6] has described Addison's reliance on parallelism or a pairing of constructions that are not strictly parallel ("The
Soul, considered abstractedly from its Passions, is of a remiss and
sedentary Nature, slow in its Resolves, and languishing in its Execu-
tions" [No. 255]), and has described a modified hypotaxis in Addison's prose, with the main clause near the beginning and the sentence extended through a succession of relative clauses ("As this is
the End of the Passions in general, so it is particularly of Ambition,
which pushes the Soul to such Actions as are apt to procure Honour
and Reputation to the Actor" [No. 255]).[7] Like Addison, Steele uses

parallelism and chiasmus, but not for the rhythmic effects that Addison achieves. Steele's parallels tend to be more rigidly schematic while, at the same time, he is more likely to write long trailing constructions of loosely linked clauses and more likely to rely on embedded or interrupted structures ("You are so excessively perplexed with the Particularities in their Behaviour, that, to be at ease, one would be apt to wish there were no such Creatures" [No. 87]). Because of such parentheses, Steele's syntax preserves a sense of interlocking observations and responses. His most convoluted sentences are often those explaining perceptual relationships ("I did not imagine these little Considerations and Coquettries could have the ill Consequence as I find they have by the following Letters of my Correspondents, where it seems Beauty is thrown into the Account, in Matters of Sale to those who receive no Favour from the Charmers" [No. 87]; "It is incredible to think how empty I have in this Time observ'd some Part of the Species to be" [No. 4]). Steele seldom separates description and interpretation; instead the two will be combined in a single paragraph or fused in a single sentence.

As a result of this style, Steele has always been seen to be more in touch with the immediate experience of observed behavior. At their best, his essays move rapidly and skillfully between levels of abstraction from generalized precepts to character sketches to dramatized scenes, although the price of Steele's immediacy is an amorphous structure that is sometimes merely chaotic. Addison has a greater suppleness of mind. It is Addison who brings its range of topics to *The Spectator*. He writes the major series on art and esthetics, and his Saturday papers, particularly, form a separate department for lectures on ethics, religion, and art. Addison is fascinated, too, by the workings of the mind as reflected in primitive tales and fables, in dreams, and in the nature of wit, genius, imagination, and memory.

The essays remind us always that they are written by different men. But we can speak purposefully of the integrity of *The Spectator* and can explore the conventions that its authors share. These include deliberately chosen strategies such as the creation of the papers' persona and the consistent contrast of affection with affectation. They also include more subtle, perhaps unconscious habits of style and description that carry the authors' assumptions about the nature of social allegiances and about the nature of communication.

The form of *The Spectator*, therefore, raises a number of critical questions. How are we to read a work like this, composed in multiple parts? What are the unifying principles and assumptions of the series? How can we describe the relationships between the internal organization of the series and the world of social communication that surrounds it? How do the essays describe their relationship with their readers, and how does a reader respond to reading a work in periodic installments? Finally, what is the relationship between *The Spectator* and other forms of social descriptions? Where does it draw techniques from other genres and how does it transform them according to its own formulas and its own conventions?

Central to many of these questions is an essential doubleness in *The Spectator*. Its mode of publication, by itself, allows the series to be seen, on the one hand, as separate pieces of paper distributed to a large reading public and, on the other hand, as a series of repeated formulas that fold back upon themselves: the essays emphatically point to an external world shared with their readers and also point back into the series itself to show the conceptual and metaphoric integrity we expect in any work of art.

This doubleness is characteristic of any literary work. Murray Krieger has set out at length the paradox in reading that any literary work exists in a historical context where it formulates values operative within its society yet forms a self-enclosed system of esthetic meanings where every element in the text defines and gives value to the others. Northrop Frye has spoken of the point at which a work "becomes no longer an object of aesthetic contemplation but an ethical instrument, participating in the work of civilization," even though it remains an esthetic object that shapes its civilization's available forms of expression according to its own internal logic.[8]

However basic it may be to our reading of any work, this doubleness becomes particularly acute in *The Spectator* because both its rhetorical purpose and its internalizing conventions are so sharply defined. Through its readers' letters and through the essayists' daily observations of manners, the essays enter into actual exchanges with their readers in a way that a novel, for instance, could not do. Yet the essays also have descriptive formulas, recurring metaphors, and conventions that make the *Spectator* series a self-contained literary universe. As a result of this dual focus, a work like *The Spectator* inevitably raises questions about the relationships between the public or rhetorical dimensions of language that address a particular audience, draw on established forms or expressions, and shape the values of a society, and the internalizing dimensions of language that make their own patterns and vocabulary, creating their own system of truth.

Particularly interesting in *The Spectator* is the fact that *The Spectator*'s social existence becomes one of the papers' themes. *The Spectator* describes a society in which it itself exists as a social object, and it presents an ideal of social communication which explains its own rhetorical power. There is an inherent mirroring in *The Spectator* where the connection between the text and its context becomes one element in the text's own system.

This interplay between the rhetorical and internalizing sides of the essays is one aspect of *The Spectator* that I will examine in the following chapters. A second is *The Spectator*'s creation of a cohesive image of society by means of its internalizing conventions. Through the course of this book I will argue that *The Spectator* is not merely a collection of observations about manners or esthetics or morality, but that the essays use a consistent set of metaphors and descriptive formulas to draw their various discussions of social and esthetic experience into a unified picture of social life. It would be impossible to argue that the *Spectator* authors deliberately chose all of these patterns or their underlying connections. But the essayists do share distinctive conventions for describing society, and these in turn carry assumptions about the nature of social life. Through the late seventeenth century, the dominant model of society had been based on a clear separation of the public realm from the private, a separation marked by the act of retirement, for example, as in Cowley's essays. *The Spectator*, however, moves toward a social model where the boundary is less clear. The public and private realms interpenetrate in manners, for instance, where the private person is revealed through his public demeanor, or in the family, where the private realm is seen as a source of social interaction. A distinction between the "inward" and "outward" man is perhaps the single most important metaphor in *The Spectator*, but this opposition is mediated through the observation of manners: the private thoughts of the social actor become public in his outward gestures; the social observer looks outward toward the behavior of others and turns inward toward his own reflections, which are his attempt to understand the actor's inward motives. Capsulized, this process is "the inward Disposition of the Mind made visible"

(No. 86), what Lionel Gossman has called "the modern 'bourgeois,' dream of intimate and inward communication."[9]

These topics overlap in various ways, but in its larger outlines the book follows a single line of argument. The main body of the book— chapters 1–5—is concerned with reconstructing the internal logic of *The Spectator*, as revealed through its recurring metaphors and formulas. Although I do discuss contemporary works that provide a context for seeing *The Spectator*, my principal concern is less to give a historical account of literary influence than to answer those questions I have asked about the internal structure of *The Spectator* and about its authors' assumptions about the structures of social life. I see this part of the book as being laid out according to two axes, or two dimensions of experience, those of space and time. The first chapter introduces an imagery of social space which defines the public and private, the outward and inward sides of social man, and examines how this imagery shapes *The Spectator*'s relationship with its readers. The second chapter examines this spatial imagery as it controls social observation in *The Spectator* and controls a general psychology of perception, including Addison's pleasures of the imagination. The third chapter examines the dimension of time by investigating *The Spectator*'s emphasis on continuity and repetition. The fourth chapter, then, discusses how the imagery of space and the imagery of time together define social groups in *The Spectator*, with particular emphasis on the family, since the family incorporates both *The Spectator*'s psychology of space and its psychology of time. With the preceding chapters as a background, the fifth chapter examines how both spatial and temporal dimensions shape *The Spectator*'s language and influence the rhetorical design of the essays. The concluding chapter is more exploratory in the sense that it deals with *The Spectator*'s relationship to other forms of social description and with changing perceptions of social life in the early eighteenth century.

CHAPTER ONE

Mr. Spectator
and His Readers

It is easiest to discuss *The Spectator* by beginning with the character of its persona. And it is easiest to see how the character of Mr. Spectator is created by seeing him in two roles, as a comic actor who occasionally appears in *The Spectator*'s scenes, and as an author who holds the variety of the world in the controlled frame of the essay. The spectator's dual role as actor and author presupposes two arenas for self-presentation, or two types of figurative space. One is a social space in which people appear as social actors; the second is the space implied in reading, an imagined space that contains both the reader and the text. The common idea is that of a frame, used in two senses. First, the writer creates an image of the social world and presents himself within it in the way that an actor presents himself on the stage. In a different way, the printed sheets of paper form a frame in which the writer presents himself between the margins of the page. In this second sense of framing, the style of the papers, the format, form of publication, and strategies of disclosure all influence how a reader imaginatively participates in the text as he reads it. In reading *The Spectator,* then, we are dealing at times with a dramatization of society (the actor on the stage) and at times with a transaction between the reader and the text (the activity framed between the margins).

As actor, Mr. Spectator is an odd and awkward version of urban man. In *Spectator* 4 we see him haunting booksellers in order to estimate the sales of his papers; during a visit to the theater he holds a conversation with Will Honeycomb about the merits of women in the audience, bewildering the man sitting next to them, since Will responds aloud to comments Mr. Spectator makes only in dumbshow;

he has been mistaken for a Jesuit, he says, because he refuses to speak in public. He has frightened his landlady's daughter simply by sitting silently in the room while she and her friends tell ghost stories (No. 12), and at dinner a superstitious woman gasps when he spills salt on the table: "I quickly found, by the Lady's Looks," he says, "that she regarded me as a very odd kind of Fellow, with an unfortunate Aspect" (No. 7).

He travels, too, in a world of performances. At times the extravagant posturing of *The Spectator*'s world explodes into threatening grotesques, as when correspondents write about nose-wringers or a tavern wager,[1] although more often *The Spectator*'s scenes take on a rarefied absurdity, as with the "Common-Place Talker" who "went on with great Facility in repeating what he talks about every Day of his Life . . . with the Ornaments of insignificant Laughs and Gestures" (No. 11), or the club of lovers who "appear like so many Players rehearsing behind the Scenes; one is sighing and lamenting his Destiny in beseeching Terms, another declaring he will break his Chain, and another in dumb-Show, striving to express his Passion by his Gesture" (No. 30).[2]

From behind this public oddity, however, Mr. Spectator preserves the privacy of the observer. Mr. Spectator says of himself, "I have acted in all the parts of my Life as a Looker-on, which is the Character I intend to preserve in this Paper" (No. 1). As I have mentioned, Mr. Spectator has a wide range of experience and a wide variety of opinions, but in a garrulous age he refuses to speak, and, although he may overhear conversations, his exchanges with the world are not primarily verbal. Instead, he enjoys a keen faculty of visual perception: "I have, methinks, a more than ordinary Penetration in Seeing; and flatter my self that I have looked into the Highest and Lowest of Mankind, and make shrewd Guesses, without being admitted to their Conversation, at the inmost Thoughts and Reflections of all whom I behold" (No. 4). "When we look round us," he says in a later paper, "and behold the strange variety of Faces and Persons which fill the Streets with Business and Hurry, it is no unpleasant Amusement to make Guesses at their different Pursuits, and judge by their Countenances what it is that so anxiously engages their present Attention" (No. 193).

By contrast to his sense of the visible man, Mr. Spectator himself fades into near invisibility. He loves the city because it shows him the spectacle of mankind. Yet he loves it, too, because he may "retire into the Town, if I may make use of that Phrase, and get into the Crowd again . . . in order to be alone. I can there raise what Speculations I please upon others without being observed my self, and at the same time enjoy all the Advantages of Company with all the Privileges of Solitude" (No. 131).

This perception of gesture and performance reflects a fundamental structure in *The Spectator*: its balance between the outward and inward, the public and private dimensions of social man. Mr. Spectator's visual acuity penetrates to the inwardness of others, and one purpose of his papers is to give his readers the same penetration with regard to themselves. Addison tells his readers that "it is not my Intention to sink the Dignity of this my Paper with Reflections upon Red-heels or Top-knots, but rather to enter into the Passions of Mankind, and to correct those depraved Sentiments that give Birth to all those little Extravagancies which appear in their outward Dress and Behaviour" (No. 16): "Discourses of Morality, and Reflections upon human Nature, are the best Means we can make use of to . . . gain a true Knowledge of our selves" (No. 215) so that the reader may be "let into the Knowledge of ones-self" (No. 10). Both the spaces of acting and reading have this same shape, since both are defined by these forms of penetration by which the observer or reader reads through outward manners to penetrate to the actors' secret selves. In both, an ideal community is defined by symmetrical responses where shared emotions form a realm of intimacy set apart from the normal commerce of the world.

In its first sentences, *The Spectator* establishes the character of Mr. Spectator and initiates its readers into its world of watchers and watching. "I have observed," Addison writes, "that a Reader seldom peruses a Book with Pleasure 'till he knows whether the Writer of it be a black or a fair Man, of a mild or cholerick Disposition, Married or a Batchelor, with other Particulars of the like nature, that conduce very much to the right Understanding of an Author." These first clauses double the subject and object ("I have observed" and "a Reader . . . peruses") so that the reader and spectator are simultaneously observer and observed: we pick up the paper out of curiosity about its author only to find that he has already observed us with a similar attention.

These opening sentences also establish an easy tone that sets out *The Spectator's* program, yet stands back from it with amused evasiveness. The first sentence reassuringly follows a standard series of parallel elements, each made up of balanced contraries, and this reassurance is reinforced by the content of the next sentence, where we learn that Mr. Spectator will provide just that information needed "to gratify this Curiosity, which is so natural to a Reader." But it is not clear that knowing these particulars conduces at all to a right understanding, and, more subversively, the author whose life is described is a fabrication. Each detail of Mr. Spectator's life is overlaid with incongruities, and the whole pervaded by self-amusement. In the end, Mr. Spectator refuses to give those details that Addison has listed because "they would indeed draw me out of that Obscurity which I have enjoy'd for many Years, and expose me in publick Places."

These uncertainties remind us of the elaborate ambiguities of the epigraph, "Not smoke after flame does he plan to give, but after smoke the light, that then he may set forth striking and wondrous tales."[3] This may suggest a writer who brings light to a subject obscured by others, as it does in Horace's original context; or it may suggest the pose of a man hiding behind a cloud of smoke, which is Mr. Spectator's characteristic disguise as he sits with his pipe in a coffeehouse; or it may suggest the peculiar eighteenth-century idiom, to smoke, meaning to penetrate a pose or disguise, as when Swift asks Stella if she has "smoakt the *Tatler* that I writ."[4]

Throughout the series, Mr. Spectator's character depends on the delicate line Addison follows here between earnestness and amused self-detachment. He sees himself, in Morris Golden's phrase, as an "idiosyncratic element acting in the world, and a reflective self which observe[s] it."[5] Thus he describes himself in his public aspect as a very peculiar person, but does so by relying on the opinions of others, on family traditions, on his reputation in school, or on how he appears in city coffeehouses. He deliberately leaves the private self hidden behind appearances:

> I have passed my latter Years in this City, where I am frequently seen in most publick Places, tho' there are not above half a dozen of my select Friends that know me; of whom my next Paper shall give a more particular Account. There is no Place of general Resort, wherein I do not often make my Appearance; sometimes I am seen thrusting my Head into a Round of Politicians at *Will*'s, and listning with great Attention to

the Narratives that are made in those little Circular Audiences. Sometimes I smoak a Pipe at *Child*'s; and whilst I seem attentive to nothing
but the *Post-Man,* overhear the Conversation of every Table in the
Room. I appear on *Sunday* nights at St. *James*'s Coffee-House, and
sometimes join the little Committee of Politicks in the Inner-Room, as
one who comes there to hear and improve. My Face is likewise very
well known at the *Grecian,* the *Cocoa-Tree,* and in the Theaters both of
Drury-Lane, and the *Hay-Market.* I have been taken for a Merchant
upon the *Exchange* for above these ten Years, and sometimes pass for a
Jew in the Assembly of Stock-Jobbers at *Jonathan*'s. In short, where-
ever I see a Cluster of People I always mix with them, tho' I never open
my Lips but in my own Club.

This paragraph exemplifies the dancelike repetition that soon becomes familiar in *The Spectator*'s prose. It plays upon a balanced separation between Mr. Spectator's public and private character, between
how he appears to others and how he observes others; and the syntax
preserves this opposition. We have, for example, three parallel sentences, each of which contrasts Mr. Spectator's appearance ("I am
seen," "I smoak a Pipe," "I appear") with his intentions and his orientation toward a physical group ("listning with great Attention to . . .
those little Circular Audiences," "overhear the Conversation of every
Table in the Room," "join the little Committee of Politicks in the
Inner-Room, as one who comes there to hear"). Although Mr. Spectator listens or overhears, any words which may be spoken leave no
impression on us. What impresses us here is a physical or spatial
disposition which represents, almost diagrammatically, Mr. Spectator's simultaneous entrance into and isolation from these conversational circles.

The balance Addison maintains between public and private in the
first paper also generates the emotional potential of the spectator club
in Steele's *Spectator* 2, where each member is seen through different
degrees of acquaintance from the common judgment of the world to
the intimate knowledge of friendship. Sir Roger de Coverley, for example, is described this way: "He is a Gentleman that is very singular
in his Behaviour, but his Singularities proceed from his good Sense,
and are Contradictions to the Manners of the World, only as he thinks
the World is in the wrong. However, this Humour creates him no
Enemies, for he does nothing with Sowrness or Obstinacy; and his
being unconfined to Modes and Forms, makes him but the readier

and more capable to please and oblige all who know him." Like Addison's sketch of Mr. Spectator, Steele's description of Sir Roger is based on a balanced syntax which contrasts Sir Roger's observable singularities with his friends' more intimate understanding of him. The turning point, of course, is Steele's understanding of the word "Gentleman," where we shift from the common conception of a gentleman as a man of fashion to the good sense, charity, and self-consistency that lie behind Sir Roger's unfashionable behavior, and that are affectionately explained for us.[6] Steele points to the word here, and again in his description of Will Honeycomb. Sir Roger had been in his youth "what you call a fine Gentleman," and of Will Honeycomb, Mr. Spectator says, "I find there is not one of the Company . . . but speaks of him as of that Sort of Man who is usually called a well-bred fine Gentleman." Here, the dimensions of meaning added by the phrase "who is usually called" indicate a shift from the common conception of a gentleman to his friends' more intimate understanding of Will's image of himself.

This balance operates in each description of the club members. The Templar is one more example: "No one ever took him for a Fool, but none, except his intimate Friends, know he has a great deal of Wit. This Turn makes him at once both disinterested and agreeable: As few of his Thoughts are drawn from Business, they are most of them fit for Conversation. His Taste of Books is a little too just for the Age he lives in; he has read all, but approves of very few. His Familiarity with the Customs, Manners, Actions, and Writings of the Ancients, makes him a very delicate Observer of what occurs to him in the present World."

Within this schematic contrast of public and private, *The Spectator* becomes itself a public gesture manifesting Mr. Spectator's private self. At the end of the first paper he explains that his essays are both a didactic address and an expression of "the Fulness of my Heart":

When I consider how much I have seen, read and heard, I begin to blame my own Taciturnity; and since I have neither Time nor Inclination to communicate the Fulness of my Heart in Speech, I am resolved to do it in Writing; and to Print my self out, if possible, before I Die. I have been often told by my Friends, that it is Pity so many useful Discoveries which I have made, should be in the Possession of a Silent Man. For this Reason therefore, I shall publish a Sheet-full of Thoughts every Morning, for the Benefit of my Contemporaries; and if I can any way contribute to the Diversion or Improvement of the Country in which I live, I shall leave it, when I am summoned out of it, with the secret Satisfaction of thinking that I have not Lived in vain.

There is an element of play with the persona here: what could Mr. Spectator, who exists only on paper, do except print himself out before he dies? And his reasons for publishing come precariously close to the stock pose of the hack or pedant who wishes to indulge himself in print. But the conjunction of thought, reading public, and the temporal limits of life is also serious. Again, this passage is structured by repetition. The contrast between Mr. Spectator's reticence in speech and volubility in writing is cut across by a psychological one which presents the same material in a radically different way. The same mental contents are referred to as "useful Discoveries" and as "the Fulness of my Heart" so that the printed sheets are published (made public) as a didactic address for "the Diversion or Improvement of the Country" while they are also associated with Mr. Spectator's inner life as a source of "secret Satisfaction." They are the spectator's way of looking into the world, and our way of looking into the spectator.

The Circle of Readers

The Spectator's relationship with its readers suggests the same intimacy that we see in the club. The *Spectator* papers are distributed to a large, public audience, yet they also sustain the illusion of an intimate circle of readers, and Addison plays on this doubleness in *Spectator* 10 with the same mixture of seriousness and self-mockery that he had used in *Spectator* 1. I have already quoted parts of *Spectator* 10 but need to look at it more closely, now, from the point of view of its metaphors and its style:

It is with much Satisfaction that I hear this great City inquiring Day by Day after these my Papers, and receiving my Morning Lectures with a becoming Seriousness and Attention. My Publisher tells me, that there are already Three Thousand of them distributed every Day: So that if I allow Twenty Readers to every Paper, which I look upon as a modest Computation, I may reckon about Threescore thousand Disciples in *London* and *Westminster,* who I hope will take care to distinguish themselves from the thoughtless Herd of their ignorant and unattentive Brethren. Since I have raised to my self so great an Audience, I shall spare no Pains to make their Instruction agreeable, and their Diversion useful. For which Reasons I shall endeavour to enliven Morality with Wit, and to temper Wit with Morality, that my Readers may, if possible, both Ways find their Account in the Speculation of the Day. And to the End that their Virtue and Discretion may not be short transient inter-mitting Starts of Thought, I have resolved to refresh their Memories from Day to Day, till I have recovered them out of that desperate State of Vice and Folly into which the Age is fallen. The Mind that lies fallow but a single Day, sprouts up in Follies that are only to be killed by a constant and assiduous Culture. It was said of *Socrates*, that he brought Philosophy down from Heaven, to inhabit among Men; and I shall be ambitious to have it said of me, that I have brought Philosophy out of Closets and Libraries, Schools and Colleges, to dwell in Clubs and Assemblies, at Tea-Tables, and in Coffee-Houses.

The governing idea of this paragraph is that of spatial distribution. *The Spectator* was, quite literally, distributed throughout the city, and Addison uses the implications of this, evident apparently after the first ten days of publication, to define the spatial field of readership. He writes about translation ("brought . . . down," "brought . . . out of") and about assimilation ("inquiring . . . after" and "receiving") that extend laterally through the reading public. In this respect, *The Spec-tator* strives for an expansiveness that will embrace a whole city. The expansive distribution, however, is countered by a process of discrim-ination, demarking one group from another and defining a limited and homogeneous circle of readers. In this respect, *The Spectator* strives for a second kind of wholeness, an integrity possible within a small community of shared values. As Philip Stevick has pointed out, the conversational familiarity of *The Spectator* is concerned, explicitly and implicitly, with membership and belonging.[7]

But Addison is clearly playing with *The Spectator*'s ambitions. In one respect this first paragraph from *Spectator* 10 is personal and conver-sational. Mr. Spectator speaks about his modest satisfaction, he shows his methods to be a considered adjustment to his readers, and he casually assumes that they will accept these methods with appropriate reactions. The very casualness of this assumption suggests a conver-sational counterpoint with both parties making appropriate adjust-ments to one another. At the same time, however, we see a creeping inflation. The argument here is clear enough: because *The Spectator* has been such a success, the author will take pains to mix instruction with delight and to publish daily to reinforce his teaching. But within this outline each sentence undergoes an unobtrusive inflation, much like that "modest Computation" of readership, through amplifying clauses, elaborate metaphors, redundancy, and hyperbole. The paragraph begins with modest sentiments, with Mr. Spectator's self-satisfaction and mild flattery of the reader ("this great City," "with a becoming Seriousness and Attention") but grows into a suggestion that the greatest passions are at issue. Those who read with a "becoming Seriousness and Attention" are transformed into those who "distinguish themselves from the thoughtless Herd of their ignorant and unattentive Brethren"; inculcation of "Virtue and Discretion" becomes recovery from "that desperate State of Vice and Folly into which the Age is fallen." The unmistakable allusion is to the Fall of Man and to a restored, although laboring and time-bound, Eden. Mr. Spectator's ambition is serious, but he protects himself from moral silliness through the hyperbole of pulpit diction.

Addison's manipulations of tone also contribute to a reader's sense of belonging. In one respect, he is let into *The Spectator*'s community if he sees this potential for comedy because he is let into the joke. But in another respect, he is brought into the community because he has this same potential for comedy in his own situation. Later in *Spectator* 10 Addison identifies four groups of readers to whom *The Spectator* is particularly addressed. The first of these is a family group: "I would therefore in a very particular Manner recommend these my Speculations to all well regulated Families, that set apart an Hour in every Morning for Tea and Bread and Butter; and would earnestly advise them for their Good to order this Paper to be punctually served up, and to be looked upon as a Part of the Tea Equipage." As Stevick says, Mr. Spectator admires the well-regulated family, but the mimetic precision of phrasing ("in a very particular Manner," "that set apart an Hour in every Morning for Tea and Bread and Butter") gives an amusing preciosity to the whole business. Next, Addison recommends *The Spectator* to "the Fraternity of Spectators," which is idle, but which "considers the World as a Theatre, and desires to form a right Judgment of those who are Actors on it," to "the Blanks of Society," who, having no ideas of their own, are urged "not to stir out of their Chambers till they have read this Paper," and, most extravagantly, to members of "the female World" who would "move in an exalted Sphere of Knowledge and Virtue." A reader can recognize himself or herself in these portraits, and recognize how closely his public self,

like Mr. Spectator's, comes to being ridiculous. He is admitted into
the circle of readership because he participates in the joke.

This persona is drawn from several traditions. One antecedent for
The Spectator is the Horatian circle of Maecenas, for which "a certain
Unanimity of Taste and Judgment . . . was the Band of this Society"
(No. 280).[8] Another is Cicero's exposition of duties in *De officiis*,
which is so often alluded to in *The Spectator* that one reader complains
"you are so great with *Tully* of late, that I fear you will contemn these
[concerns in this letter] as Matters of no Consequence" (No. 154). A
third is Tillotson's sermon style, which Irene Simon has described as
giving "his congregation the impression that they were hearing from
the pulpit the same kind of language as they were using in everyday
life."[9] For Steele, Tillotson argues "in Words and Thoughts so natural, that any Man who reads them would imagine he himself could
have been Author of them" (No. 103).

Two antecedents, however, are particularly important in creating
Mr. Spectator's social self. The first is his Socratic self-image, the
second his Lockean empiricism. Together, these models suggest his
public oddity and private reflectiveness along with the techniques of
disguise and self-disclosure that create for his readers the illusion of
an intimate community.

According to critical tradition, Socratic dialectic with its indirection
and subtle control of argument was the origin for both Cicero's colla-
tion of precepts and Horace's careful manipulation of exempla.[10] It is,
in particular, a model for the effect Cicero called dissimulation,
"when we say one thing and mean another, the most effective of all
means of stealing into the minds of men and a most attractive device,
so long as we adopt a conversational rather than a controversial tone":
"We may confer with our audience," according to Quintilian, "admitting them as it were into our deliberations . . . , may describe the
results likely to follow some action, introduce topics to lead our hearers astray, move them to mirth or anticipate the arguments of our
opponent." We "may describe the life and character of persons either
with or without mention of their names . . . [and] by the introduction
of fictitious personages we may bring into play the most forcible form
of exaggeration."[11]

Along with drawing on this battery of styles, *The Spectator* adopts
both the oddness of Socrates' public character and the ideal of So-

cratic teaching: reminding men of truths they already know through the common language of conversation. This is the "recovery" Addison speaks of in *Spectator* 10, not the restoration of an historical period but the rediscovery of genetic truths in human nature. As a character, Socrates appears in *Spectator* essays on physiognomy, on marriage, and on dancing (Nos. 479, 86, 67). He also appears as "The Divine *Socrates*" who purposefully leads his listeners to insights into immortality and prayer (Nos. 146, 207). Addison can thus defend the humor of *The Spectator* in a later periodical (*Free-Holder* 45), by arguing that a Socratic insinuation made it possible to "increase the Number of Readers": "I need not remind this learned Gentleman [Defoe, who had criticized *The Spectator*'s levity], that *Socrates*, who was the greatest Propagator of Morality among the Heathens, and a Martyr for the Unity of the Godhead, was so famous for the Exercise of this Talent among the politest People of Antiquity, that he gained the Name of (ὅ῎Εἰρων) *the Drole.*" For Shaftesbury, too, in his *Characteristics*, the scope of the Socratic dialogue—its capacity to incorporate dialogue, formal exposition, fable, and satire—is a function of Socrates' public idiosyncracy: "[Socrates] was in himself a perfect character; yet in some respects so veiled and in a cloud, that to the unattentive surveyor he seemed often to be very different from what he really was; and this chiefly by reason of a certain exquisite and refined raillery which belonged to his manner, and by virtue of which he could treat the highest subjects and those of the commonest capacity both together, and render them explanatory of each other."[12] By bringing together the trivial and philosophical the dialogues become both illustrations of the manners of the age and discourses on wisdom: "by this means they not only taught us to know others, but, what was principal and of highest virtue in them, they taught us to know ourselves."

This instruction succeeds because Socratic raillery allows opinions to be insinuated into a reader's consciousness before he is aware of what is happening. And it succeeds because it manipulates the poses in which we see ourselves. It plays with the social languages which surround us so that we may more clearly see ourselves. Thus Shaftesbury analyzes the self-consciousness which *The Spectator* also fosters, distinguishing "two faces which would naturally present themselves to our view," that of the actor and that of the Socratic teacher who forces the actor to look at himself: "Whatever we were employed in, whatever we set about, if once we had acquired the habit of this mirror we should, by virtue of the double reflection, distinguish ourselves into two different parties. And in this dramatic method, the work of self-inspection would proceed with admirable success."[13] This is the doubleness Golden speaks of, where we see ourselves both as actors and as reflective observers. Like Shaftesbury, *The Spectator* poses the question of our two selves that so intrigued the eighteenth century. It also suggests a characteristically eighteenth-century solution: an awareness of ourselves in social situations where we attend both to the movements of manners in which we participate and to the movements of our own consciousness.

This Socratic split between the public and private selves leads to one of the most comic and pregnant presentations of Mr. Spectator as impostor. "When I want Materials for this Paper," he says, "it is my Custom to go abroad in quest of Game; and when I meet any proper Subject, I take the first Opportunity of setting down an Hint of it upon Paper. . . . By this Means I frequently carry about me a whole Sheet full of Hints, that would look like a Rhapsody of Nonsense to any Body but my self: There is nothing in them but Obscurity and Confusion, Raving and Inconsistency. In short, they are my Speculations in the first Principles, that (like the World in its Chaos) are void of all Light, Distinction, and Order" (No. 46). Mr. Spectator has forgotten the list in a coffee-house, and when he returns to recover it he finds it being read aloud: it must be a code, one man suggests, used by a spy: another man, closer to the mark, suggests it is the work of a lunatic taking notes from *The Spectator.* As it is passed around the table, Mr. Spectator takes up the sheet of paper, rolls it, holds it to a candle, lights his pipe, and casually puts the remainder in his pocket: "My profound Silence, together with the Steadiness of my Countenance, and the Gravity of my Behaviour during this whole Transaction, raised a very loud Laugh on all Sides of me: but as I had escaped all Suspicion of being the Author, I was very well satisfied, and applying my self to my Pipe and the *Postman*, took no further Notice of any thing that passed about me."

This is a classic form of comedy—the man watching himself as comedian—and it shows how *The Spectator* is conceived. Mr. Spectator is struggling with the contingent world in which *The Spectator* exists (he explains, of course, that he has been able to work up and publish only those hints not burned off the end). In itself, however,

The Spectator forms a self-contained order. It is a reflective ordering of random experience.

While Mr. Spectator represents the Socratic doubleness of our social selves, he is also the perfect Lockean observer, balancing his mental life between experience and reflection.[14] Locke's ambition had been Socratic, too. He speaks with humility of "my own coarse thoughts" (1:11), and he is well known for abandoning jargon and bringing philosophy, in his own way, out of closets and schools into clubs and assemblies. The "uncouth, affected, or unintelligible terms" of the schools had brought philosophy to the point that it "was thought unfit or incapable to be brought into well-bred company and polite conversation" (1:14). The stylistic premises of *The Spectator*, in fact, can as reasonably be said to come from Locke's remarkable "Epistle to the Reader" from the *Essay Concerning Human Understanding* as from Socrates, Cicero, or Tillotson: "Were it fit," Locke writes, "to trouble thee with the history of this *Essay*, I should tell thee, that five or six friends meeting at my chamber, and discoursing on a subject very remote from this, found themselves quickly at a stand. . . . [Thus] some hasty and undigested thoughts, . . . which I set down against our next meeting, gave the first entrance into this Discourse; which having been thus begun by chance, was continued by intreaty; written by incoherent parcels; and after long intervals of neglect, resumed again, as my humour or occasions permitted" (1:9–10).

The style of the *Essay* is the popular style of *The Spectator*, and its epistemology is that of *The Spectator*. Rosalie Colie has described Locke's explorations into the idea of the public and private in his style, political thought, and epistemology.[15] "Locke takes ordinary men, or men of ordinary common sense, both as subjects of his philosophical descriptions and formulations, and as the audience for whom his books were designed" (p. 32), and his analysis of the common man considers both the privacy of our thoughts and the demands of the community. Here we find a second antecedent to *The Spectator*'s exploration of the inward and the outward. Because our ideas, for Locke, are the products of experience, they are the products of a constant flux of sensations. They are part of a world of contingent things. But Locke emphasizes two constraints. First, the words we use to express them must be communal; that is, the language we use to express our private thoughts is subject to public negotiation. And second, both within our selves and in discourse with others, our thoughts must be examined and ordered according to internal standards of clarity and distinctness, and they must be consistently assigned to words or other signs to form true propositions (*Essay*, 2.29.1–10). To shift terminology, they must be methodized.

Shaftesbury had noted that the most conspicuous features of Socratic address are its obvious respect for the reader and its carefully structured argument, disguised by a familiar style: "the concealment of order and method in this manner of writing," he says, "makes the chief beauty of the work."[16] Addison, too, applauds method. He says that his own papers include both those "written with Regularity and Method" and those "that run out into the Wildness of those Compositions, which go by the Name of *Essays*," but he clearly approves more of the ordered style:

> When I read an Author of Genius, who writes without Method, I fancy my self in a Wood that abounds with a great many noble Objects, rising among one another in the greatest Confusion and Disorder. When I read a Methodical Discourse, I am in a regular Plantation, and can place my self in its several Centers, so as to take a view of all the Lines and Walks that are struck from them.
>
> Method is of Advantage to a Work, both in respect to the Writer and the Reader. . . . When a Man has plann'd his Discourse, he finds a great many Thoughts rising out of every Head, that do not offer themselves upon the general Survey of a Subject. . . . The Advantages of a Reader from a Methodical Discourse, are correspondent with those of the Writer. He comprehends every thing easily, takes it in with Pleasure, and retains it long. (No. 476)

Introducing No. 99, Addison briefly describes how reflections become ordered discourse: "The Club, of which I have often declared my self a Member, were last Night engaged in a Discourse upon that which passes for the chief Point of Honour among Men and Women, and started a great many Hints upon the Subject which I thought were entirely new. I shall therefore methodize the several Reflections that arose upon this Occasion, and present my Reader with them for the Speculation of this Day." In No. 46 he describes the ordering procedure more diffusely when he introduces us to Mr. Spectator's list, with its "Obscurity and Confusion." In the revised and finished essays, *The Spectator* retains all the features of the world which may be recorded in random hints but gives them light, distinction, and order, in effect creating a cosmos within itself, the Edenic garden which Addison envisions in No. 10 and which is his metaphor for method.

Mr. Spectator and His Readers

We have seen the same sets of relationships reenacted at various levels in *The Spectator*: Mr. Spectator's face is publicly known, but he expresses his thoughts only in the privacy of the club; *The Spectator* is distributed to a large and expanding readership, but its style suggests intimacy and shared values; Socrates is publicly a comedian, but his disguised wisdom leads us into a knowledge of ourselves; Locke's empirical observer turns outside of himself toward a world of physical, shared experience, and turns inside toward a cognitive, internal reflectiveness.

The Spectator presupposes what Steele in No. 4 calls "the Commerce of Discourse," a commerce of words and gestures in which social actors present themselves through a succession of postures and Mr. Spectator presents himself through the signs on the page. But through the processes of enclosure these public signs are marked off as a special region. The symmetries of reading, the symmetry suggested by the balance of "observing" and "perusing," make *The Spectator* a closed world, even with its commerce of words and gestures: while reading *The Spectator* we step out of the unformed world of random experience into a controlled world of play.

The public world is morally ambiguous. It is in the public world that Mr. Spectator's disinterested observation tends to look ridiculous. On a radically different level, it is in the public world that Richard Steele, the moralist, is also the polemicist and defaulted debtor, and Joseph Addison, the consummate stylist, is also the secretive party factotum. But the world of public behavior, the middle ground of gestures through which *The Spectator* reads its readers and its readers read *The Spectator*, is also a field of raillery and play, and a closed world of intimate community. Play, as Huizinga has explained it, demands "temporary worlds within the ordinary world, dedicated to the performance of an act apart"; "into the confusion of life it brings a temporary, a limited perfection"[17]—it exists within a frame, since the rules of play mark off a stage in which the actor assumes a role. The world of play allows for a repeated succession of postures or roles,

like the verbal forms repeated through *The Spectator*'s repeated publication. Furthermore, play demands the self-consciousness of the
player who watches himself as player. Through this self-consciousness he internalizes the rules (in the "play" of manners, these are the
rules of behavior) which are in turn expressed in the repeated postures of the game. The world of play, then, becomes a social world.
The individual "I" shades into the communal "we" of membership;
individual attitudes are expressed in gestures which have public
meaning.[18] The world of play establishes the community that
Huizinga calls being "apart together," the club which stands apart
from the world.[19]

In the final paper, No. 555, of the original *Spectator* series, Richard
Steele, in his own voice, closes *The Spectator*. He separates its artificial
world from the real world of moral ambivalence—including the ambivalence of his own position as moralist—and points to Mr. Spectator as a mask: "It is much more difficult to converse with the World
in a real than a personated Character. That might pass for Humour,
in the *Spectator*, which would look like Arrogance in a Writer who sets
his Name to his Work. The Fictitious Person might contemn those
who disapproved him, and extoll his own Performances, without giving Offence. He might assume a mock-Authority, without being
looked upon as vain and conceited." When Steele speaks "in my own
private Sentiments, I cannot but address my self to my Readers in a
more submissive manner, and with a just Gratitude." The final paper
disengages the reader from the self-enclosed, theatrical world of *The
Spectator* to return him to the ambiguous world of common life. The
final words of Steele's address to the reader are the actors' *Vos valete
& plaudite*, and the theatrical world of *The Spectator* vanishes. But
while we read it we are enwrapped in a comedy, in a vision of order, in
a moral universe; and we are caught in a suspension of time, like the
original readers who found at the end of the series that there was
"nothing to interrupt our Sips in a Morning, and to suspend our
Coffee in mid-air, between our Lips and right Ear" (No. 553).

CHAPTER TWO

"The Inward Disposition of the Mind Made Visible"

Whereas *Spectator* 1 introduces Mr. Spectator as author, *Spectator* 4 introduces him as actor. Here he does not take on the distant pose of a "Spectator of Mankind" but records the immediate impressions and encounters that drive *The Spectator*'s vision of urban life. Rather than being the figure framed by the margins of the page, he is surrounded by the theater of the world.

One would think [Steele writes] a silent Man who concerned himself with no one breathing, should be very little liable to misinterpretations; and yet I remember I was once taken up for a Jesuit, for no other Reason but my profound Taciturnity. It is from this Misfortune, that to be out of Harm's Way, I have ever since affected Crowds. He who comes into Assemblies only to gratify his Curiosity, and not to make a Figure, enjoys the Pleasures of Retirement in a more exquisite Degree, than he possibly could in his Closet; the Lover, the Ambitious, and the Miser, are follow'd thither by a worse Crowd than any they can withdraw from. To be exempt from the Passions with which others are tormented, is the only pleasing Solitude. I can very justly say with the antient Sage, *I am never less alone than when alone.* As I am insignificant to the Company in publick Places, and as it is visible I do not come thither as most do, to shew my self; I gratify the Vanity of all who pretend to make an Appearance, and have often as kind Looks from well dressed Gentlemen and Ladies, as a Poet would bestow upon one of his Audience. There are so many Gratifications attend this publick sort of Obscurity, that some little Distastes I daily receive have lost their Anguish; and I did the other Day, without the least Displeasure, overhear one say of me, *That strange Fellow,* and another answer, *I have known the Fellow's Face these twelve Years, and so must you; but I believe you are the first ever asked who he was.* There are, I must confess, many to whom my Person is as well known as that of their nearest Relations, who give themselves no further Trouble about calling me by my Name or Quality, but speak of me very currently by Mr. *what-d'ye-call-him.*

This is a very different role for the spectator than we see in the first paper, although the two versions are not far apart since, for both, *The Spectator's* metaphors create an imagery of inwardness and penetration. In the theater of the world, the spectator is subject to the apparatus of social judgments that subject him to multiple interpretations and misinterpretations. For his part, gestures, stance, and facial expressions for Mr. Spectator become media of interpretation through which he sees an intimate link between the outward and inward, the physical and psychological, the public and private sides of the social man: the actor's behavior becomes a signature for the movements of his mind.

This passage from *Spectator* 4 thus introduces a range of themes that recur throughout the series. The first is the attention to gesture, itself, as in the visible relationships between Mr. Spectator and the "well dressed Gentlemen and Ladies." Interpreting gestures creates a framework of comparisons whereby the spectator measures gratification, satisfaction, or pleasure. This paragraph, for instance, is based on a contrast between public fame and the pleasures of "our own Minds." Interlaced through this governing contrast are forms of quantification ("more exquisite Degree, than," "worse Crowd than," "as most do," "so many Gratifications . . . that," "little Distastes," "without the least Displeasure") that make *The Spectator's* world one of continual assessment and measurement.

Finally, such comparisons support a modified ideal of retirement, derived from classical morality as filtered through the seventeenth-century essayists. Specifically, it is Cowleyan. "The great dealers in the world," Cowley explained, "may be divided into the Ambitious, the Covetous, and the Voluptuous"; the obscure man "deceives" the world by passing through it unnoticed along *secretum iter*; and Scipio's tag, *Nunquam minus solus, quam cum solus,* opens his essay "Of Solitude."[1] Through Cowley's interpretation of this last sentence, however, we may see a crucial shift in the concept of the retired man. "His meaning," Cowley says of Scipio, "no doubt was this, That he found more satisfaction to his mind, and more improvement of it by Solitude then by Company, and to shew that he spoke not this loosly or out of vanity, after he had made *Rome*, Mistriss of almost the whole World, he retired himself from it by a voluntary exile, and at a private house in the middle of a wood near *Linternum*, passed the remainder of his Glorious life no less Gloriously." This, however, is not Steele's meaning when he uses the phrase. He does not write about the glorious man, but about the man in common life whose retirement is not a removal from the world but a disinterestedness sustained within it. His description of Mr. Spectator fuses into the oxymoron of a "publick sort of Obscurity" the complementary pleasures of retirement and social observation.

While an attention to gesture, therefore, is at the heart of *The Spectator*'s image of social man, that image develops in these and other directions through a network of themes, topics, and arguments that criss-cross and overlap in various ways. Three nodes in this network prove particularly important. The first is the importance *The Spectator* assigns to the perception of gesture and to the related arts of physiognomy, painting, and theater. The second is the framework of moral judgments supported by this perception of gesture, including the endorsement of an urban retirement. The third is a language of esthetics that spans both these accounts of social life and Addison's papers on esthetics. Social life comes to be represented in the language of esthetics because it shares with esthetics the same structures of perception and the same capacities for spontaneous assent and critical discrimination.

THE ARTS OF GESTURE

Because of his faculties of visual perception, gestures for Mr. Spectator take on the status of language. Through them he may, as he says, enter into "the inmost Thoughts and Reflections of all whom I behold," "without being admitted to their Conversation" (No. 4). As he walks along London streets he watches a woman who "hangs on her Cloaths, plays her Head, varies her Posture, and changes Place incessantly," coachmen who "make Signs with their Fingers as they drive by each other, to intimate how much they have got that Day," the shops in the City "adorn'd with contented Faces," and "Men in the Crowds . . . pleased with their Hopes and Bargains" (No. 454). While at the theater, he and Will Honeycomb judge the characters of women by considering their choices of ribbons or the qualities of personality manifest in their faces. Will says of one woman, somewhat rhapsodically, that "Good-Nature, and Affability are the Graces that play in her Countenance. . . . Her Air has the Beauty of Motion, and her Look the Force of Language." In this case, the gesture is an immediate presence, since "there is a strict Affinity between all Things that are truly laudable and beautiful, from the highest Sentiment of the Soul, to the most indifferent Gesture of the Body" (No. 466). Yet there is also the potential for an imitative regress, a play of exteriors where the interior self is lost. Other women "move a knowing Eye no more than the Portraitures of insignificant People by ordinary Painters, which are but Pictures of Pictures" (No. 4).

In this world of appearances other figures, like Mr. Spectator and Will Honeycomb, devote their attention to gesture. One correspondent ("Orator" Henley, in the character of Tom Tweer) explains that "there is a very close Correspondence between the Outward and the Inward Man; that scarce the least Dawning, the least Parturiency towards a Thought can be stirring in the Mind of Man, without producing a suitable Revolution in his Exteriors, which will easily discover it self to an Adept in the Theory of the Phiz" (No. 518). Another correspondent recommends himself as an expert in the language of the eyes (No. 354); another is enraptured by the eloquence of a glance (No. 252). A fourth correspondent proves himself adept at both theory and practice. "In Relations," he explains, "the Force of the Expression lies very often more in the Look, the Tone of Voice, or the Gesture, than the Words themselves." He explains, too, that even in dull conversations "good Breeding obliges a Man to maintain the Figure of the keenest Attention, the true Posture of which in a Coffee-house I take to consist in leaning over a Table, with the Edge of it pressing hard upon your Stomach; for the more Pain the Narration is received with, the more gracious is your bending over" (No. 521). One woman writes about young men who "examine our Eyes with a Petulancy in their own, which is a downright Affront to Modesty" (No. 528), and a shop girl complains of customers who "loll at the Bar staring just in my Face, ready to interpret my Looks and Gestures, according to their own Imaginations" (No. 155).

The Spectator thus resolves itself into a succession of scenes, a shadow play of gestures in the theater of the world, where words may be spoken but where the drama is in the accompanying action.

In *Spectator* 86 Addison explains Mr. Spectator's visual acuity in more detail:

> We are no sooner presented to any one we never saw before, but we are immediately struck with the Idea of a proud, a reserved, an affable, or a good-natured Man; and upon our first going into a Company of Strangers, our Benevolence or Aversion, Awe or Contempt, rises naturally towards several particular Persons before we have heard them speak a single Word, or so much as know who they are.
>
> Every Passion gives a particular Cast to the Countenance, and is apt to discover itself in some Feature or other. I have seen an Eye curse for half an Hour together, and an Eye-brow call a Man Scoundrel. Nothing is more common than for Lovers to complain, resent, languish, despair and dye, in dumb Show. For my own Part, I am so apt to frame a Notion of every Man's Humour or Circumstances by his Looks, that I have sometimes employed my self from *Charing-Cross* to the *Royal-Exchange* in drawing the Characters of those who have passed by me. When I see a Man with a sour rivell'd Face, I cannot forbear pittying his Wife; and when I meet with an open ingenuous Countenance, think on the Happiness of his Friends, his Family, and Relations.
>
> I cannot recollect the Author of a famous Saying to a Stranger who stood silent in his Company, *Speak that I may see thee*: But with Submission, I think we may be better known by our Looks than by our Words; and that a Man's Speech is much more easily disguised than his Countenance. In this Case however, I think the Air of the whole Face is much more expressive than the Lines of it: The Truth of it is, the Air is generally nothing else but the inward Disposition of the Mind made visible.

In speaking of the countenance as a register of the passions, Addison draws upon a well-established although heterogeneous theory of physiognomy. An understanding of physiognomy requires that distinctions be made between inborn and acquired features, and between permanent features (whether inborn or acquired) and changing expressions. (Interestingly, with regard to Addison as an amateur collector of medals, John Evelyn appended to his *Numismata* a "Digression Concerning Physiognomy" which toyed with and entangled these distinctions.) Physiognomy, properly, deals with the permanent structures of the face and contours of the body which supposedly display innate qualities of mind. Pathognomy, by contrast, studies the changing expressions which indicate the movements of emotion. This is the distinction Addison makes between the lines of the face, which have no value as measures of character because they are purely fortuitous, and the more indefinite qualities of the air, which register both changing emotions and a general attitude toward the world. Through habitual use, an expression may be fixed upon the face as a permanent signature of a mental attitude, but it is acquired as part of a way of living and thus marks an intimate connection between character and behavior.[2]

Addison's passage from No. 86 illustrates this system of distinctions, which constitutes a more or less formal notion of physiognomy. But it also goes beyond the theory of physiognomy toward a theory of sentiment. Judgment and feeling arise spontaneously and simultaneously. Upon seeing a person we are "immediately struck" with an "Idea" of his character, and a responsive emotion "rises naturally" within us. The spectator draws for himself "Characters" of those he encounters and immediately skips from noting a single feature to feeling pity or thinking about happiness. Addison provides no details about physical appearance, in a way begging the question. To describe a face as "sour" or "open" already presupposes those qualities of mind. Yet E. H. Gombrich has described just such an indefiniteness as an essential element in esthetic empathy: "We respond to a face as a whole," Gombrich has explained; "we see a friendly, dignified, or eager face, sad or sardonic, long before we can tell what exact features or relationships account for this intuitive impression."[3] In a manner characteristic of sensibility, then, perception and response are inseparable. So, in the last sentences of the second paragraph, we are presented, through skillful abbreviation, with typically sentimental elements, with Mr. Spectator's heightened awareness of his own feelings in response to the visible passions of others, especially with respect to the domestic circle of the family. Out of the confusion of the street, Mr. Spectator isolates an individual and places him into two emotional contexts, one existing within an imagined family group, and the second created through the spectator's own feelings in response to the individual he sees only momentarily. We are given a double portrait of the good man of sentimental literature, first in the portrait of the man whose family is happy because he is open and ingenuous, and second in the portrait of the spectator with his own generous sympathy.

With this sentimental interaction as background, Addison makes a

general proposition about social knowledge. Again the spatial metaphor dominates the epistemology: "the Air," we are told, "is generally
nothing else but the inward Disposition of the Mind made visible."
This proposition is set against Socrates' (the author is unacknow-
ledged, but understood) *Speak that I may see thee.* Again Addison alludes to the Socratic model, with this difference—the visible man is
the spectator's contact with the marketplace.

Even this assertion about the "Air" must be qualified, however,
since throughout the essay Addison backs away from his initial proposition. Every passion is "apt" to discover itself "in some Feature or
other"; the air is "generally" the disposition of the mind made visible.
Outward postures do not correspond with the inward man in any
simple way. To perceive the inward man, an observer must get around
the element of disguise Addison mentions, which is not only the intentional disguise of hypocrisy or affectation but also the uninten-
tional disguise whereby the private man is hidden behind appearances, very liable to misinterpretation.

Other essays question the link between appearance and character,
and still others deny that there is a link at all (compare Nos. 95, 206,
257). But, without trying to reconcile all of *The Spectator*'s various
statements about the visible man, we can assert that they all assume
the same orientation toward social knowledge by attempting to correlate outward behavior with inward character. What we learn from Addison's qualifications in No. 86 (or elsewhere, as in No. 257) is that
more than the countenance or gesture by itself must be considered to
read the gesture accurately. Addison's qualifications anticipate the
later skepticism of Fielding and Hogarth, both of whom held that
"the Passions of Men do commonly imprint sufficient Marks on the
Countenance," but that these marks can be read only against the circumstances in which they appear.[4] The gesture or expression has no
value when taken in isolation. It must be interpreted, both with reference to the actor and with reference to the situation in which the act
occurs. As one critic has said, pathognomy is only a factor in a moral
drama.[5]

The Geometry of Perception

The Spectator's moral drama is found in its narrative scenes. These
scenes are related to the other arts that explore the visible passions of

men: the arts of physiognomy, painting, and the theater. They also
suggest a geometry of perception that corresponds to these three arts.
The simplest structure is a one-dimensional line, where the observer
recognizes signatures of character in those he sees, as in physiognomy. A more complex structure is triangular, two-dimensional perception, where the observer watches one person react to another, as in
a history painting or conversation picture. The most complex structure is three-dimensional, whereby the observer may see the degree
to which the inward person corresponds with his outward postures, as
a member of the audience at a theater may distinguish between an
actor and his role. This most complex form of perception leads to a
distinction between affectation and sincerity that is the basis for *The
Spectator*'s system of moral comparisons.

Addison's proposal that the "Air" is "the inward Disposition of the
Mind made visible" had been anticipated in a chapter heading to a
1699 translation of Cicero's *De officiis*: "Outward Carriage discovers
the inward Dispositions of the Mind."[6] This verbal coincidence (if it
is one) points to one set of traditions behind *The Spectator*'s attention
to gesture, the classical traditions of rhetoric and conduct. Both
Cicero in *De oratore* (3.57.215–17) and Quintilian in the *Institutes*
(11.3.66) had given advice on how an orator should use his eyes,
voice, and gesture to reinforce the passions he discusses, and John
Hughes in *Spectator* 541 quotes Cicero's instructions for the orator as
advice to the actor: "Nature her self," Hughes says, in paraphrase,
"has assigned, to every Emotion of the Soul, its peculiar Cast of the
Countenance, Tone of Voice, and Manner of Gesture; and the whole
Person, all the Features of the Face and Tones of the Voice answer . . . to the Impressions made on them by the Mind." Hughes
calls this "the Speech of the Features and Limbs," "a kind of Universal Tongue."

Cicero integrates this sense of gesture into the ideals of reason,
harmony, correctness, and beauty which so profoundly influenced *The
Spectator*. Thus Steele, in a crucial statement of *The Spectator*'s values
in No. 104, translates from *De officiis* (1.28), employing a balanced
phrasing that mirrors the harmonies advocated in the argument:

It would be a noble Improvement, or rather a Recovery of what we call
good Breeding, if nothing were to pass amongst us for agreeable which
was the least Transgression against that Rule of Life called Decorum, or
a Regard to Decency. . . . *Tully* says Virtue and Decency are so nearly

related, that it is difficult to separate them from each other but in our Imagination. As the Beauty of the Body always accompanies the Health of it, so certainly is Decency Concomitant to Virtue: As Beauty of Body, with an agreeable Carriage, pleases the Eye, and that Pleasure consists in that we observe all the Parts with a certain Elegance are proportioned to each other; so does Decency of Behaviour which appears in our Lives obtain the Approbation of all with whom we converse, from the Order, Constancy, and Moderation of our Words and Actions. This flows from the Reverence we bear towards every good Man, and to the World in general.

Linking consistency in virtue with visible harmonies of the body is not an explanatory analogy, but a crucial connection in Cicero's thought of *pulchrum* and *honestum*. The finest details of manners, gesture, or expression become signatures of the inward man. Cicero's observation in *De oratore* that every emotion has its proper signature is elevated in *De officiis* to a principle of social judgment:

> We might from the least and most trivial Matters, make several Observations that would be much to our Advantage. From the moving of our Eyes, for Example; from our way of smoothing or wrinkling our Brows; from the merry or sorrowful Air of our Contenances; from our Laughter, freedom or reservedness in Discourse; from the raising or falling the Tone of our Voices, and a great many other such little kind of Circumstances, we might easily judge what is Handsom and Becoming us, and what is repugnant to the Rules of Duty, and to that which our Nature or Character requires.[7]

A second tradition behind *The Spectator*'s attention to gesture is Descartes's mechanistic physiology, which gave new impetus to physiognomy and put it on a "scientific" basis. The body, Descartes had argued, is a machine, a piece of clockwork, connected with the soul through the flux of animal spirits. Stimuli presented to the body are communicated to the soul, where they give rise to emotions, and these in turn influence the muscles of the body so that they are displayed in physical features. Both the emotions and their expressions, then, may be systematically categorized according to the types of stimuli that inspire them.[8] As we shall see, Descartes's physiology, along with Cicero's ideal of the *honestus vir*, influenced the continental conduct tradition of La Bruyère, Bellegarde, and Courtin, and the characters sketched by these writers have their counterparts in *The Spectator*. But Descartes's physiology is in the background of *The Spectator* in other ways as well. Addison in No. 86 leaves to the consideration of the curious "whether or no the different Motions of the Animal Spirits in different Passions, may have any Effect on the Mould of the Face," but elsewhere he accepts the prevailing physiology of his day: man, he insists, is a "Compound" of body and mind; the body influences the mind and is influenced by it through the animal spirits (Nos. 115 and 387). Descartes's physiology also has a more interesting, although more indirect, connection with the visual world of *The Spectator*: it lies behind the academic theory of expression in painting, as best represented by Charles le Brun's *Expression des passions*, which includes, as Gombrich describes it, a series of "schematic heads" illustrating the decisive signatures of the passions.[9]

This attention to physiognomy, or a variant of physiognomy, is apparent in *The Spectator*'s character sketches (such as the sketch of an Idol in No. 73), but it can be illustrated most concisely through Mr. Spectator's precursor, Isaac Bickerstaff, from Steele's *Tatler*. Bickerstaff, too, had enjoyed a visual acumen. For him "the Motive of a Man's Life is seen in all his Actions" (*Tatler* 49): "A Cane upon the Fifth Button shall from henceforth be the Type of a Dapper; Red-heeled Shoes, and an Hat hung upon one Side of the Head, shall signify a Smart; a good Periwig made into a Twist, with a brisk Cock, shall speak a Mettled Fellow; and an Upper-Lip covered with Snuff, denotes a Coffee-house Statesman" (*Tatler* 96).[10] Something of Bickerstaff's way of reading character is carried over for Mr. Spectator, who can, for example, easily recognize a "Woman's Man": "His Garb is more loose and negligent, his Manner more soft and indolent; that is to say, in both these Cases there is an apparent Endeavour to appear unconcerned and careless" (No. 156). But for Mr. Spectator, more typically, manners are not "signs" that "denote" character types. Perhaps to contrast *The Spectator* with the earlier *Tatler*, Addison insists that he (as Mr. Spectator) does not concern himself with "Red-heels or Top-knots," but "enter[s] into the Passions of Mankind" (No. 16). Social observation is a more intricate process of interpretation, looking at the interaction between inward and outward, so the spatial metaphor ("penetration," "looked into," "inmost," "enter into," "outward") dominates *The Spectator*'s descriptions of the social man. Specifically, the gesture must be interpreted with respect to the situation in which it occurs, as in a painting, and with respect to the inward character which lies behind the gesture, as in the theater.

Le Brun's catalogue of heads corresponds in the arts to the one-dimensional characterizations of Isaac Bickerstaff, or Mr. Spectator on occasion: one mark equals one meaning. This is the one-dimensionality of simple physiognomy. But the art of painting also corresponds with the two-dimensional scenes in which the spectator sees a man's actions within the circumstances which give them meaning. Alleviating somewhat the mechanism of Le Brun's handbook is the element of drama in those history paintings most admired by the academies, those that successfully arrange several figures, each of whom illustrates a different emotion felt in response to some central action. Such paintings also elicit various responses from the observer. This is the attitude Steele adopts in *Spectator* 226 when he praises Raphael's cartoons for representing "almost all the different Tempers of Mankind." In response to St. Paul's oratorical authority, "You see one credulous of all that is said, another wrapt up in deep Suspense, another saying there is some Reason in what he says, another angry that the Apostle destroys a favourite Opinion . . . another wholly convinced and holding out his Hands in Rapture."[11]

The pictorial possibilities of pathognomy are not limited to the technical work of the academy, although Steele admired these styles and was a member of Kneller's Academy of Painting and Drawing. Later in the century, Hogarth was to argue that depicting character and emotion in the moral dramas of daily life was equivalent in artistic value to the grand patterns of history painting, and in Hogarth's prints we are closer to the visual world of *The Spectator* with its histrionics of cursing and making love. Mr. Spectator does not see "the different Tempers of Mankind" in the panoply of historical events, but in the streets of London during his curious walks between Charing Cross and the Exchange. From the dramas of daily life, Mr. Spectator draws his own scenes, scenes which may be described as triangular perception.

Triangular scenes depict a posed relationship between two characters, usually combining words and actions, with the spectator standing back as an audience, while participating in the scene through a movement of heart. The scenes which punctuate *The Spectator*'s narratives about Sir Roger de Coverley use this configuration to capture, in a pictorial form, Sir Roger's memorable personality:

> I could not but observe with a great deal of Pleasure the Joy that appeared in the Countenances of these ancient Domesticks upon my Friend's Arrival at his Country-Seat. Some of them could not refrain

from Tears at the Sight of their old Master; every one of them press'd forward to do something for him, and seemed discouraged if they were not employed. . . . [His] Humanity and good Nature engages every Body to him, so that when he is pleasant upon any of them, all his Family are in good Humour, and none so much as the Person whom he diverts himself with: On the Contrary, if he coughs or betrays any Infirmity of Old Age, it is easy for a Stander-by to observe a secret Concern in the Looks of all his Servants. (No. 106)

I was touched with a secret Joy at the Sight of the good old Man, who before he saw me was engaged in Conversation with a Beggar Man that had asked an Alms of him. I cou'd hear my Friend chide him for not finding out some Work; but at the same time saw him put his Hand in his Pocket and give him Six-Pence. (No. 269)

While the Sir Roger episodes may produce the most memorable scenes in *The Spectator*, probably no sentence so compactly presents the intricate patterns of perception possible in the essays as the first sentence of Steele's No. 19: "Observing one Person behold another, who was an utter Stranger to him, with a Cast of his Eye, which, methought, expressed an Emotion of Heart very different from what could be raised by an Object so agreeable as the Gentleman he looked at, I began to consider, not without some secret Sorrow, the Condition of an Envious Man."

This kind of extravagant embedding allows Steele to express a complex pattern of observations and responses in a single syntactic unit. But, although all of the elements in this sentence are pertinent, and in some respects inseparable, the sentence does need some unpacking. There are a number of similarities among the three people presented to us. Two reveal aspects of their character in their physical appearance: one man appears agreeable; by looking at him in a peculiar way, the second appears envious. Two have mental responses triggered by observation: one man responds with envy; the spectator responds with sorrow and begins to reflect on the nature of envy. By means of the amplifying clauses, our attention shifts repeatedly among the people presented to us, like the eye moving between figures in a painting. Taking one fragment as an example— "who was an utter Stranger to him, with a Cast of his Eye, which, methought, expressed an Emotion of Heart very different from what could be raised by an Object so agreeable"—we move from the agreeable man, to the envious man, to the spectator, to the envious man, and again to the agreeable man. Through the grammar of the sentence, Steele sketches a picture, the basic configuration of which is that of a triangle based on two acts of seeing: "Observing one Person behold another."

A triangular structure of this type allows Mr. Spectator to turn in three directions in order to "translate" the scene into a discourse: he may look into the character of the actor; he may look into the environment which causes him to act as he does; or he may look into his own responses. Seen with respect to the actor, the gesture is a "stance," a "posture," an "attitude" taken toward the world, all these terms playing on the metaphor which pairs a mental "attitude" with a physical "attitude." In the case of No. 19, the spectator follows a typical maneuver and turns from his immediate response to consider the general condition of the envious man, examining the psychology of envy according to "His Pains, His Reliefs, and His Happiness." Seen with respect to its environment (its circum-stances), the gesture can be seen as part of a complex system of actions, including the habits and values of a whole society. Any one gesture, any detail of dress or turn of manners, may become a wedge by which the spectator may enter into the society's system of values, and from which he may abstract the several social forms embedded in the gesture. Or, seen with respect to the spectator, his response may be taken as a measure of his judgment and sensibility.[12] These alternative directions for enlarging on particular instants of perception are illustrated in other essays.

A different kind of scene based on similar responses is the vivid scene in No. 266 when Mr. Spectator is accosted by a prostitute: "I was jogged on the Elbow as I turned into the Piazza, on the right Hand coming out of *James-street*, by a slim young Girl of about Seventeen, who with a pert Air asked me if I was for a Pint of Wine." Mr. Spectator is careful to reassure the reader "that I am wholly unconcerned in any Scene I am in, but meerly as a Spectator," and explains that he would invite the girl inside except that "the Man of the *Bumper* knows me" and might misunderstand his curiosity.

> This Impediment being in my Way, we stood under one of the Arches by Twilight; and there I could observe as exact Features as I had ever seen, the most agreeable Shape, the finest Neck and Bosom, in a Word, the whole Person of a Woman exquisitly beautiful. She affected to allure me with a forced Wantonness in her Look and Air; but I saw it checked with Hunger and Cold: Her Eyes were wan and eager, her Dress thin and tawdry, her Mein genteel and childish. This strange

Figure gave me much Anguish of Heart, and to avoid being seen with her I went away, but could not forbear giving her a Crown. The poor thing sighed, curtisied, and with a Blessing, expressed with the utmost Vehemence, turned from me.

Through this momentary encounter, visually framed by the archway, Mr. Spectator may see into the character of the girl through her response to him. As spectator he sees through the "forced Wantonness" to the contradictions which motivate the woman, a sympathetic access to the inner person made possible by the details of behavior. This movement of sympathy has physical expression as Mr. Spectator gives her a coin. She in turn curtsies, blesses him, and turns away.

From this one scene, Mr. Spectator is able to reconstruct the girl's history: she is "what they call *newly come upon the Town*"; she has probably been seduced and abandoned, managed by a succession of bawds, and reduced to soliciting in the street. In this case, the spectator turns from the girl's character to examine the environment that has made her what she is. In a subsequent paper on "the present State of Fornication" (No. 274), he explains that to condemn women like this girl without considering "their Circumstances when they fell"—the importunities of parents, poverty, and passion—"would be to act like a Pedantick Stoick, who thinks all Crimes alike, and not like an impartial SPECTATOR, who looks upon them with all the Circumstances that diminish or enhance the Guilt." The "circumstances" Steele speaks of are less casuistic details than an environing condition which surrounds the woman, and which is, figuratively, indicated by the gesture, the "stance" that points us toward its "circum-stances." The girl's approach to Mr. Spectator, which constitutes the immediate "circumstances" of her appearance, contains both the wantonness and the suffering that, together, reflect upon the "circumstances" of her history, which the spectator then discloses by inferring the social forces that are at once revealed and concealed by the gesture.

So, Mr. Spectator's enlargement of the gesture may turn toward the character of the actor, or may turn toward the environment that surrounds him. Or, it may turn toward the third point of the triangle, toward the spectator himself. In one respect the character of the spectator is already obvious as he reflects on the gesture he sees. By tracing the connections between an actor and his environment, the spectator translates the visual into the rhetorical, the specific into the universal, the fortuitous into the systematic. By interpreting it, the essayist absorbs the gesture into the verbal fabric of *The Spectator*. Thus his encounter with the young prostitute is absorbed into an essay, and the essay is absorbed into a series of several essays on prostitution.

At the end of No. 19, for another example, Mr. Spectator says that he has managed to escape envy, since if any man envies Mr. Spectator's wit he may comfort himself that the spectator never uses it in public, or if any man envies his morality he may comfort himself that Mr. Spectator's face is "none of the longest." This admission earns Mr. Spectator membership in the Ugly Club, mentioned again in No. 87, which alludes to No. 86, where Addison proposes that the air is the disposition of the mind made visible. Such a string of allusions, cross-references, and shared themes forms a network of topics enclosing *The Spectator*'s miniature world, where every scene, every encounter has its place within a schematic portraiture. The encounter with the prostitute, for instance, has an interesting analogue much later in the series, in much different circumstances. In No. 536 Mr. Spectator meets a young woman in a bookstore, who has just left a letter for him:

> As I was the other Day standing in my Bookseller's Shop, a pretty young Thing, about Eighteen Years of Age, stept out of her Coach, and brushing by me, beck'ned the Man of the Shop to the further End of his Counter, where she whispered something to him with an attentive Look, and at the same time presented him with a Letter: After which pressing the End of her Fan upon his Hand, she delivered the remaining Part of her Message, and withdrew. I observed, in the midst of her Discourse, that she flushed, and cast an Eye upon me over her Shoulder, having been informed, by my Bookseller, that I was the Man of the short Face whom she had so often read of. Upon her passing by me, the pretty blooming Creature smiled in my Face, and dropp'd me a Curtsie. She scarce gave me time to return her Salute, before she quitted the Shop with an easie Scuttle, and stepp'd again into her Coach, giving the Footmen Directions to drive where they were bid.

The two scenes illustrate the degree to which fixed patterns and modes of repetition control the contents of *The Spectator*.

The spectator responds to gestures by translating them into discourse, but he also responds emotionally through sentimental feeling, and this pairing of sentiment and judgment combines two attitudes toward moral perception that become increasingly important during the eighteenth century. It anticipates what Adam Smith, fifty years later, was to call "moral sentiment": "Upon some occasions sympathy may seem to arise meerly from the view of a certain emotion in another person. The passions, upon some occasions, may seem transfused from one man to another, instantaneously and antecedent to any knowledge of what excited them in the person principally concerned. Grief and joy, for example, strongly expressed in the look and gestures of any one, at once affect the spectator with some degree of a like painful or agreeable emotion."[13] This sympathy, however, is imperfect, Smith explains, until we are more thoroughly "informed of its cause": "Sympathy, therefore, does not arise so much from the view of the passion, as from the situation which excites it." Seen against its situation, a passion may give rise to passions in the spectator that the actor himself does not feel. He may, for instance, feel a secret sorrow at the sight of an envious man. But this is only one of a complex of possible emotions: "As Love is the most delightful Passion, Pity is nothing else but Love softned by a degree of Sorrow: In short, it is a kind of pleasing Anguish, as well as generous Sympathy, that knits Mankind together, and blends them in the same common Lot" (No. 397). Love and admiration, joy and sorrow are the bonds that draw men into communities.

But examining the situations in which emotions appear also requires a second, critical faculty of judgment. The spectator's sensitivity to character acknowledges the mediation of socially learned behavior, which carries with it both a system of values learned in society and also the possibility of imposture. The spectator's sensitivity to character anticipates the psychology of sentimentality with its immediate or intuitive access to the inner man, registered in the observer's own feelings, in a "secret Joy," or "secret Sorrow." But examining an artificial system of values and separating imposture from sincerity demands a moral discrimination much like that Fielding requires of his readers.

The spectator's pairing of sentiment and judgment also leads to the third dimension of his perceptual geometry, the dimension of depth that distinguishes the inward and outward man. This dimension is illustrated by a third art, that of the theater. In the theatrical play between actor and role we may see a confusion of pretense and reality

which must be prized apart, and we may also see the origins of intimate sympathy, the bond of sentiment.

More than physiognomy or painting, the theater in *The Spectator* is
a persistent and flexible analogue to social life. "The Word *Spectator*,"
Steele remarks, is "most usually understood as one of the Audience at
Publick Representations" (No. 22); Addison speaks of "the Fraternity
of Spectators" as "every one that considers the World as a Theatre,
and desires to form a right Judgment of those who are the Actors on
it" (No. 10). Characters, scenes, and intrigues are patterned after
stage comedy (as in Nos. 175, 318, 320, 423); illustrations from plays
are scattered casually through the papers ("If the Reader has a mind
to see a Father of the same Stamp represented in the most exquisite
stroaks of Humour, he may meet with it in one of the finest Comedies
that ever appeared upon the *English* Stage"—No. 189); and the theater is absorbed into the vocabulary of description ("behold *Gloriana*
trip into a Room with that theatrical Ostentation of her Charms"—
No. 206). Inevitably, Addison paraphrases Epictetus's aphorism, "We
are here, says he, as in a Theatre, where every one has a Part allotted
to him" (No. 219).

As an audience for "publick Representations," the spectator wavers
between art and life, since stage action and the artifice of manners are
equally public representations. The spectator's world ranges through
all degrees of histrionics and disguise. He watches women nod to one
another in the theater (No. 270) and watches beaux strut on the stage
(No. 240). Outside of the theater he watches the performances, the
moments of self-presentation, which make up our experience of the
social world: "I had the Honour the other Day," Mr. Spectator says,
"to sit in a publick Room, and saw an inquisitive Man look with an Air
of Satisfaction upon the Approach of one of those Talkers. The Man
of ready Utterance sat down by him; and rubbing his Head, leaning
on his Arm, and making an uneasy Countenance, he began" (No.
228). He has an opportunity to admire the play-acting of a coquette:
"She asks a Question of one [admirer], tells a Story to another,
glances an Ogle upon a third, takes a Pinch of Snuff from the fourth,
lets her Fan drop by accident to give the fifth an occasion of taking it
up" (No. 73). And in another coffeehouse encounter he watches the
father of a young Templar come in dressed in "a thread-bare loose
Coat" to sit, ignored, while his son ostentatiously displays the wit and
finery purchased with his father's money: "At last one of the Lads

presented him with some stale Tea in a broken Dish, accompanied
with a Plate of brown Sugar; which so raised his Indignation, that
after several obliging Appellations of Dog and Rascal, he asked him
aloud before the whole Company *Why he must be used with less Respect
than that Fop there?* pointing to a well-dress'd young Gentleman who
was drinking Tea at the opposite Table" (No. 150, Budgell). The
father is rightly offended at his son's attempts to win the admiration of
"a Parcel of Rascals," but, twisting the effect of the scene, Mr. Spectator remarks that "I cannot but think the old Gentleman was in some
Measure justly served for walking in Masquerade."

In this world of masquerade, Mr. Spectator asks (his reflection
prompted by his thoughts about the inquisitive man in No. 228),
"Would it not be the most pleasing Entertainment imaginable to enjoy
so constant a Farce, as the observing Mankind much more different
from themselves in their secret Thoughts and publick Actions, than
in their Night-Caps and long Periwiggs," an image that appears again
in one paper on the theater: "I am never less at a Play than when I am
at the Theatre . . . for most Men follow Nature no longer than while
they are in their Night-Gowns, and all the busy part of the Day are in
Characters which they neither become or act with pleasure to themselves or their Beholders" (No. 270).

The theater emphasizes such postures and impostures in three
ways. First, it emphasizes the frame that encloses the gesture (like the
archway that frames Mr. Spectator's encounter with the prostitute).
The theater is a confined space or condensed world of acting and
observing, bounded by the physical limits of the stage, and, in only a
slightly larger compass, by the theater building. Actors playing together create between them a stage space like that created in *The
Spectator*'s descriptive scenes (we need only look at contemporary illustrations of stage action to see how momentary postures can cap-
sulize the action of the play), and the spectator's visual distance from
the stage permits both critical disinterestedness and emotional prox-
imity. Mr. Spectator looks at the world and the theater in the same
way. "I confess," Steele writes in *Tatler* 182, "it is one of my greatest
Delights to sit unobserved and unknown in the Gallery, and entertain
my self either with what is personated on the stage, or observe what
Appearances present themselves in the Audience. If there were no
other good Consequences in a Playhouse, than that so many Persons
of different Ranks and Conditions are placed there in their most
pleasing Aspects, that Prospect only would be very far from being

below the Pleasures of a wise Man." Although this is written in *The Tatler* through the persona of Isaac Bickerstaff, it also applies to Mr. Spectator. The theater is a microcosm. Like the city, it is an assembly of all social types engaged in related activities. Still more, it is like the Exchange ("so rich an Assembly of Country-men and Foreigners consulting together upon the private Business of Mankind") that Addison finds to be an "infinite Variety of solid and substantial Entertainments" (No. 69). The theater is commerce, but a commerce of manners: it is quintessentially a place of self-presentation.

Second, the theater emphasizes the spectator's perceptual triangle within its self-enclosed world, with actors and audience playing in response to each other while the spectator takes the same distanced perspective that he has toward the world of affairs, watching actors and observers together. Having learned well a lesson from Restoration comedy, Mr. Spectator observes that while the actors on the stage imitate the manners of the audience, the audience imitates the manners of the actors in a complex mirroring.[14] Accordingly, he watches scenes played out in the audience which may be as vivid as those enacted on the stage, with people taking on roles meant to be observed by others.

Finally, the theater adds an analogy between the stage actor and the social actor, which goes beyond the framing and the triangular perception that are analogous to painting. In *Spectator* 370 Steele takes as his epigraph and starting point "from the Top of the Stage in *Drury-Lane* a Bit of *Latin* which . . . signifies that *the whole World acts the Player*":

> It is certain that if we look all round us and behold the different Employments of Mankind, you hardly see one who is not, as the Player is, in an assumed Character. . . . Consider all the different Pursuits and Employments of Man, and you will find half their Actions tend to nothing else but Disguise and Imposture; and all that is done which proceeds not from a Man's very self is the Action of a Player. For this Reason it is that I make so frequent mention of the Stage: It is, with me, a Matter of the highest Consideration what Parts are well or ill performed, what Passions or Sentiments are indulged or cultivated, and consequently what Manners and Customs are transfused from the Stage to the World, which reciprocally imitate each other.

Steele offers two reasons for *The Spectator*'s repeated consideration of the theater: first, that passions and sentiments are learned from the stage; and second, that the stage is an explanatory model for social existence. The connection between the world and the stage is due not only to an imitative correspondence between the manners of the actors and the manners of the audience, but also to a metaphysical similarity.

Eighteenth-century manuals for the actor gave two complementary types of advice. On the one hand they provided instructions in the artificial management of the body and voice, identifying the postures that would signify the passions of the character. On the other hand they urged the actor to feel his part, because through emotional identification the appropriate gestures would follow spontaneously.[15] When artificiality is carried too far, the actor merely imitates the outward postures of the passions, a degenerate acting that parallels a degeneration of theatrical production into mere spectacle. Addison remarks in his papers on tragedy, "For my own part, I prefer a noble Sentiment that is depressed with homely Language, infinitely before a Vulgar one that is blown up with all the Sound and Energy of Expression" (No. 39). He expresses nothing but contempt for the opera. The spectacle and posturing of opera are a bizarre confusion of artifice and reality, creating a stage world of monsters and grotesques. Genuine sentiment has been replaced by "Dresses and Decorations," absurd attempts to manufacture illusion: "How would the Wits of King *Charles*'s Time have laughed to have seen *Nicolini* exposed to a Tempest in Robes of Ermin, and sailing in an open Boat upon a Sea of Paste-Board" (No. 5). Moreover, just as the opera empties the theater of all meaning, turning it into incongruous display, the popular stage has its "Corporeal Actors" (No. 141), rope dancers and contortionists, who physically represent a vacant distortion of human nature.

By contrast, a good actor, a Betterton, Wilks, or Cibber, plays so that the passions of the mind are truly represented in his gestures. Betterton is supposed to have said that "the Stage ought to be the *Seat of Passion* in its various Kinds, and therefore the *Actors* ought to be thoroughly acquainted with the whole Nature of the Affections, and Habits of Mind, or else they will never be able to express them justly in their Looks and Gestures, as well as in the Tone of their Voice, and Manner of Utterance."[16] Steele in *Tatler* 201 goes further in advising the actor: "In the General I observed to him, That tho' Action was his Business, the Way to that Action was not to study Gesture, for the Behaviour would follow the Sentiments of the Mind . . . and if the Actor is well possessed of the Nature of his Part, a proper Action will necessarily follow." The actor should feel in himself the passions he represents, entering into the role in order to conform to its outward signatures.

As in poetry and painting, Horace's maxim—

> We weep and laugh as we see others do,
> He only makes me sad, who shews the way,
> And first is sad himself . . .
> . . . .
> For Nature forms and softens us within,
> And writes our Fortune's changes in our Face[17]

—becomes a rudimentary principle of empathy. Thus while the stage is inherently a place of pretense and illusion, it is also a source of true sentiment felt equally in the actor and audience, and therefore a model of true social community. "*Comedy,*" Rapin had said, "is as it should be, when the Spectator believes himself really in the company of such persons as he has represented, and takes himself to be in a Family whilst he is at the Theatre."[18] The impression, moreover, of real presence is not limited to comedy. In one of *The Spectator*'s series of essays on Ambrose Philips's *Distrest Mother,* Mr. Spectator has gone to a rehearsal of the play, and finds, to his own gratification, an expression of true feeling in the actors themselves: "It was a most exquisite Pleasure to me, to observe real Tears drop from the Eyes of those who had long made it their Profession to dissemble Affliction; and the Player who read, frequently throw down the Book, till he had given Vent to the Humanity which rose in him at some irresistible Touches of the imagined Sorrow" (No. 290).[19]

Although the puffery for *The Distrest Mother* may say little for Steele's critical integrity, such a passage is an excellent illustration of the structures of perception implied in the theater. Thus, while Steele in No. 370 appeals to the traditional defense of the theater—that it laughs us out of our follies or raises in us "a thorough Detestation" of more intractable vices—he adds a characteristically spectatorial defense: the theater is an education in sensibility. It not only presents, as Steele urges, examples of the good man, but, particularly in the intimacy of the English theater, teaches the audience to recognize movements of feeling in response to the successive actions on the stage. He describes the physical grace of an actress as a succession of postures, each of which will raise an appropriate reaction:

An amiable Modesty in one Aspect of a Dancer, an assumed Confidence in another, a sudden Joy in another, a falling off with an Impatience of being beheld, a Return towards the Audience with an unsteady Resolution to approach them, and a well-acted Sollicitude to please, would revive in the Company all the fine Touches of Mind raised in observing all the Objects of Affection or Passion they had before beheld. Such elegant Entertainments as these, would polish the Town into Judgment in their Gratifications; and Delicacy in Pleasure is the first Step People of Condition take in Reformation from Vice.

Reformation from vice may be the ultimate justification for theatrical excellence, but the process by which it takes place is what is important here: the theater is a refinement in sensibility, a refinement achieved through the play of gesture.[20]

Gestures and Signs

Each of *The Spectator*'s three ways of representing gesture (by analogy to physiognomy, painting, and the theater) reveals different assumptions about the way in which signs get their meanings, different notions about how we can read gestures as signs of character. Each also carries ethical implications in *The Spectator*.

In physiognomy there is a one-to-one link between sign and meaning ("an Upper-Lip covered with Snuff denotes a Coffee-house Statesman"). The meanings of gestures can, therefore, be transcribed into some kind of external catalogue of meanings, such as Le Brun's handbook (a lexicon) so that someone sufficiently familiar with the catalogue and sufficiently observant can readily translate from a sign to its meaning. But this is overly simple. This notion of meaning does violence to the complex ways in which signs obtain meaning and to the complex ways in which people manifest themselves. Instead, an observer must interpret a gesture according to the circumstances in which it appears (a sign must be seen according to its context), and he must respond to the gesture with a degree of sympathy which will allow him access to the actor's inward character (a sign must be seen according to some kind of inner meaning hidden behind the sign).

If an observer examines a gesture according to the circumstances in which it occurs, he needs to analyze the gestures that surround it, and he needs to analyze the system of social values that are implicit within the gesture. Ultimately, he has to analyze the whole society of which that gesture forms a part. Ethically, this means that he must see the gesture as an expression of social values and as a response to social forces that are often external to the actor but that influence his performances and his concept of himself. In practice, this means that the perception of gesture is not translated into a word (an item chosen from the lexicon), but into an essay that begins to explain the complex circumstances surrounding the gesture. In a theory of signs, this means that we do not find the meaning by examining the form of the sign itself, but by looking at its context: an observer is constantly drawn out away from the sign to ever-expanding circles of context that contribute to his understanding of it.

Examining the gesture according to the correlation between the inward actor and the outward role (as in the theater) leads in the opposite direction. Whereas judging a gesture according to its circumstances leads centrifugally outward, away from the sign, judging the gesture according to the disposition that motivates it leads centripetally inward, trying to penetrate to the core of meaning hidden within the gesture. This division of interior and exterior leads to a crucial division in *The Spectator*'s social ethics. A disjunction between sign and reality, where the gesture does not correspond to inward character, leads to a realm of affectation, as can be seen in the polite nods and giggles of the wit and beauty in No. 38. (In such cases, the gesture is derived only from other gestures, and such people "move a knowing Eye no more than the Portraitures of insignificant People by ordinary Painters, which are but Pictures of Pictures"—No. 4.) Where the gesture corresponds with inward character, we have a realm of sincerity which is, ideally, a presentation of the natural self. But as an observer tries to penetrate to the inner meaning of the sign (the inner meaning of the gesture), he finds that meaning within himself, in his inward responsiveness. So, as Mr. Spectator contemplates the condition of an envious man, for example, he feels in himself a "secret Sorrow." Ultimately, *The Spectator*'s image of an ideal society depends on a doubling or symmetry of inward meanings, just as the ideal form of reading is based on a symmetry of responses, where the observer's willingness to penetrate into the meaning of a gesture raises in him the same feelings as those which motivate it.

The Spectator's interpretation of gesture moves away from a correspondence theory of meaning (one sign equals one meaning) toward a theory of interpretation based on the double nature of the sign. *The*

Spectator marks a transition away from the implicit physiognomy of conduct books and character sketches, where the meaning of a sign may be found in some kind of external catalogue of meanings, toward a more complex, more novelistic reading of social performances whereby the meaning of a sign must be read according to its context, and toward a theory of sentiment where the meaning of the sign resides in the observer's responses.

SOCIAL JUDGMENT

In addition to these arts of gesture, the French conduct tradition of the seventeenth century forms an antecedent for *The Spectator*'s perception of gesture. Like the other arts, the arts of conduct share analogous structures with *The Spectator*. The French writers introduce into the analysis of gesture a system of dualisms which is carried over into *The Spectator*, although there is a crucial difference between the mechanisms of gesture that the conduct writers describe and the psychology of gesture in *The Spectator*. As we will see later in this section, *The Spectator*'s psychology of gesture makes inward sentiment a foundation for social cohesiveness.

The French conduct writers, among them La Bruyère, the Abbé Bellegarde, and Antoine de Courtin, drew generously from Cicero's portrait of the *honestus vir (l'honnête homme)* and from Descartes's physiology, and turned the signatures of character into a proto-behaviorism. Using Descartes's revealing metaphor, Bellegarde observes in his *Reflexions upon the Politeness of Manners* that "there's so great a Correspondence betwixt those Springs that move the Heart, and those that move the Countenance; that we may judge by this outward Dial-plate, how the Clock-work goes in the Soul."[21] The various forms of behavior, in the hands of the conduct writers, can suffer through intricate distinctions recognizable only to the most polite sensibilities, but, following from the correspondence of body and mind, the conduct writers distinguish two major modes of behavior— affectation, which is a disjunction between behavior and character, and politeness or modesty, which is their ideal union. "Affectation," Bellegarde writes, "is *the falsification of the whole Person, which deviates from all that is Natural, whereby it might please to put on an ascititious Ayre, wherewithal to become Ridiculous. . . .* People corrupted with this

Vice, have nothing natural in their way of Talking, Walking, Dressing, turning their Eyes or Head, these are Motions unknown to other Men" (*Reflexions upon Ridicule*, p. 58); an affected person "seems to be acted with Wheels and Pullies like a Machine; 'tis a Piece of Clockwork" (*Ridicule*, pp. 59–60). Modesty, like affectation, is "diffus'd thro' all our Words and Actions"; "this Virtue," however, "consists not merely in Surface and Exterior, but must have its Principle in the Soul, as being the Product of an accomplish'd Mind, centring on it self, and Master of its Thoughts and Words" (*Politeness*, p. 2). (Cicero had chosen to illustrate this same contrast through the decorum of the theater: "For all People hate the affected Motions and Carriage of those, who would be taken as Masters of a gentile Air; and your Actors on the Stage have a great many Foolish impertinent Gestures, which are very displeasing and offensive to the Spectators; and in each of these kinds what is simple and unaffected, is always best lik'd of and approv'd by the World.")[22]

In *The Spectator* the representation of character has radically changed from that of the conduct books. For Bellegarde there is no ground of society except in the counterpoint of postures. Although he may speak of modesty as residing in the self-possessed mind, Bellegarde belies this assertion in the descriptions he actually gives of polite behavior, which conform more closely to a further definition of politeness: through "a sincere Desire of pleasing," the polite man "puts on all Appearances, and transforms himself into all Shapes, the better to gain his Point" (*Politeness*, p. 2). A person's social existence becomes a succession of motions meant to influence others, motions which are a commercial display of one's talents intended to "purchase the Esteem and Affection of Men" (*Politeness*, p. 39). For *The Spectator*, the ground of society exists in the private movements of consciousness. Social life includes complex processes of self-reflection and perceptual sensitivity, both of them indispensable parts of social life.

The difference may be illustrated in a detail. Bellegarde's Damon prefigures almost literally Steele's Cinna from *Spectator* 206:

> *Damon* can't be denied to have Wit, and fine Qualities; but the Fault is, he knows it too well. He is full of it on all Occasions; and is his own Panegyrist, where others will not be at the Pains to praise him. He has a wonderful Faculty for Poetry; but he stuns all that come near him, with the Recital of his Verses. He shews how he relishes them himself, when he reads them, and every Word puts him into an Extasy: But the Plea-

sure he takes, hinders that of others; and the Applauses he bestows on himself, excuses them from the Trouble of applauding him. That which would make him courted, if he made a good Use of it, is the Cause of his being shunn'd as an impertinent Scribbler. (*Politeness*, pp. 39–40).[23]

There is no one living would deny *Cinna* the Applause of an agreeable and facetious Wit; or could possibly pretend that there is not something inimitably unforced and diverting in his Manner of delivering all his Sentiments in Conversation, if he were able to conceal the strong Desire of Applause which he betrays in every Syllable he utters. But they who converse with him, see that all the Civilities they could do to him, or the kind things they could say to him, would fall short of what he expects; and therefore instead of shewing him the Esteem they have for his Merit, their Reflexions turn only upon that they observe he has of it himself.

Bellegarde's passage remains entirely on the level of observed behavior (Damon's victims physically turn away—"*on le fuit comme un importun*"); Steele's passage turns from observable manners to the listeners' reflections—reflections, moreover, about Cinna's concept of himself.

Steele shows the social world to be a continual process of acting, observing, and evaluating, an intricate process of measuring other people according to their behavior and adjusting our responses to them. For example:

Orbicilla is the kindest poor thing in the Town, but the most blushing Creature living. . . . If she had more Confidence, and never did any thing which ought to stain her Cheeks, would she not be much more modest without that ambiguous Suffusion which is the Livery both of Guilt and Innocence? Modesty consists in being conscious of no Ill, and not in being ashamed of having done it. When People go upon any other Foundation than the Truth of their own Hearts for the Conduct of their Actions, it lies in the Power of scandalous Tongues to carry the World before them, and make the rest of Mankind fall in with the Ill for Fear of Reproach. (No. 390)

As intricate as these process of social evaluation may be, *The Spectator* retains the conduct writers' division between affectation and politeness and their sense of the social world as a system of behavioral exchanges, with the addition of its own conceptualism. *The Spectator* is concerned not only with the outward forms of manners, but also with the forms of mind which are implied by them; it is concerned with an actor's behavior not only as it is directed outward toward others, but also as it is a measure of his image of himself. All forms of social behavior are mirrors: our gestures reveal our self-images, as reflected in our reactions toward other people. The processes of social response become a system of mirrors, a system of self-reflections. The problem in moral evaluation is to understand to what extent these mirrors are accurate reflections or distortions of the self.[24]

In *Spectator* 38 Steele shows "meer Beauty" and "meer Wit" (the phrase is from No. 172) to be an extravagance of behavior running to rarefied absurdity:

> A Late Conversation which I fell into, gave me an Opportunity of observing a great deal of Beauty in a very handsome Woman, and as much Wit in an ingenious Man, turned into Deformity in the one, and Absurdity in the other, by the meer Force of Affectation. The Fair One had something in her Person upon which her Thoughts were fixed, that she attempted to shew to Advantage in every Look, Word, and Gesture. The Gentleman was as diligent to do Justice to his fine Parts, as the Lady to her beauteous Form: You might see his Imagination on the Stretch to find out something uncommon, and what they call bright, to entertain her; while she writhed herself into as many different Postures to engage him. When she laugh'd, her Lips were to sever at a greater Distance than ordinary to shew her Teeth: Her Fan was to point to somewhat at a Distance, that in the Reach she may discover the Roundness of her Arm; then she is utterly mistaken in what she saw, falls back, smiles at her own Folly, and is so wholly discompos'd, that her Tucker is to be adjusted, her Bosom expos'd, and the whole Woman put into new Airs and Graces. While she was doing all this, the Gallant had Time to think of something very pleasant to say next to her.[25]

In a thoroughly familiar way, Steele shifts the grounds of the essay from the dramatized scene to an abstract reflection on affectation: "These unhappy Effects of Affectation, naturally led me to look into that strange State of Mind which so generally discolours the Behaviour of most People we meet with."

> Every Thought is attended with Consciousness and Representativeness; the Mind has nothing presented to it, but what is immediately followed by a Reflection or Conscience, which tells you whether that which was so presented is graceful or unbecoming. This Act of the Mind discovers it self in the Gesture, by a proper Behaviour in those

whose Consciousness goes no further than to direct them in the just Progress of their present Thought or Action; but betrays an Interruption in every second Thought, when the Consciousness is employ'd in too fondly approving a Man's own Conceptions; which sort of Consciousness is what we call Affectation.

Steele acknowledges that the idea of immediate "Consciousness and Representativeness" is borrowed from Thomas Burnet, but the application is entirely his own, including the suggestion that we immediately apprehend what is "graceful or unbecoming." Gesture reveals movement of thought, particularly movement of thought with respect to ourselves: affectation, while being a mannerism, is a particular kind of self-reflection. The affected person suffers an unwitting self-dissociation. He looks upon himself as an object and measures this removed self against external standards, against what he takes to be the approval of other people. His gestures, then, are vacant. They are mechanical imitations of social fashions, performed only to display the external qualities of wit, beauty, or wealth. Because they are dissociated from the true resources of character, they are incongruous and ridiculous. Thus, the studied poses of affectation undergo a comic metamorphosis in *The Spectator* by which they "turn into" an absurd range of social intercourse, as beauty and wit in No. 38 "turn into" deformity. This is not the bemused comedy through which Mr. Spectator sees his own ridiculousness, but a critical comedy which makes disguised nonsense into patent nonsense.

This is a favorite comic mode, especially for Addison. Obviously, Steele does not forego comedy or satire, but he writes more conventional and often sentimental character sketches, and he tends to argue more strictly than Addison for distinctions between proper and improper behavior. Steele's dualisms are important to *The Spectator*'s educational purpose, as we will see, but Addison is readier to play with *The Spectator*'s program, as when a serious paper on Sappho (No. 223) turns a week later into a bill of mortality from Lover's Leap (No. 227), and he is readier to transform manners into a fabulous artifice, as in his papers on valetudinarians, party-patches, the anatomy of female orators, the dissections of a beau's head and coquette's heart, and the history of pin money. Through a *reductio ad absurdum* (Addison's comedy is above all rational comedy), social pretensions are transformed into a manipulation of vacant symbols. His insistence that the customs he satirizes are not "Fantastick Conceits of my own"

(No. 435) only reinforces their basis in social fictions. In No. 102, for example, *The Spectator* receives a letter from a man purporting to instruct young ladies in the use of a fan, to replace the expressions with studied exercises. Addison notes by way of a preface that "I do not know whether to call the following Letter a Satyr upon Coquets, or a Representation of their several fantastical Accomplishments, or what other Title to give it." "There is the angry Flutter, the modest Flutter, the timorous Flutter, the confused Flutter, the merry Flutter, and the amorous Flutter. Not to be tedious, there is scarce any Emotion in the Mind which does not produce a suitable Agitation in the Fan; insomuch, that if I only see the Fan of a disciplin'd Lady, I know very well whether she laughs, frowns, or blushes." Such signatures of the fan are to be answered by elegant gentlemen with appropriate snaps of their snuff boxes.

In No. 15 Addison describes a woman seduced not by a man but by an embroidered coat—"A Pair of fringed Gloves may be her Ruin." Eustace Budgell describes an automaton, a necessity in time of war, which imports not only the latest fashions but also "the various Leanings and Bendings of the Head, the Risings of the Bosome, the Curtesy and Recovery, the genteel Trip, and the Agreeable Jet, as they are now practised at the Court of *France*" (No. 277).[26] On one occasion Steele brings about an almost metaphysical collision of person and persona in the character of a Pict, startled with one half of her face painted and the other in its natural condition. "The Muscles of a real Face," he reminds us, "sometimes swell with soft Passion, sudden Surprize, and are flushed with agreeable Confusions, according as the Objects before them, or the Ideas presented to them, affect their Imagination. But the *Picts* behold all things with the same Air, whether they are Joyful or Sad; The same fix'd Insensibility appears upon all Occasions" (No. 41). Will Honeycomb has told Mr. Spectator of once interrupting a Pict while she was applying "that Complexion, for which he had so long languished": "The *Pict* stood before him in the utmost Confusion, with the prettiest Smirk imaginable on the finish'd side of her Face, pale as Ashes on the other."[27]

Although affectation can be reduced through the logic of comedy to mere physical mechanism, affectation begins with that ignorance of the self described by Steele, the subordination of self to external standards of behavior. Affectation is yet more extrinsic because it is imposed from without. In one paper on the theater, Steele laments the suppression of "the Innocent or Unaffected" in the audience: "You may sometimes see one of these sensibly touched with a well wrought Incident; but then she is immediately so impertinently observed by the Men, and frowned at by some insensible Superiour of her own Sex, that she is ashamed, and loses the Enjoyment of the most laudable Concern, Pity. Thus the whole Audience is afraid of letting fall a Tear, and shun as a Weakness the best and worthiest Part of our Sense" (No. 208). Social coercion through the pressures of fashion, money, or parental insistence is one of Steele's more common topics. Education, particularly, is a medium of coercion.

In No. 66 Steele concentrates on the education of women. This essay also illustrates the balance of familiar address and controlled discourse which together make up *The Spectator*'s own form of education. A letter from Celimene complains about her "young Country Kinswoman":

> Dear Mr. SPECTATOR, help me to make her comprehend the visible Graces of Speech, and the dumb Eloquence of Motion; for she is at present a perfect Stranger to both. She knows no Way to express her self but by her Tongue, and that always to signify her Meaning. Her Eyes serve her yet only to see with, and she is utterly a Forreigner to the Language of Looks and Glances. In this I fancy you could help her better than any Body.

Our amusement is spontaneous. Gesture is a matter of social presence, communication, and taste, and Celimene misunderstands completely. Steele, however, takes the letter as an occasion to discuss a girl's education:

> When a Girl is safely brought from her Nurse, before she is capable of forming one simple Notion of any thing in Life, she is delivered to the Hands of her Dancing-Master; and with a Collar round her Neck, the pretty wild thing is taught a fantastical Gravity of Behaviour, and forced to a particular Way of holding her Head, heaving her Breast, and moving with her whole Body; and all this under Pain of never having an Husband, if she steps, looks, or moves awry. This gives the young Lady wonderful Workings of Imagination, what is to pass between her and this Husband that she is every Moment told of, and for whom she seems to be educated. Thus her Fancy is engaged to turn all her Endeavours to the Ornament of her Person, as what must determine her Good and Ill in this Life; and she naturally thinks, if she is tall enough she is wise enough for any thing for which her Education makes her

think she is designed. To make her an agreable Person is the main Purpose of Her Parents; to that is all their Cost, to that all their Care directed; and from this general Folly of Parents we owe our present numerous Race of Coquets.

Throughout the passage education is described as coercion absorbing all energies in a grotesque pursuit of false values. The expected conduct for a woman becomes "a particular Way of holding her Head, heaving her Breast, and moving with her whole Body," the product of "wonderful Workings of Imagination," "Fancy," and "this general Folly of Parents."

This central passage from No. 66 illustrates one facet of *The Spectator*'s rhetoric, the system of dualisms that attempts to measure or weigh moral attitudes.[28] Addison does use these techniques, but we find them most commonly in Steele's work as he balances opposing spheres of behavior. Such dualisms assign new values to words within these dualisms in order to present a new definition of beauty.

The rhetoric of this essay is also typical in that it disengages the reader from the moral argument and returns him to his own arena of experience. Returning to Celimene's letter, Steele adopts a personal voice which admits that "these Reflections puzzle me"; "sure there is a middle Way to be followed; the Management of a young Lady's Person is not to be overlooked, but the Erudition of her Mind is much more to be regarded." The advice to follow moderation is not unexpected. It takes its character, however, from the fact that it is spoken through the "I" of the spectator rather than through the impersonal voice of the main body of the paragraph. The reader is moved outside of the moral lesson back into a realm of social communication.

The essay as a whole ends with an idealized portrait, one of the abstract characters common in *The Spectator* as a way of bringing moral reflections back into the world of manners: "*Cleomira* dances with all the Elegance of Motion imaginable; but her Eyes are so chastised with the Simplicity and Innocence of her Thoughts, that she raises in her Beholders Admiration and good Will, but no loose Hope or wild Imagination. The true Art in this Case is, To make the Mind and Body improve together; and if possible, to make Gesture follow Thought, and not let Thought be employed upon Gesture."

The Spectator's positive exempla and its insistent rhetoric of evaluation are, of course, a counter-education, an attempt to realign a universe of values. Occasionally we may see a character in transition from one side of the division to the other. No. 306, for instance, begins with a letter from Parthenissa, who has been disfigured by the smallpox and who tries to explain her attitudes toward herself: "It goes to the very Soul of me to speak what I really think of my Face; and tho I think I did not over-rate my Beauty while I had it, it has extremely advanced in its Value with me now it is lost." The opposition of possession and loss, of greater and lesser is repeated with appropriate variations in Mr. Spectator's reply: "If *Parthenissa* can now possess her own Mind, and think as little of her Beauty as she ought to have done when she had it, there will be no great Diminution of her Charms; and if she was formerly affected too much with them, an easy Behaviour will more than make up for the Loss of them"; "Good-Nature will always supply the Absence of Beauty, but Beauty cannot long supply the Absence of Good-Nature." The paper as a whole aligns terms on one side or the other of this division, generating a pattern of associations where possession of mind, easy behavior, cheerfulness, agreeability, and good nature are contained in a single redefinition of beauty.

The positive exemplum for this paper is a more humble and more immediate version of Cleomira:

> The fondest Lover I know, said to me one Day in a Crowd of Women at an Entertainment of Musick, You have often heard me talk of my Beloved; That Woman there, continued he, smiling when he had fixed my Eye, is her very Picture. The Lady he showed me was by much the least remarkable for Beauty of any in the whole Assembly; but having my Curiosity extremely raised, I could not keep my Eyes off of her. Her Eyes at last met mine, and with a sudden Surprize she looked round her to see who near her was remarkably handsome that I was gazing at. This little Act explain'd the Secret: She did not understand her self for the Object of Love, and therefore she was so. The Lover is a very honest plain Man; and what charmed him was a Person that goes along with him in the Cares and Joys of Life, not taken up with her self, but sincerely attentive with a ready and chearful Mind to accompany him in either.

With admirable economy, Steele sketches a scene in which every detail implies a social whole. The scene is based on two movements we have seen before in the spectator's attention to gesture: the first isolates the gesture within its context; the second explains that gesture as a reflection of mind. From out of the "Crowd of Women," with its suggestion of conspicuous display, Steele isolates a nuclear triangle based on acts of seeing: "smiling when he had fixed my Eye," "he showed me," "I could not keep my Eyes off of her," "Her Eyes at last met mine." The woman is isolated by the lover's designation, by Mr. Spectator's special attention, and by her own action as she "looked round her to see who near her was remarkably handsome." As she is isolated, a small community is created out of the intimacy of friendship, sympathetic interest, and love. That she is modest (the word *modest* being a shadowy approximation to the dynamics of the scene) and that he is "a very honest plain Man" are mutual recommendations describing a symmetrical balance, a self-enclosed emotional unit.

The circumstances surrounding the woman's action thus form a setting, or frame, for the gesture. Seen by itself, the gesture is access to the woman's character; seen with respect to those gestures which surround it, it opens out a system of values. One accompanying gesture is the lover's act of pointing out the woman who shares the qualities of the woman he loves. Other accompanying gestures are suggested by the crowd of women, with their expected vanity. By an opposition between her gesture and the gestures that surround her, her "little Act" participates in a redefinition of beauty based on self-reflection. Just as the self-concept of the beloved woman is apparent in the "little Act," so the self-importance of beauties is revealed in their gestures. Again, it leads to the absurd: "An apparent Desire of Admiration, a Reflexion upon their own Merit, and a precious Behaviour in their general Conduct, are almost inseparable Accidents in Beauties"; "They pray at publick Devotions as they are Beauties; they converse on ordinary Occasions as they are Beauties. Ask *Bellinda* what it is a Clock, and she is at a Stand whether so great a Beauty should answer you."

The polarities in No. 306 are part of a systematic redefinition of beauty that we have seen in No. 66 and that extends throughout *The Spectator.* The mechanics of this redefinition go back to the distinction Addison makes in No. 86 between the lines and the air of the face. Following the lines of his Socratic example, Addison establishes the perception of gesture on a new foundation:

I think nothing can be more glorious, than for a Man to give the Lie to his Face, and to be an honest, just, good-natured Man, in spite of all those Marks and Signatures which Nature seems to have set upon him for the Contrary. This very often happens among those, who instead of being exasperated by their own Looks, or envying the Looks of others, apply themselves entirely to the cultivating of their Minds, and getting those Beauties which are more lasting and more ornamental. I have seen many an amiable Piece of Deformity, and have observed a certain Chearfulness in as bad a System of Features as ever was clap'd together, which hath appeared more lovely than all the blooming Charms of an insolent Beauty.

What the spectator sees in the physical person is not a set of features, but a close connection between one's self-concept, physical appearance, and social presence. The connection is made more explicit when Steele takes up the topic in *Spectator* 87. He emphasizes that an "unconcerned Behaviour" derives from one's concept of one's self and emphasizes its social benefits: "Diffidence and Presumption, upon account of Our Persons, are equally Faults; and both arise from the want of knowing, or rather endeavouring to know, our selves, and for what we ought to be valued or neglected"; "It has therefore been generally my Choice to mix with chearful Ugly Creatures, rather than Gentlemen who are Graceful enough to omit or do what they please; or Beauties who have Charms enough to do and say what would be disobliging in any but themselves."

If, as *The Spectator* essayists assume, false values are learned through false education, then they can be corrected through the careful discrimination of values represented in *The Spectator*'s style. A corrective such as Cleomira or the principles she represents is always held explicitly as a model to be followed, carefully balanced against the corresponding folly. The Pict in No. 41 is ameliorated by the figure of Lindamira, who is punished sufficiently simply in "chusing to be the worst Piece of Art extant, instead of the Masterpiece of Nature"; "In the mean time, as a Pattern for improving their Charms, let the Sex study the agreeable *Statira*. Her Features are enlivened with the Chearfulness of her Mind, and good Humour gives an Alacrity to her Eyes. She is Graceful without Affecting an Air, and Unconcerned without appearing Careless. Her having no manner of Art in her Mind, makes her want none in her Person." No. 38 includes a more abstract recommendation coming to the same point. Steele describes how "Persons, Dress, and bodily Deportment" will "naturally be winning and attractive if we think not of them": "when our Consciousness turns upon the main Design of Life, and our Thoughts are employ'd upon the chief Purpose either in Business or Pleasure, we shall never betray an Affectation, for we cannot be guilty of it"; "It is only from a thorough Disregard to himself in such Particulars, that a Man can act with a laudable Sufficiency: His Heart is fix'd upon one Point in view; and he commits no Errours, because he thinks nothing an Errour but what deviates from that Intention."

The Unity of Retirement

These recommendations reflect the awareness of gesture that is part of *The Spectator*'s social world, but they distinguish from affectation a mode of consciousness that is not concerned with gesture at all, but with what is graceful and becoming in thought. In No. 75 Steele represents Mr. Spectator returning home to reflect on what it is to be a fine gentleman after being ridiculed about "the Air, the Height, the Face, the Gesture of him who could pretend to Judge so arrogantly of Gallantry": "[I] could not help revolving that Subject in my Thoughts, and setling, as it were, an Idea of that Character in my own Imagination." He rejects the fashionable Vocifer who "is Loud, Haughty, Gentle, Soft, Lewd, and Obsequious by turns, just as a little Understanding and great Impudence prompt him at the present Moment" ("every Reader will have in his Eye from his own Observation" many such fashionable gallants), and advances instead the figure of Ignotus: "The Change of Persons or Things around him do not at all alter his Situation, but he looks disinterested in the Occurences with which others are distracted, because the greatest purpose of his Life is to maintain an Indifference both to it and all its Enjoyments." In part, the ideal state of life is a type of retirement, a harmony and completeness in one's self, isolated from and indifferent to the demands of the public world. But this form of retirement returns to society, becoming apparent in an easy and natural grace. In the figure of Ignotus, retired indifference becomes part of those manners "exposed to common Observation": "Being firmly Established in all Matters of Importance, that certain Inattention which makes Mens Actions look easie, appears in him with greater Beauty: By a thorough Contempt of little Excellencies, he is perfectly Master of them"; "It is thus with the State of the Mind; he that governs his Thoughts with the everlasting Rules of Reason and Sense, must have something so inexpressibly Graceful in his Words and Actions, that every Circumstance must become him." In this way, the psychology of retirement returns to the social world; the true values of the mind afford social graces; judgment and reflection are manifested in manners and discourse. In a figure like Ignotus, then, we find a merger of several patterns: the retired man and the agreeable man coalesce; the public and the private come together in an ideal form of beauty.

Steele in these essays has adapted and modified the traditional forms of retirement, as seen in Cowley. *The Spectator*'s retirement is living "in the World, and out of it, at the same time." "Let us not stand upon a Formal taking of Leave," Steele writes, "but wean our selves from them [the allurements of the world], while we are in the midst of them" (No. 27). In No. 264 he cautions against "an Affectation to love the Pleasure of Solitude," and, in a distinctively spectatorial way, suggests that retirement is not an isolation but an accommodation of our individual and singular lives to the graces of social life:

> But when we consider the World it self, and how few there are capable of a religious, learned, or philosophick Solitude, we shall be apt to change a Regard to that sort of Solitude, for being a little singular in enjoying Time after the Way a Man himself likes best in the World, without going so far as wholly to withdraw from it. I have often observed, there is not a Man breathing who does not differ from all other Men, as much in the Sentiments of his Mind, as the Features of his Face. The Felicity is, when any one is so happy as to find out and follow what is the proper bent of his Genius, and turn all his Endeavours to exert himself according as that prompts him.

Taken a step further, this language of retirement allows Steele to describe a pervasive tolerance of the idiosyncrasies of others (that tolerance that "gives to every Character of Life its due Regards"), and allows him to admonish his readers to follow the personal harmonies of their own lives:

> Instead of going out of our own complectional Nature into that of others, 'twere a better and more laudable Industry to improve our own, and instead of a miserable Copy become a good Original; for there is no Temper, no Disposition so rude and untractable, but may in its own peculiar Cast and Turn be brought to some agreeable Use in Conversation, or in the Affairs of Life. A Person of a rougher Deportment, and less tied up to the usual Ceremonies of Behaviour, will, like *Manly* in

the Play, please by the Grace which Nature gives to every Action wherein she is complied with. (No. 238)

The Structures of Social Life

These patterns of description, woven throughout *The Spectator*, yield a definite model of social life. The first structure in this model is the dichotomy between outside and inside, with the corresponding distinction between affectation and politeness. This structure may be seen with special clarity in *Spectator* 172 and *Spectator* 280, where Steele makes a seemingly absolute division of social types:

> The Desire of Pleasing makes a Man agreeable or unwelcome to those with whom he converses, according to the Motive from which that Inclination appears to flow. If your Concern for pleasing others arises from innate Benevolence, it never fails of Success; if from a Vanity to excell, its Disappointment is no less certain. What we call an agreeable Man, is he who is endowed with that natural Bent to do acceptable things, from a Delight he takes in them meerly as such; and the Affectation of that Character is what constitutes a Fop. Under these Leaders one may draw up all those who make any Manner of Figure.

These are the dichotomies on which all of *The Spectator*'s rhetoric stands. But this paragraph from No. 280 also takes us a step toward understanding a second structure defining *The Spectator*'s model of social life: this is the ideal symmetry between the behavior of the actor and the responses of an observer. Steele's definition of the agreeable man (and it is a definition rather than a description—Steele is weaving a fabric of equivalent ideas) can be transcribed this way: the agreeable man is one who takes pleasure in giving pleasure; there is a symmetry between the emotions of the actor and the emotions of the observer.[29] This symmetry can be described further. The actor's "Talent of Pleasing" derives from "a Delicacy of Sentiment," and, although it is not made explicit here (as it is in No. 386), the pleasure the observer feels in the presence of the agreeable man derives from a similar delicacy of sentiment. (This may be compared to the "refinement of Sensibility" through which the stage action in the theater raises corresponding emotions in the audience.) Since this is a symmetrical pattern, the relationship between the agreeable man and the observer can be inverted: the agreeable man pleases because he is pleased by others—"the true Art of being agreeable in Company, (but there can be no such thing as Art in it,) is to appear well pleased with those you are engaged with"; "A Man must be sincerely pleased to become Pleasure" (No. 386).

It is precisely this balance between giving and receiving pleasure that allows society to absorb all types of characters: "It is certainly a very happy Temper," Steele writes, "to be able to live with all Kinds of Dispositions, because it argues a Mind that lies open to receive what is pleasing to others, and not obstinately bent on any Particularity of its own"; "The Companion who is formed for such by Nature, gives to every Character of Life its due Regards, and is ready to account for their Imperfections, and receive their accomplishments as if they were his own" (No. 386). In contrast to the conflict involved in "a Vanity to excell," social pleasure is bounded by symmetrical responses, by a harmonious correspondence between minds which supports both the pleasure the observer feels in the presence of the agreeable man and the pleasure the agreeable man feels in himself.

This principle of symmetry defines three levels of social cohesion. The greatest discrepancy between actor and observer comes when the actor performs only to gain the approval of the crowd; the two correspond most nearly in the testimony of conscience, where actor and observer are the same. At the third, intermediate level, at the level of social life, the actor and observer correspond because their "inward dispositions" correspond.

These levels of cohesiveness are illustrated in No. 172. After distinguishing the outward behavior of an actor from his inward motives, and distinguishing a false response in an observer which honors outward manners from a true response which honors inward character, Steele considers another traditional and perplexing problem, that of the great man. At this point he shifts from considering how we assess the characters of others to considering how we can assess our own, contrasting the approval of the crowd with the approval of conscience:

> But those Men only are truly great, who place their Ambition rather in acquiring to themselves the Conscience of worthy Enterprizes, than in the Prospect of Glory which attends them.
>
> He only is a great Man who can neglect the Applause of the Multitude, and enjoy himself independent of its Favour. This is indeed an arduous Task; but it should comfort a glorious Spirit that it is the highest Step to which humane Nature can arrive. Triumph, Applause, Acclamation,

are dear to the Mind of Man; but it is still a more exquisite Delight to say to your self, you have done well, than to hear the whole humane Race pronounce you glorious, except you your self can join with them in your own Reflexions. A Mind thus equal and uniform may be deserted by little fashionable Admirers and Followers, but will ever be had in Reverence by Souls like it self.

As he recasts the division between fame and conscience, Steele touches on an underlying core of values, defining the "truly great" by aligning words within a dominant conceptual scheme. The "great Man" and "a Mind thus equal and uniform" become functional synonyms, interchangeable within the valuative syntax of these paragraphs. Like the retired man, the great man enjoys the "Conscience" of worthy enterprises. He is content in his judgment of himself. But the great man also enjoys the "reverence of souls like itself," and here Steele describes a symmetrical harmony of minds as the basis for social community. The retired man (content in the satisfactions of his own mind) and the agreeable man (who gives pleasure to minds like his own) are themselves "synonymous" within this basic model of social life. The retired man is the agreeable man, although retirement and agreeableness represent complementary aspects of social existence.

These structures are shown yet more schematically in the opening of No. 188, where the man who "is set rather to do Things laudable than to purchase Reputation" values only minds like his own: "Where there is that Sincerity as the Foundation of a good Name, the kind Opinion of virtuous Men will be an unsought but a necessary Consequence" (No. 188). This is why Steele can speak of "a Man of Spirit" as a retired figure disinterested in the world and say also that "A generous Mind is of all others the most sensible of Praise and Dispraise" (No. 238). The polarities of public and private are reconciled in an ideal symmetry: the good man values opinions that mirror his reflections of himself.

The two structures I have just outlined—the dichotomy between politeness and affectation, and the symmetry of social feelings—yield a cluster of related words created out of *The Spectator*'s rhetorical syntax. The original terms are "Nature" (within the structure of dichotomies) and "Pleasure" (within the structure of symmetries). George Berkeley, writing in *Guardian* 49, has absorbed Steele's and Addison's conceptual vocabulary from *The Spectator* and schematically sets out the oppositions implicit in the term *nature*: "*Natural Pleasures* I call those, which not depending on the Fashion and Caprice of any particular Age or Nation, are suited to Humane Nature in general, and were intended by Providence as Rewards for the using our Faculties agreeably to the Ends for which they were given us. *Fantastical Pleasures* are those which having no natural Fitness to delight our Minds, presuppose some particular Whim or Taste accidentally prevailing in a Sett of People, to which it is owing that they please."

Natural pleasures are free from ambition, from predatory love, and from covetousness (Steele's triad from No. 4). These false pleasures originate in a realm of symbols which are the products of imagination or chimera: attempts to win the admiration of others become lost in displays of wit or power or wealth; love becomes lost in flirtation and adornment; the self becomes lost in an infinite regress of imitations. It becomes lost in a bizarre world of artifice. Nature therefore entails retirement, because it is free from these false forms of self-display. But the retired self is also the source of pleasure, which is the key term in a second cycle of terms based on the symmetry of social feeling. Steele's model of an ideal society is based on a symmetrical mirroring of pleasure in the actor and in the observer, a pleasure apparent in the silent communication of gesture. (Steele's vision of society, for all its emphasis on reason and morality, is utilitarian at its root; it is a calculus of pleasure.) The man who lives according to his nature is cheerful, because he has all the resources of pleasure within himself; this cheerfulness becomes evident in good-nature and in a redefined form of beauty, because the disposition of the mind is visible in gesture; this beauty becomes the foundation for communal affection, of love, in those who can discern it. So, through this cycle of terms, society completes nature, and community completes retirement.

These structures of discourse, along with their special semantics, coalesce in Steele's portrait of the retired man in *Spectator* 206:

> There is a Call upon Mankind to value and esteem those who set a moderate Price upon their own Merit; and Self-denial is frequently attended with unexpected Blessings, which in the End abundantly recompence such Losses as the Modest seem to suffer in the ordinary Occurences of Life. The Curious tell us, a Determination in our Favour or to our Disadvantage is made upon our first Appearance, even before they know any thing of our Characters, but from the Intimations Men gather from our Aspect. A Man, they say, wears the Picture of his

Mind in his Countenance; and one Man's Eyes are Spectacles to his who looks at him to read his Heart. But tho' that Way of raising an Opinion of those we behold in Publick is very fallacious, certain it is, that those who by their Words and Actions take as much upon themselves as they can but barely demand in the strict Scrutiny of their Deserts, will find their Accompt lessen every Day. . . . It were therefore a just Rule to keep your Desires, your Words, and Actions, within the Regard you observe your Friends have for you. . . .

. . . But if there were no such Considerations as the good Effect which Self-Denial has upon the Sense of other Men towards us, it is of all Qualities the most desirable for the agreeable Disposition in which it places our own Minds. . . . He that is moderate in his Wishes from Reason and Choice . . . doubles all the Pleasures of his Life. The Air, the Season, a Sun-shine Day, or a fair Prospect, are Instances of Happiness; and that which he enjoys in common with all the World, (by his Exemption from the Enchantments with which all the World are bewitched) are to him uncommon Benefits and new Acquisitions. . . . He knows there is in such a Place an uninterrupted Walk; he can meet in such a Company an agreeable Conversation. He has no Emulation; he is no Man's Rival, but every Man's Well-wisher; can look at a prosperous Man, with a Pleasure in reflecting that he hopes he is as happy as himself; and has his Mind and his Fortune (as far as Prudence will allow) open to the Unhappy and to the Stranger.

Lucceius has Learning, Wit, Humour, Eloquence, but no ambitious Prospects to pursue with these Advantages; therefore to the ordinary World he is perhaps thought to want Spirit, but known among his Friends to have a Mind of the most consummate Greatness. He wants no Man's Admiration, is in no Need of Pomp. His Cloaths please him if they are fashionable and warm, his Companions are agreeable if they are civil and well-natured. There is with him no Occasion . . . in a Word, for any thing extraordinary to administer Delight to him. Want of Prejudice and Command of Appetite, are the Companions which make his Journey of Life so easy, that he in all Places meets with more Wit, more good Chear, and more Good-Humour, than is necessary to make him enjoy himself with Pleasure and Satisfaction.

The themes are familiar. This passage illustrates *The Spectator*'s attention to gesture, with its characteristic qualifications; it illustrates the distinction between modesty and self-display; it illustrates the circle of friendship with its intimate access to others' minds; and, moving further inward, it illustrates the satisfactions felt within one's self, the quiet possession of pleasure. This circle of retirement (which is also a circle of intimacy) is defined by a paradoxical inversion. The ordinary world exists outside the circle of intimacy. In the ordinary world, the retired man "is perhaps thought to want Spirit," although within the circle he is seen "to have a Mind of the most consummate Greatness." Yet the ordinary world requires extraordinary entertainments; it requires spectacle, show, and self-display. For the retired man (the great mind), those things held "in common with all the World" become "uncommon Benefits and new Acquisitions." The ordinary world requires extraordinary display; the extraordinary man is content with ordinary things. Finally, throughout the portrait, the retired man duplicates the position of the spectator, as it was defined seven months earlier, in *Spectator* 4. The world of commonplace things holds the attention and demands the reflections of the spectator, as well.

The place of the retired man in this system of values is important to *The Spectator*'s idea of time, as we shall see in the next chapter. And it is important, too, because Steele's language in No. 206 prefigures Addison's descriptions of the pleasures of the imagination in Nos. 411 and 412. Addison's descriptions of the imagination are not an isolated set of essays somehow dropped into *The Spectator*, something new and philosophical in the midst of transient reflections on manners. Instead, they grow out of the system of perceptions, the implicit epistemology which permeates *The Spectator*.

ESTHETIC JUDGMENT

Addison's essays on criticism and esthetics have received a good deal of critical attention, principally because Addison systematically formulates many of the tenets of eighteenth-century criticism, and, in formulating them, advances them. His *Spectator* essays on wit, genius, opera, tragedy, *Paradise Lost,* folk ballads, criticism, and imagination adopt neoclassical dualisms: art is to instruct and delight; it is the product of natural genius but may be learned through rules; it conforms to universal standards but also appeals to the taste of the age; it may be judged objectively but raises passions; taste is an educated sensibility but also an innate emotional responsiveness. In each instance Addison shifts the emphasis within these pairs away from traditional formalism toward a psychology of artistic creation and esthetic perception. Accordingly, Addison's essays on criticism, especially his papers on the Pleasures of the Imagination, are among the earliest attempts to give a systematic analysis of esthetic experience.[30]

For these reasons, Addison's papers on criticism have often, at least tacitly, been regarded as a separate collection of essays somehow inserted into *The Spectator*. Here, however, I am interested in these papers less as expositions of critical theory than as parts of *The Spectator* as a whole, because they share, first, rhetorical tactics and, second, psychological assumptions established throughout the series. Thus when Addison writes about tragedy that "I prefer a noble Sentiment that is depressed with homely Language, infinitely before a Vulgar one that is blown up with all the Sound and Energy of Expression" (No. 39) he reiterates the distinction between show and substance that is a staple principle of judgment in *The Spectator*'s essays on social behavior. When he says that a critic "ought to dwell rather upon Excellencies than Imperfections, to discover the concealed Beauties of a Writer, and communicate to the World such things as are worth their Observation" (No. 291), he echoes Steele's description of the agreeable man as one who discovers the concealed beauties of those with whom he converses.[31]

Wit, Genius, and the Dualities of Behavior

Addison's essays on Wit (Nos, 58–63) illustrate the rhetorical tactics that his papers on literary criticism share with the papers of social criticism. Addison is careful to announce in No. 58 that the series on wit has been prompted by his readers' attention to earlier papers on criticism, as gauged by his bookseller's sales records, and he is careful to announce that the series itself will be adjusted from day to day so that if readers find one paper "a little out of their Reach . . . they may assure themselves the next shall be much clearer." The whole undertaking is carefully adapted to his readers' interests.

Like his concern for his readers' reactions, Addison's opening formulas are also familiar from other *Spectator* essays. In examining wit, he sets out, as he has done before, to provide a correct definition of a word which has been misunderstood. He intends to enter "into the Bottom of the Matter," just as he had announced in No. 16 that he would "enter into the Passions of Mankind." Since he aims "to banish Vice and Ignorance out of the Territories of *Great Britain*," he "shall endeavour . . . to establish among us a Taste of polite Writing," in the way that he has aimed to recover his readers from "that desperate State of Vice and Folly into which the Age is fallen" (No. 10) through the balance of wit and morality. We learn in No. 61 that "The Seeds of Punning are in the Minds of all Men, and tho' they may be subdued by Reason, Reflection and good Sense, they will be very apt to shoot up in the greatest Genius, that is not broken and cultivated by the Rules of Art," just as "the Mind that lies fallow but a single Day, sprouts up in Follies that are only to be killed by a constant and assiduous Culture" (No. 10).

The reader who recognizes these formulas knows that the papers on wit are not a new departure, but an extension of an old design. In fact, the tone of No. 58 is the now-familiar combination of decorum ("I treat at large upon this Subject . . . in a Manner suitable to it") and self-mockery: "I dare promise my self, if my Readers will give me a Week's Attention, that this great City will be very much changed for the better by next *Saturday* Night." (We might remember "this great City inquiring Day by Day after these my Papers" from No. 10.)

With this last sentence we have been inducted into Addison's typical array of ironic possibilities: Mr. Spectator is partly amused at himself for his presumption, and partly amused at his readers because he knows they will not give these matters even a week's serious attention. Later, Addison's wit again turns for a moment against Mr. Spectator as he struggles to understand a piece of nonsense written in the form of an egg: "I would endeavour to hatch it, or, in more intelligible Language, to translate it into *English,* did not I find the Interpretation of it very difficult" (No. 58). Such a "hatching" is typical of Addison's ironic indirection: he does not condemn the egg, but shows Mr. Spectator struggling with it in a naive attempt to understand. Still, the comedy is not only at Mr. Spectator's expense. We have stepped into the world of satiric mechanisms where literalized metaphors (hatched eggs) dictate that form override substance. The next sentence takes us further into a reductive satire: "The Pair of Wings consist of twelve Verses, or rather Feathers." In poetical wigs made out of Bible verses, virtuosity (or pretentiousness) has turned into a vacant mechanism, literally an empty form: an "eminent Writing-Master" has "designed this Wig originally for King *William,* having disposed of the two Books of *Kings* in the two Forks of the Foretop; but that glorious

Monarch dying before the Wig was finished, there is a Space left in it for the Face of any one that has a mind to purchase it."

This icon of false wit leads an analysis in two directions. In one direction, it leads back to the world of social posturings, to the world of Budgell's mannequin or Steele's pict. In the second direction, it leads to Addison's definitions of true and false wit: "*true Wit* consists in the Resemblance of Ideas, and *false Wit* in the Resemblance of Words" (No. 62). False wit resides in exteriors, in letters, in syllables, in words, or in postures; that is, in the mannequin's wit: "Some carry the Notion of Wit so far, as to ascribe it even to external Mimickry; and to look upon a Man as an ingenious Person, that can resemble the Tone, Posture, or Face of another" (No. 62). Borrowing from Bouhours, Addison concludes with regard to true wit that "it is impossible for any Thought to be beautiful which is not just, and has not its Foundation in the Nature of things: . . . the Basis of all Wit is Truth; and . . . no Thought can be valuable, of which good Sense is not the Ground-work." We are not far at all from Celimine and Cleomira.

Addison uses four methods for defining wit, techniques he uses in other critical essays as well. The first method is analytic, separating true, false, and mixed wit. The second is historical, tracing the history of wit from classical through Gothic and modern times. The third applies the conventional categories of neoclassical criticism. Thus in wit "the first Race of Authors, who were the great Heroes in Writing, were destitute of all Rules and Arts of Criticism; and for that Reason, though they excel later Writers in Greatness of Genius, they fall short of them in Accuracy and Correctness" (No. 61).

Because he follows conventional categories of this type, Addison's papers on ballads and on *Paradise Lost* are among the most formulaic of his critical essays, adhering to the Aristotelian separation of action, character, sentiment, and language as categories for critical analysis. Addison's defense of these poems in the end, however, does not rest on their formal integrity within these categories but on their impact on the reader's sentiments: *Chevy Chase* deserves the respect of any sensitive reader "because the same Paintings of Nature which recommend it to the most ordinary Reader, will appear beautiful to the most refined" (No. 70); *Two Children in the Wood* "is a plain simple Copy of Nature, destitute of all the Helps and Ornaments of Art . . . and yet, because the Sentiments appear genuine and unaffected, they are able to move the Mind of the most polite Reader with inward Meltings of Humanity and Compassion" (No. 85). These papers on ballads continue the argument regarding taste that Addison had begun in the series on wit but take the argument a step further. They search for psychological universals that will explain both the origins and the impact of literary techniques. The poet of *Chevy Chase* has not been influenced by Virgil, but "he was directed . . . in general by the same Kind of Poetical Genius" (No. 74). Similarly, the ballad's popularity can be explained because "it is impossible that any thing should be universally tasted and approved by a Multitude, tho' they are only the Rabble of a Nation, which hath not in it some peculiar Aptness to please and gratify the Mind of Man" (No. 70).

This is the fourth of Addison's methods for defining wit—the search for psychological explanations. Addison contrasts his own definitions with Dryden's definition of wit as "a Propriety of Words and Thoughts adapted to the Subject" (No. 62). George Williamson has pointed out that Addison misquotes Dryden,[32] but the misquoting emphasizes the opposition between Addison's position and earlier perceptions of wit. For Dryden, according to Addison's misreading, wit can be tested by looking at the work by itself, by assessing the proportions between words and thoughts. For himself, Addison turns to Locke's definition of wit as *"lying most in the Assemblage of Ideas, and putting those together with Quickness and Variety, wherein can be found any Resemblance or Congruity thereby to make up pleasant Pictures and agreeable Visions in the Fancy"* (quoted in No. 62). Addison modifies this definition, as well, to further emphasize an affective psychology: "every Resemblance of Ideas is not that which we call Wit, unless it be such an one that gives *Delight* and *Surprize* to the Reader" (No. 62). Addison appeals beyond the formal qualities of the work to the mechanisms of the mind.

In general, Addison's essays on criticism move from specific issues to general principles of esthetic psychology, moving, for example, from *carmen figuratum* to the psychology of wit, or from the essays on wit to the essays on the pleasures of the imagination. The notion of assembling ideas into *"pleasant Pictures and agreeable Visions in the Fancy"* is crucial to this movement. Addison's essay on Genius, No. 160, is based on a distinction between natural genius ("that divine Impulse which raises the Mind above it self") and genius trained through art, a distinction that contrasts different ways in which writers assemble ideas. The results of these different types of genius are different types of "Pictures" or "Visions" for the reader: the one is "a whole Wilderness of noble Plants rising in a thousand beautiful Landskips"; the other "is the same rich Soil . . . laid out in Walks and Parterres, and cut into Shape and Beauty." In both cases, as Addison explains in No. 417, the artist retains vivid associations which he can rapidly assemble into images, but different styles can be explained according to different arrangements of ideas in the imagination.

Like the artist, the observer must also train his mind to assemble ideas rapidly and vividly. In No. 409, his last paper immediately preceding the series on the imagination, Addison presents an analysis of taste which, like his analysis of genius, follows traditional guidelines: "notwithstanding this Faculty must in some measure be born with us, there are several Methods for Cultivating and Improving it." As in the paper on genius, this distinction leads Addison to an affective psychology of art. Taste is *that Faculty of the Soul, which discerns the Beauties of an Author with Pleasure, and the Imperfections with Dislike.*" Thus a person can test his own taste by finding himself "delighted" by a passage or by finding "a Coldness and Indifference in his Thoughts." Or, he can train and channel his sensibilities, since he "either discovers new Beauties, or receives stronger Impressions from the Masterly Stroaks of a great Author every time he peruses him: Besides that he naturally wears himself into the same manner of Speaking and Thinking." A man of polite taste should be "affected" by the skill of one author differently than by that of another because he will discover for each author "the several Ways of thinking and expressing himself, which diversify him from all other Authors." Equally, each reader "forms several Reflections that are peculiar to his own manner of Thinking," because, as we learn in *Spectator* 416, of differences in readers' capacities for holding associated ideas: "We find one transported with a Passage, which another runs over with Coldness and Indifference, or finding the Representation extremely natural, where another can perceive nothing of Likeness and Conformity. This different Taste must proceed, either from the *Perfection of Imagination* in one more than in another, or from the *different Ideas* that several Readers affix to the same Words"— "the Fancy must be warm, to retain the Print of those Images it hath received from outward Objects; and the Judgment discerning, to know what Expressions are most proper to cloath and adorn them to the best Advantage."

As Lee Andrew Elioseff has pointed out, Addison's thinking about wit, genius, and the imagination arises out of a single set of psychological assumptions, indebted to Locke's notion that ideas can be assembled into pictures or visions in the fancy.[33] From this point of view, Addison's essays on wit, on ballads, on *Paradise Lost*, and on taste all illustrate how this esthetic psychology influences various issues in practical criticism. Taking No. 409 as a transition, these essays become one long series leading up to the papers on the pleasures of the imagination as a *terminus ad quem*. But we must remember that the papers on wit are the *terminus a quo*. In the final paragraph of No. 409, Addison reviews his earlier papers on criticism and describes each of them as an additional step advancing the argument he had begun in the papers on wit. "Our general Taste in *England*," he says in No. 409, "is for Epigram, turns of Wit, and forced Conceits," but "I have endeavoured in several of my Speculations to banish this *Gothic* Taste . . . and at the same time to shew wherein the nature of true Wit consists." All of the papers on criticism follow one another as a series devoted to this one enterprise. While the series may end in the psychology of the imagination, it begins by discriminating types of wit in the same way that Steele discriminates between forms of social behavior. Furthermore, the psychology of imagination, itself, is not very different from the psychology of social life, as can be seen in a second series of essays leading up to the papers on the pleasures of the imagination.

Pleasures of the Imagination
and the Pleasures of the Retired Man

Addison's essays on criticism and taste form a series of essays preparing for his papers on the imagination. But I have shown that the ideas in these essays cannot be seen fully unless they are seen in the context of *The Spectator*'s essays on the psychology of social life: Addison's argument in the essays on wit mirrors the argument of many papers on social behavior, and, as I hope to demonstrate in the next chapter, the process of assembling ideas in imagination is not only an

esthetic phenomenon for Addison but a fundamental way of organizing our experience in time.

Similarly, the papers on the pleasures of the imagination have analogues in other essays. Keeping this in mind, it is instructive to look at
another series of essays preceeding those on the imagination, Addison's three essays on cheerfulness, Nos. 381, 387, and 393. These
essays develop a psychology integrating social and esthetic experience. Together, the series on cheerfulness and the series on imagination form what might be called the intellectual backbone of *The Spectator*. Before I can give a full picture of cheerfulness, however, I need
to discuss a companion term, good-nature.

Good-nature and cheerfulness are complements, the first a public
benevolence and the second a private contentment. Both arise from
The Spectator's model of social life, with its metaphor of beauty and its
sense of the symmetry that pairs a person's inner disposition with his
effect on others. Together, as a balance of public and private, good-
nature and cheerfulness are at the center of *The Spectator*'s moral
system: "Virtue in general is of an amiable and lovely Nature," Addison writes in No. 243, and "The two great Ornaments of Virtue,
which shew her in the most advantageous Views, and make her altogether lovely, are Chearfulness and Good-nature"; "These generally go together, as a Man cannot be agreeable to others who is not
easie within himself."

In his most important discussion of good-nature, *Spectators* 169
and 177, Addison describes it as the origin of society. Our social life
ameliorates man's frightening existence in the world, subject to "innumerable Pains and Sorrows" both from "the very Condition of Humanity" and from the violence men do to one another.

> Half the Misery of Human Life might be extinguished, would Men
> alleviate the general Curse they lye under, by mutual Offices of Com-
> passion, Benevolence and Humanity. There is nothing therefore which
> we ought more to encourage in our selves and others, than that Dis-
> position of Mind which in our Language goes under the Title of Good-
> nature. . . .
> There is no Society or Conversation to be kept up in the World
> without Good-nature, or something which must bear its Appearance,
> and supply its Place. For this Reason Mankind have been forced to
> invent a kind of artificial Humanity, which is what we express by the
> Word *Good-Breeding*. For if we examine thoroughly the Idea of what we

call so, we shall find it to be nothing else but an Imitation and Mimickry of Good-nature, or in other Terms, Affability, Complaisance and Easiness of Temper reduced into an Art.

Again, an observer must discriminate between imitative and genuine forms of behavior. The formalities of good-breeding (which is, here, something like the fine-breeding of Steele's *Spectator* 66) threaten to degenerate into "exterior Shows and Appearances," or into "Imitation and Mimickry." The true form of good-nature, Addison says, "is more agreeable in Conversation than Wit, and gives a certain Air to the Countenance which is more amiable than Beauty." Moreover, the true form of good-nature creates the self-supporting symmetry of "mutual Offices" where a certain "Disposition of Mind" leads us to be concerned equally with "our selves and others."

The first of Addison's series on cheerfulness, No. 381, has the same purpose as does No. 169, to identify the satisfactions possible even in the face of our tenuous existence. But No. 381 works in the opposite direction, locating the source of contentment not in social life but in the private individual. At the beginning of the paper, Addison makes a well-known distinction between cheerfulness and mirth: "I have always preferred Chearfulness to Mirth. The latter I consider as an Act, the former as an Habit of the Mind. Mirth is short and transient, Chearfulness fixt and permanent. . . . Chearfulness keeps up a kind of Day-light in the Mind, and fills it with a steady and perpetual Serenity." The body of the essay then considers "Chearfulness in three Lights, with regard to our selves, to those we Converse with, and to the great Author of our Being." Examining man according to these headings is a conventional formula used in any number of sermons, treatises, and moral tracts. But it is, significantly, a model of *The Spectator*'s moral universe. *The Spectator* seeks to describe an inclusiveness which will contain our lives in an integral whole. This inclusiveness moves in two directions, toward the completeness of self-enclosure, and toward the completeness of infinite extension. Addison's division of man's three relations graphically points in these two directions. It turns inward, at one extreme, toward the self-contained equanimity of the retired man, speaking of an "inward Chearfulness" or "a secret Delight in the Mind." And it extends outward toward God, and, through God, to all of creation. The "Being of a God," Addison says, is "such a Truth as we meet with in every Object, in every Occurence, and in every Thought." The cheerful man appreciates "all those Goods which Nature has provided," "all the Pleasures of the Creation which are poured about him," and "all its Dispensations." At the center is the social man:

> If we consider him in relation to the Persons whom he converses with, it naturally produces Love and Good-will towards him. A chearful Mind is not only disposed to be affable and obliging, but raises the same good Humor in those who come within its Influence. A Man finds himself pleased, he does not know why, with the Chearfulness of his Companion: It is like a sudden Sun-shine that awakens a secret Delight in the Mind, without her attending to it. The Heart rejoices of its own accord, and naturally flows out into Friendship and Benevolence towards the Person who has so kindly an effect upon it.

The cheerful man is an intersection, in social life, of the self-contained wholeness of privacy and the expansive wholeness of public existence. Addison uses the metaphor of sight, along with the immediate response that accompanies sight, to balance the inward and outward, the private and the social. Cheerfulness is a private disposition of the mind that moves into the social world, being "affable and obliging" and stimulating in others an inevitable response that is itself at once "a secret Delight in the Mind" and a natural flowing out "into Friendship and Benevolence." Meeting with the cheerful man, we are immediately struck by a sensation of pleasure and an overflowing of good-will, at once a consciousness of our own state of mind and a heightened awareness of the other. This paragraph is, in short, the summation of *The Spectator*'s image of society. It mirrors Steele's description of the retired man in No. 206, and, notably, it mirrors Addison's description of the esthetic observer in his papers on the pleasures of the imagination.

Addison's papers on the pleasure of the imagination made two major contributions to critical thinking. First, Addison pointed out that an observer may have several different types of esthetic response. The primary pleasures of the imagination, which we feel when we are immediately confronted with an esthetic object, are different from the secondary pleasures, which we feel when we imaginatively reconstruct an object; the secondary pleasures are related to the pleasures of the understanding, the pleasures we take in critically examining a work of art. The primary pleasures themselves fall into three types:

beauty, novelty, and greatness, terms which for a century gave critics and poets a standard vocabulary for describing esthetic responses.

Addison's first contribution, then, was this analysis of esthetic responses. His second contribution was his description of an esthetic stance. If an esthetic response is genuine, it must hit the observer immediately, and the observer must have no extraneous interest in the sensation beyond the pleasure it gives. That is, beauty is not a utilitarian or moral sensation; we are not instructed by beauty.[34]

This principle of esthetic disinterestedness is the basis for Addison's description of the man of polite imagination. But notice, too, that Addison places the pleasures of the imagination within a social framework. The man of polite imagination is, after all, a version of the spectator:

> A Man of a Polite Imagination, is let into a great many Pleasures that the Vulgar are not capable of receiving. He can converse with a Picture, and find an agreeable Companion in a Statue. He meets with a secret Refreshment in a Description, and often feels a greater Satisfaction in the Prospect of Fields and Meadows, than another does in the Possession. It gives him, indeed, a kind of Property in every thing he sees, and makes the most rude uncultivated Parts of Nature administer to his Pleasures: So that he looks upon the World, as it were, in another Light, and discovers in it a Multitude of Charms, that conceal themselves from the generality of Mankind.
> . . . A Man should endeavour, therefore, to make the Sphere of his innocent Pleasures as wide as possible, that he may retire into them with Safety, and find in them such a Satisfaction as a wise Man would not blush to take. (No. 411)

The metaphors are familiar: the "Man of a Polite Imagination" removes himself from "the generality of Mankind" into a retired "Sphere of innocent Pleasures"; he enjoys a true possession of things through the personal appropriation of feeling; he is "let into" concealed beauties invisible to the eyes of the world. The esthetic stance, with its disinterestedness and spontaneous esthetic sense, mirrors the spectator's social perspective. We can, with justification, recall Steele's description of the theater in *Tatler* 182 as a "Prospect" which "would be very far from being below the Pleasures of a wise Man"; Addison, in fact, remarks in *Spectator* 387 that "the whole Universe is a kind of Theatre filled with Objects that either raise in us Pleasure, Amusement or Admiration." And we can recall Steele's description of the retired man from *Spectator* 206: "The Air, the Season, a Sun-shine Day, or a fair Prospect, are Instances of Happiness; and that which he enjoys in common with all the World . . . are to him uncommon Benefits and new Acquisitions."

This similar stance is one link, among many, connecting the pleasures of the imagination with the pleasures of social communion. A second link is Addison's emphasis, in discussing the primary imagination, on the spontaneous sensations of sight: "It is but opening the Eye, and the Scene enters. The Colours paint themselves on the Fancy, with very little Attention of Thought or Application of Mind in the Beholder. We are struck, we know not how, with the Symmetry of any thing we see, and immediately assent to the Beauty of an Object, without enquiring into the particular Causes and Occasions of it" (No. 411). Within his threefold analysis of esthetic experience (into experience of greatness, novelty, and beauty), Addison attributes this immediacy particularly to the perception of beauty: "But there is nothing that makes its way more directly to the Soul than *Beauty*, which immediately diffuses a secret Satisfaction and Complacency thro' the Imagination, and gives a Finishing to any thing that is Great or Uncommon. The very first Discovery of it strikes the Mind with an inward Joy, that spreads a Chearfulness and Delight through all its Faculties" (No. 412).

Again, this spontaneous assent to beauty has already been described as a social phenomenon when Addison in No. 86 speaks of how "we are immediately struck" by the air of a countenance. The parallel, however, is most impressive in his description of the cheerful man: "A Man finds himself pleased, he does not know why, with the Chearfulness of his Companion: It is like a sudden Sun-shine that awakens a secret Delight in the Mind, without her attending to it."

A spontaneous response is certainly part of Addison's concept of the pleasures of the imagination, and, by analogy to the cheerful man, part of the pleasures of the social world. Both social and esthetic perception, however, also involve objective judgment. The intuitive immediacy of the primary imagination is complemented by the secondary pleasures of the imagination and by the pleasures of the understanding that assess how well a work of art corresponds to a natural object. This is, of course, the pleasure derived from artistic imitation, that is, from a social artifact.

This Secondary Pleasure of the Imagination proceeds from that Action of the Mind, which compares the Ideas arising from the Original Objects, with the Ideas we receive from the Statue, Picture, Description, or Sound that represents them. . . . The *final Cause*, probably, of annexing Pleasure to this Operation of the Mind, was to quicken and encourage us in our Searches after Truth, since the distinguishing one thing from another, and the right discerning betwixt our Ideas, depends wholly upon our comparing them together, and observing the Congruity or Disagreement that appears among the several Works of Nature. (No. 416)

Here, therefore, we must enquire after a new Principle of Pleasure, which is nothing else but the Action of the Mind, which *compares* the Ideas that arise from Words, with the Ideas that arise from Objects themselves. (No. 418)

This same possibility for comparing nature and artifice exists, of course, in the social world when the spectator compares inward character with the socially conditioned forms of manners. This is the basis for a further link between social and esthetic perceptions in *The Spectator*: just as the observer takes a similar "stance" in both realms, he participates in the same two modes of experience, pairing subjective immediacy with objective discrimination. Like the pleasures of the imagination, the pleasures of society are in part an intuitive or suprarational sense of rightness, the product of a mind that does not concern itself with social graces but which is a perfect master of them for this very reason. But social exchanges can also be observed, described, and judged, and this is the work of *The Spectator.* The moral scheme that distinguishes between disinterestedness and affectation involves an epistemology that distinguishes between a spontaneous or intuitive sensibility and an objective or evaluative judgment.

Esthetic experience and social experience have the same form; and they are represented in the same language. For this reason we can begin to discern a social basis for esthetics, when we see, for example, that the man of polite imagination is one version of *The Spectator*'s retired man. We can also discern the esthetic basis of society. Social experience in *The Spectator* is represented in the language of esthetics because *The Spectator*'s psychology of social life is esthetic: it is a psychology of spontaneous sensation, of responses to beauty, and of critical discriminations between primary and secondary realities.

The network of related themes traced in this chapter has several important implications. First, *The Spectator*'s sense of gesture carries with it a notion of signs, and along with this a notion of how signs are to be interpreted: the meaning of a gesture, like a view of a landscape, can be grasped by a spontaneous intuition of its inward nature, or it can be explicated according to its surrounding circumstances. This pairing of intuition and explication leads to larger structures of social and esthetic thought, these being represented in characteristic verbal formulas that I have also begun to outline in this chapter. This pairing also suggests two modes of thought that become increasingly important during the eighteenth century. *The Spectator*'s psychology of spontaneous sensation anticipates the later psychology of sensibility, both in Addison's description of the esthetic stance and in *The Spectator*'s descriptions of social sensibility. Its psychology of critical judgment also anticipates Fielding's commentaries in his novels, where a scene will be paired with a commentary which will explain its ramifications and which will discriminate between inward motives and outward manners.

This chapter, however, deals with only one dimension of experience in *The Spectator*. It deals only with instantaneous perceptions. A gesture is a momentary encounter between two or three individuals; it is a picture, a static scene. Esthetic perception is "but opening the Eye, and the Scene enters." We have yet to see the dimension of time in *The Spectator*, a dimension that encompasses both the continuity of an observer's perceptions and the continuity of *The Spectator*'s publication.

CHAPTER THREE

The Psychology of Time

The scenes of *The Spectator* epitomize its notion of social space. They are static tableaux, literally arrays in space, that can be analyzed according to *The Spectator*'s psychology of inwardness. But these scenes are also emblems of time in *The Spectator* since they capture a paradox in our sensation of time. In one respect our sensations are continually changing; yet in another, any one sensation can be lifted from the flow of time to be a suspended or timeless object of consideration. This is a paradox that Locke suggests in his discussion of the succession of ideas. Our concept of time, he says, is drawn from "the constant train of *ideas* in our minds whilst we are waking," but we can see, too, "that one who fixes his thoughts very intently on one thing, so as to take but little notice of the succession of ideas that pass in his mind, whilst he is taken up with that earnest contemplation, lets slip out of his account a good part of that duration."[1] Contemplation is one form of "retention" for Locke, "keeping the idea which is brought into [the mind], for some time actually in view." A second form of retention is memory, where, again, our attention is abstracted from the flow of events as the mind turns toward internally generated images which "we *can* bring in sight, and make appear again . . . , without the help of those sensible qualities which first imprinted them there."[2]

The Spectator in effect dramatizes Locke's account of duration. It is referred to and quoted in Addison's *Spectator* 94 and is illustrated more indirectly in the stream of impressions attributed to Mr. Spectator. Such impressions affirm a temporal continuity as speculation leads to speculation, imitating the succession of ideas. But the essays also capture the paradox of time, since they suggest Locke's forms of retention. *The Spectator*'s scenes allude to our succession of perceptions as one essay follows the next in a kinematographic image of social life,[3] but they can be lifted out of time, isolated, and moved into a form of timelessness. Later in the century, this paradox of time also became a feature of novelistic renderings of time and of the serpentine path in gardening.[4] The path continually opens new vistas for someone walking along it, mimicking the changing ideas which make us aware of time; but a visitor can pause at any one of these vistas and figuratively suspend time as he gazes at the scene before him. In the same way, *The Spectator* affirms both the continuity of time and the value of moments of suspended attention. While *The Spectator*'s imagery of space, therefore, provides one axis along which the essayists organize their descriptions of social life, an imagery of time provides a second axis, equally important for its readers and for its renderings of experience.

Simply raising the subject of time, however, raises questions about the multiple dimensions of time. For any written work, we must distinguish time as it is represented in the text from the impression of time a reader has as he reads it. The time presented in the text can itself be divided into the time attributed to events and the time attributed to the narrating consciousness. In considering *The Spectator* we have to keep in mind, too, that the essays can be (or could have been) read in two quite different ways. They could be read, as they first appeared, as a series of daily essays. Or they can be read, as most readers have read them, as a bound collection. Each method of reading has its own effects on the process of reading and on the reader's perceptions.

Like time in a written text, our consciousness of time in life has several dimensions, among them memory, anticipation, and that sense of the moment that William James termed the specious present.[5] Locke's account of time similarly suggests a durational present, since our sense of time depends not only on changing sensations but also on a dimension of consciousness that monitors the flow of ideas, unifying them and providing a sense of duration: "by reflecting," Locke says, "on the appearing of various ideas one after another in our understandings, we get the notion of succession"; "All that is in a man's power in this case, I think, is only to mind and observe what the ideas are that take their turns in his understanding."[6] Just the opposite of this awareness of change is an awareness of changelessness in our daily lives, an awareness of unchanging habits and routines, very prominent in *The Spectator*. This is the perpetual present that makes a character sketch possible, since a character is marked by a timeless attitude.[7] Finally, beyond these secular dimensions of time is a religious consciousness in which each moment is measured against eternity and the prospect of judgment.

For these reasons, asking about time in *The Spectator* in fact means asking several questions that point to various aspects of temporality. What statements do the essays make about the nature of time? What awareness of time is attributed to the spectator? What are a reader's impressions of time as he or she reads the essays? Even these questions suggest only a few of the considerations that color our awareness of time,[8] although they do point, first, toward the consciousness of time described in the essays and, second, toward the perception of time *The Spectator* imparts to its readers through its own publication.

The Spectator's Consciousness of Time

The spectator's succession of perceptions is best illustrated in a remarkable essay, Steele's *Spectator* 454, in which Mr. Spectator resolves to wander about London and Westminster for a full day "till the many different Objects I must needs meet with should tire my Imagination." Reminding his readers that "the greatest Pleasure I know I receive at my Eyes," he watches the movements of crowds and exchanges of gesture, the meanings given to fashionable dress and the visible satisfaction of commerce, recording his observations in rich detail according to time of day and districts of the city. This paper is *The Spectator* in epitome, showing minute gestures that remain almost invisible until they are given meaning through Mr. Spectator's attentive eye. Most commonly, Mr. Spectator will choose one incident from out of the panoply of city life and pair it with a commentary to stand as a reflection on a static scene. He typically isolates a scene or character so that the act of composition stops the flow time: the essay is a crystalized or static version of the movement of the mind. No. 454, however, emphasizes the flow of experience that lies behind the individual papers. Appropriately, the commentary does not deal with the meanings of the scenes themselves, but with the movement of experience that the essay records:

> When I came to my Chamber I writ down these Minutes; but was at a
> Loss what Instruction I should propose to my Reader from the Enu-

meration of so many insignificant Matters and Occurrences; and I thought it of great Use, if they could learn with me to keep their Minds open to Gratification, and ready to receive it from any thing it meets with. This one Circumstance will make every Face you see give you the Satisfaction you now take in beholding that of a Friend; will make every Object a pleasing one; will make all the Good which arrives to any Man, an Encrease of Happiness to your self.

This commentary is important because it suggests the essays' concept of time. For Mr. Spectator, as for the retired man, common things are a source of continuous gratification. For the retired man, "the Air, the Season, a Sun-shine Day, or a fair Prospect, are Instances of Happiness" and "uncommon Benefits" (No. 206). For Mr. Spectator, "to be ever unconcerned, and ever looking on new Objects with an endless Curiosity, is a Delight known only to those who are turned for Speculation: Nay they who enjoy it, must value things only as they are the Objects of Speculation" (No. 454). In *Spectator* 100, Steele urges every man to "place himself in a constant Aptitude for the Satisfactions of his Being," and in No. 143 he urges us to "arrive at an Equality of Mind" so that we can "enjoy Life and Health as a constant Feast." In this way, the spectator's openness to sensation ensures a psychological continuity from moment to moment. Yet it also suggests that individual moments may stand out as sources for complex reflections. For Addison, particularly, they can become sources of esthetic response. Just as the essays, for a reader, become vehicles for a continuity of perceptions, the commonplaces of daily life, for the spectator, can become vehicles for a succession of ideas, for the continuity of habit, and for moments of sublime attention.

Esthetic Perception and the Metaphor of the Garden

Both the continuity and the intensity of time are elaborated in Addison's imagery of the garden. "The Air, the Season, a Sun-shine Day, or a fair Prospect" shade into the esthetic realm where some type of imaginative pleasure can be found in "almost every thing about us" (No. 413). "All that variety of Scenes which diversifie the Face of Nature . . . fill the Mind with a perpetual Succession of beautiful and pleasing Images" (No. 387); "the Creation is a perpetual Feast to the Mind of a good Man, every thing he sees chears and delights him"

(No. 393). The esthetic psychology of time, however, is characterized less by a consciousness of succession than by a consciousness of the moment that Addison typically represents through the image of the garden. He uses the garden as a metaphor in his paper on memory (No. 417), in his papers on composition and style (Nos. 417 and 476), and in his papers on the pleasures of a wise man (Nos. 93 and 94), in addition to papers on esthetics and on gardening itself (Nos. 414 and 477). Because of these multiple contexts, the garden brings together a consciousness of time, the moral psychology of the wise man, and the compositional order of *The Spectator* into a single system of ideas.

Addison's essays on gardens express an English attitude that emphasizes "naturalness" and psychological impact; they describe the new eighteenth-century garden, laid out according to prospects and described according to its effects on the perceiving mind.[9] Presenting this idea of the garden meant altering two traditions, the traditional imagery of the garden as an Eden or *hortus conclusus,* and the practical traditions of the parterre and topiary styles that had been imported from France and Holland. At the end of No. 477, an essay published as a letter, although presumably written by Addison, the author rehearses these associations: the garden was "the Habitation of our First Parents"; it fills "the Mind with Calmness and Tranquility"; it is an image of Providence, and thus "suggests innumerable Subjects for Meditation."[10] But the man in the garden, as described in the body of the letter and in Addison's other essays on gardens, is no longer the man in contemplative retirement. Instead, he is the figure of the spectator whom we see in No. 206—the man who enjoys a walk on a sunshiny day, and who attends to the movements of his mind. The imagination, Addison had argued, "loves to be filled with an Object," "to range abroad, to expatiate at large on the Immensity of its Views, and to lose it self amidst the Variety of Objects that offer themselves to its Observation" (No. 412), and the garden exploits this expansiveness through natural prospects: "in the wide Fields of Nature, the Sight wanders up and down without Confinement, and is fed with an infinite variety of Images" (No. 414).

Addison's image of the garden systematically exploits the language of the pleasures of the imagination. The garden has the expansive greatness just described; it encourages a spontaneous assent to its beauty, and a delight in its surprises. Like the Chinese garden, the ideal English garden would have "the particular Beauty of a Plantation that thus strikes the Imagination at first Sight, without discovering what it is that has so agreeable an Effect" (No. 414).[11] It would "hit the Eye with so uncommon and agreeable a Scene" by "compos-[ing] a Picture of the greatest Variety," and it would allow plants to "run into as great a Wildness as their Natures will permit" so that the gardener would be "pleased when I am walking in a Labyrinth of my own raising, not to know whether the next Tree I shall meet with is an Apple or an Oak" (No. 477).

Such an idea of the garden will have consequences in garden design.[12] Formal parterres and topiary work will be replaced by natural perspectives, or by perspectives which are contrived to appear natural: a "little wandring Rill," for example, would "run in the same manner as it would do in an open Field, so that it generally passes through Banks of Violets and Primroses, Plats of Willow, or other Plants, that seem to be of its own producing" (No. 477). The garden will alternate open prospects with forests, native plants will be clustered according to their natural habitats and seasons of growth, and trees will be allowed their "Luxuriancy and Diffusion of Boughs and Branches" (No. 414). The result will be a union of luxuriance, practical benefit, and esthetic delight:

> A Marsh overgrown with Willows, or a Mountain shaded with Oaks, are not only more beautiful, but more beneficial, than when they lie bare and unadorned. Fields of Corn make a pleasant Prospect, and if the Walks were a little taken care of that lie between them, if the natural Embroidery of the Meadows were helpt and improved by some small Additions of Art, and the several Rows of Hedges set off by Trees and Flowers, that the Soil was capable of receiving, a Man might make a pretty Landskip of his own Possessions. (No. 414)

Such an idea of the garden will also change how gardens are used as metaphors, so that Addison's image of the garden is notable too because it becomes part of a more comprehensive system of imagery. The garden which Addison describes is laid out to provide the visitor with changing perspectives and with a variety of psychological effects that both stimulate and mirror the movements of the mind. The garden thus becomes an emblem of time not as continuity but as a psychological expansion of a single moment. As it scans the garden, the eye pursues the "Immensity of its Views." Or, the observer may take one detail from his view of the garden as a trigger for reconstructing a complex emotional state through the processes of association.

Addison's analysis of memory illustrates how he uses the garden as a metaphor. In the sixth of his papers on the imagination, No. 417, Addison explains memory in what he calls a "Cartesian" fashion as a network of traces left in the brain by experience,[13] and chooses a garden to illustrate these processes of memory. Once a trace has been etched in the mind, any subsequent experience can initiate an expanding array of associations. A color or configuration of objects once seen in the garden will, when encountered again, lead to an associative reconstruction until at last

> We may observe, that any single Circumstance of what we have formerly seen often raises up a whole Scene of Imagery, and awakens numberless Ideas that before slept in the Imagination; such a particular Smell or Colour is able to fill the Mind, on a sudden, with the Picture of the Fields or Gardens where we first met with it, and to bring up into View all the Variety of Images that once attended it. . . .
> . . . At last the whole Sett of them is blown up, and the whole Prospect or Garden flourishes in the Imagination.

Along a somewhat different track, more sentimental than psychological, Addison publishes a letter from a young woman who tells *The Spectator,* her husband being absent, that "I look over the several Prospects and Points of View which we used to survey together, fix my Eye upon the Objects which he has made me take Notice of, and call to mind a thousand agreeable Remarks which he has made on those Occasions" (No. 241). In both psychological and sentimental examples, memory is an array laid out before the mind (through the image of the prospect it is literally an array in space) simultaneously holding together many mental objects that are made accessible through the experience of the moment. It is a sensation isolated from the stream of experience, which reconstructs elaborate emotional patterns.

The essayist's process of composition is analogous to these processes by which an observer reconstructs a "whole Prospect or Garden" from a "single Circumstance." As we may remember from *Spectator* 476, Addison uses the metaphor of a garden to describe the effects of composition: "When I read an Author of Genius, who writes without Method, I fancy my self in a Wood that abounds with a great many noble Objects, rising among one another in the greatest Confusion and Disorder. When I read a Methodical Discourse, I am in a regular Plantation, and can place my self in its several Centers, so

as to take a view of all the Lines and Walks that are struck from them."
In No. 417, drawing from his representation of memory, Addison explains that a writer must be able to "receive lively Ideas from outward
Objects, to retain them long, and to range them together, upon occasion, in such Figures and Representations as are most likely to hit the
Fancy of the Reader." With a methodized discourse, where objects
are "ranged together," the reader "comprehends every thing easily,
takes it in with Pleasure, and retains it long": "your Eye commands
the whole Prospect, and gives you such an Idea of it, as is not easily
worn out of the Memory" (No. 476).

The link between landscape and consciousness is made all the
stronger because of Addison's emphasis on design in his descriptions
of the garden. The garden is expansive, but it is a controlled expanse.
It has "that Vastness and Immensity, which afford so great an Entertainment to the Mind of the Beholder," yet Addison quickly qualifies
this immensity by emphasizing the control of art that must accompany
nature: "For in this case our Pleasure arises from a double Principle;
from the Agreeableness of the Objects to the Eye, and from their
Similitude to other Objects" (No. 414). He balances the primary and
secondary pleasures of the imagination and in so doing balances mental movement and compositional stasis. The essayist—if we keep in
mind Addison's analogy to the gardener—creates a fruitful garden.
Like the gardener he "range[s] in the same Quarter the Products of
the same Season, that they may make their Appearance together, and
compose a Picture of the greatest Variety" (No. 477). But the essayist
methodizes this variety, designing a plantation.

Finally, Addison's comments on gardens link the psychology of the
spectator with the pleasures of the wise man, since both may recover
this full and fruitful garden out of time. In No. 417 Addison assigns
gardening styles to the styles of classical poets. Homer has the sub-
limity of wild rocks and deserts. Ovid has the novelty of enchanted
ground. "The *Aeneid* is like a well-ordered Garden, where it is impossible to find out any Part unadorned, or to cast our Eyes upon a
single Spot, that does not produce some beautiful Plant or Flower."
The *Aeneid* may be too high to stand as representative of *The Spectator*,
but within Addison's triad of esthetic effects, the effect of *The Spectator* is that of beauty—the well-ordered garden where each detail fits
the whole and prompts spontaneous assent. When the spectator (or
essayist) reconstructs a scene through memory or through the com-

positional order of an essay, it has the psychological effect of the well-ordered garden with its controlled plenitude. This is precisely the effect that a wise man enjoys when he reconstructs his own life in recollection, since Addison's description of the wise man in *Spectator* 94 uses the image of the garden and exactly the phrasing that he has used to describe the effects of Virgil's poem.

In an early pair of papers, Nos. 93 and 94, Addison notes our "Inconsistency with our selves," complaining that life is too short while leaving time unused. He suggests three "Methods" for "filling up [the] empty Spaces of Life" that people, unaccountably, find to be idle. The third of these methods, reserved for the second paper, is "the Pursuit of Knowledge." The topic is one of Cowley's, who, in his essay "Of Solitude," argues that a man must prepare himself through education to enjoy a contemplative retirement: "Now because the soul of Man is not by its own Nature or observation furnisht with sufficient Materials to work upon; it is necessary for it to have continual recourse to Learning and Books for fresh supplies"; "a very small portion of any Ingenious Art will stop up all those gaps of our Time."[14] Addison, to make the same point, draws upon the new psychology. He quotes from Locke's explanation of duration "that we get the Idea of Time, or Duration, by reflecting on that Train of Ideas which succeed one another in our Minds," and adopts a corollary from Malebranche that experienced time may be lengthened "by employing [our] Thoughts on many Subjects, or by entertaining a quick and constant Succession of Ideas."[15]

The paper concludes with a description of the pleasures available to the wise man through activity of mind:

> The Hours of a wise Man are lengthened by his Ideas, as those of a Fool are by his Passions: The Time of the one is long, because he does not know what to do with it; so is that of the other, because he distinguishes every Moment of it with some useful or amusing Thought; or in other Words, because the one is always wishing it away, and the other always enjoying it.
>
> How different is the View of past Life, in the Man who is grown old in Knowledge and Wisdom, from that of him who is grown old in Ignorance and Folly? The latter is like the Owner of a barren Country, that fills his Eye with the Prospect of naked Hills and Plains which produce nothing either profitable or ornamental; the other beholds a beautiful and spacious Landskip divided into delightful Gardens, green Mead-

ows, fruitful Fields, and can scarce cast his Eye on a single Spot of his Possessions, that is not covered with some beautiful Plant or Flower.

This is the imagery of the new garden that Addison takes up again in No. 414 when he describes how "a Man might make a pretty Landskip of his own Possessions"; and it is the imagery of time and memory.

The Ethical Use of Time

As we would expect, *The Spectator*'s rendering of psychological time shades into what is inseparable from it, the ethical use of time, although the emphasis now shifts from our ability to reconstruct a scene in memory to our ability to sustain a psychological continuity over time. Here, Steele and Addison draw on conventional religious advice. A person should examine each moment of his life because the most trivial details may indicate his spiritual condition; and he should prudently use each moment in active industry because that moment may be his last, and because a constant exercise of virtue will sustain itself through habit. "Lay hold then upon the present opportunities," Tillotson had said, "and look upon every action thou dost, and every opportunity of doing any, as possibly thy last. . . . It is not certain how much or how little is remaining; therefore be sure to make the best of that little which may be left, and wisely to manage the last stake."[16] Or, "We must not only make conscience of our ways by fits and starts, but in the general course and tenour of our lives and actions, without any balks and intermissions. . . . Religion should be a constant frame and temper of mind, discovering it self in the habitual course of our lives and actions."[17]

The *Spectator* essayists adopt this religious perspective on time. For Addison, "the great Art and Secret of Christianity" is conducting our lives "in such a manner, that every thing we do may turn to Account at that great Day, when every thing we have done will be set before us" (No. 213). He recommends that we "possess our Minds with an habitual Good Intention, and . . . aim all our Thoughts, Words and Actions at some laudable End," because if "we apply a good Intention to all our most indifferent Actions, we make our very Existence one continued Act of Obedience." Steele argues the value of each moment in absolute terms: "Last Night is certainly gone, and to Morrow may never arrive: This Instant make use of" (No. 374); "since the Duration of Life is so incertain . . . how is it possible that we should defer a Moment the beginning to Live according to the Rules of Reason" (No. 27). Or, "The great Rule, methinks, should be to manage the Instant in which we stand with Fortitude, Aequanimity, and Moderation" (No. 374).

There is no profound theology here. Christianity slides imperceptibly into a generalized psychology where religion is subsumed under the broader themes of habit and cheerfulness. The stability of habit becomes necessary to maintain our personal continuity in time. "The Man who lives under an habitual Sense of the Divine Presence," Addison writes in No. 93, "keeps up a perpetual Cheerfulness of Temper, and enjoys every Moment." He repeats this observation in Nos. 381 and 441: an "habitual Trust" in God is the source of "Patience, Hope, Chearfulness, and all other Dispositions of Mind that alleviate those Calamities which we are not able to remove" (No. 441). Steele makes the same connection between cheerfulness and easiness of temper in his character of Ignotus in No. 75, and in his character of Uranius in No. 143, for whom religious faith becomes a social grace ("*Uranius* has arrived at that Composure of Soul, and wrought himself up to such a neglect of every thing with which the generality of Mankind is enchanted, that . . . his being [is] one uniform and consistent Series of chearful Diversions and moderate Cares").

Uniformity, constancy, and habit take on special value in *The Spectator* because of man's tenuous existence in the world, where he is constantly threatened with physical or psychological fragmentation. Death is always imminent, as the adaptations of religious advice remind us, and the distractions of the world may blast our psychological selves: "When Ambition pulls one Way, Interest another, Inclination a third, and perhaps Reason contrary to all, a Man is likely to pass his Time but ill who has so many different Parties to please"; "There is scarce a State of Life, or Stage in it, which does not produce Changes and Revolutions in the Mind of Man," and such change "in a Manner destroys our Identity" (No. 162, Addison).

Preserving our identity (ensuring duration) depends on habit and on cheerfulness, the two qualities Addison and Steele draw out of the Protestant anxiety about time. A long line of ethical thought, derived from classical ethics and preserved through generations of commonplaces, saw character and habit to be essentially equivalent, since character creates habit, and habit creates character.[18] Drawing on this wealth of commonplaces, Addison in *Spectator* 447 reconstructs what had come to be a standard argument: habit can render any experience pleasurable because we naturally follow accustomed activities (habit is a second nature); the constant exercise of virtue, therefore, while remaining a duty, becomes a constant source of delight. (Thus Steele, as well, in *Tatler* 49: "Life without the Rules of Morality is a wayward, uneasy Being, with Snatches only of Pleasure; but under the Regulation of Virtue, a reasonable and uniform Habit of Enjoyment.")[19]

No. 447 is *The Spectator*'s only essay on habit as such, but the idea permeates *The Spectator*'s morality. Habit suggests the familiar actions of everyday life, what one scholar has called "acquired, repeated and uniform behavior,"[20] and in part explains how a single gesture can indicate a way of living. What Steele calls "the Instant in which we stand" may contain only a single gesture, but it is an epitome of our lives because such gestures are repeated throughout them: "That which was, at first, the effect of Instruction, is grown into an Habit; and it would be as hard for *Eudosia* to indulge a wrong Suggestion of Thought, as it would be to *Flavia*, the Fine Dancer, to come into a Room with an unbecoming Air" (No. 79). The prominence of the word itself—"an Habit of Mind," "a constant and habitual Gratitude"—suggests its importance to *The Spectator*. Its function is to preserve identity in time.

The continuity of habit is allied to cheerfulness through several connections, some of which we have already seen. For Steele's retired man and for Addison's esthetic observer, an appreciation of commonplace things is a source of continual happiness. For both Steele and Addison cheerfulness is an ideal union of body and mind because it preserves the harmony of both (as in Steele's No. 143, or Addison's No. 387). And, for both, cheerfulness implies a temporal constancy. Addison seeks to describe the "two perpetual Sources of Cheerfulness"; he speaks of it as "an Habit of the Mind," as "fixt and permanent," "a steady and perpetual Serenity," "a constant habitual Gratitude." The consciousness of his own existence "spreads a perpetual Diffusion of Joy through the Soul of a virtuous Man, and makes him look upon himself every Moment as more happy than he knows how to conceive" (No. 381). Steele's No. 100 argues for "a constant Aptitude for the Satisfactions of [our] Being," which "seasons all the Parts and Occurences we meet with in such a Manner,

that there are no Moments lost; but they all pass with so much Satisfaction, that the heaviest of Loads (when it is a Load) that of Time, is
never felt by us."

We come again to the retired man's appreciation of the commonplace: "It is therefore the Duty of every Man that would be true
to himself, to obtain, if possible, a Disposition to be pleased, and
place himself in a constant Aptitude for the Satisfactions of his
Being" (No. 100, Steele). Without this appreciation of the commonplace, men suffer a "loose State of the Soul," "a certain Inca-
pacity of possessing themselves, and finding Enjoyment in their own
Minds" (No. 228, Steele). The alternative is fragmentation, or, in
Steele's phrase, "Inexistence" (No. 100). A man will cease to exist as
himself, falling into an entropic existence which is either the haphaz-
ard "Vicissitude of Motion and Rest, which we [mistakenly] call Life"
(No. 143) or an indolence which is "the meer Encrease and Decay of
a Body" (No. 100). This pursuit of habit and its sensitivity to the
commonplace has a definite place in *The Spectator*'s moral system. It is
the retired man who finds delight in commonplace things, a delight
that guarantees psychological permanence.

Addison's esthetic sense of the moment carries rather different implications. For Addison, an observer enlarges moments of perception
by tracing expanding lines of association, so the present instant is less
satisfying in itself than as the origin for mental excursions in time:
"The *Time present* seldom affords sufficient Employment to the Mind
of Man. . . . In order, therefore, to remedy this Defect, that the Mind
may not want Business, but always have Materials for thinking, she is
endowed with certain Powers, that can recall what is passed, and anticipate what is to come" (No. 471). Similarly, succession for Addison
is not only a medium of continuity, but a medium for "the perpetual
Progress which the Soul makes toward the Perfection of its Nature"
(No. 111): "To look upon the Soul as going from Strength to
Strength . . . [to consider] That she will be still adding Virtue to Virtue, and Knowledge to Knowledge, carries in it something wonderfully agreeable to that Ambition which is natural to the Mind of
Man." These two versions of time, however, are not far apart: the first
is the observer's delight in commonplace things; the second is the
esthetic enlargement of the moment we have seen before. In both, a
constant activity of mind ensures a genuine existence in time.

A more intricate representation of the impact of time takes place in

Spectators 316 and 317. No. 316 publishes a letter from "Samuel Slack," written by John Hughes, a collaborator in seven issues who has clearly absorbed *The Spectator*'s conventions. In No. 316 the author describes the ingenious but unsuccessful stratagems by which he has tried to jolt himself out of a torpor "which gives a Tincture of its Nature to every Action of ones Life." No. 317, in reply, is a tightly woven paper built on parallelism and parody, an excellent example of Addison's control of comic absurdity and serious admonition in a single essay. It begins with a description of Augustus Caesar's death: "*Augustus,* a few Moments before his Death, asked his Friends who stood about him, if they thought he had acted his Part well; and upon receiving such an Answer as was due to his extraordinary Merit, *Let me then,* says he, *go off the Stage with your Applause*; using the Expression with which the *Roman* Actors made their *Exit.*"[21]

In the third paragraph, Addison sets up in the *Spectator* club a modern analogue to Augustus' deathbed scene: "My Friend, Sir ANDREW FREEPORT, as we were sitting in the Club last Night, gave us an Account of a sober Citizen, who died a few Days since. This honest Man being of greater Consequence in his own Thoughts, than in the Eye of the World, had for some Years past kept a Journal of his Life. Sir ANDREW shewed us one Week of it." The disposition of the club members mirrors the audience surrounding Augustus, but where Augustus appeals to his friends for their opinion of his life, the deceased businessman was "of greater Consequence in his own Thoughts, than in the Eye of the World." His life, as represented in the journal, is neither appropriate for a rational being nor of any use to mankind. Mr. Spectator quotes one week of the journal (insisting that he gives "a faithful Copy of it") devoted entirely to dressing in the morning, smoking a pipe in his club, and vacant admiration of Mr. Nisby's opinions in politics.[22] One entry exemplifies the whole: "*Six.* Went to the Club. Like to have faln into a Gutter. Grand Vizier certainly Dead." Like fashionable attachment to external things, idleness is reduced to comically absurd mechanism; the life recorded in the journal is a mechanical imitation of the active life which Augustus represents. Every action is absorbed into an entropic dullness, dissolving into nonentity. The "Face of Indolence," in Hughes's phrase, "overspreads the whole."[23]

Pivoting on the reader's surprise "to find the above-mentioned Journalist taking so much care of a Life that was filled with such inconsiderable Actions," Addison turns to the reader with a serious proposal:

> If we look into the Behaviour of many whom we daily converse with, we shall find that most of their Hours are taken up in those three Important Articles of Eating, Drinking and Sleeping. I do not suppose that a Man loses his Time, who is not engaged in Publick Affairs, or in an Illustrious Course of Action. On the contrary, I believe our Hours may very often be more profitably laid out in such Transactions as make no Figure in the World, than in such as are apt to draw upon them the Attention of Mankind. . . . I would, however, recommend to every one of my Readers, the keeping a Journal of their Lives for one Week, and setting down punctually their whole Series of Employments during that Space of Time. This kind of Self-Examination would give them a true State of themselves, and incline them to consider seriously what they are about. One Day would rectifie the Omissions of another, and make a Man weigh all those indifferent Actions, which, though they are easily forgotten, must certainly be accounted for.

This is a secular adaptation of that advice given equally by Puritan and orthodox divines that a man should reflectively rehearse each day's events, and, if possible, record them in a diary for the dual purpose of measuring his spiritual state and improving his life.[24] Tillotson traces the idea back to Pythagoras's advice to his pupils "every night before they slept, to call themselves to account for the actions of the day past; enquiring wherein they had transgressed, what good they had done that day, or omitted to do."[25] Somewhat surprisingly, Swift in a sermon on "The Difficulty of Knowing One's-Self" came to make a recommendation very close to the tone and temper of Addison's: "But a Man must rather sit down and unravel every Action of the past Day into all its Circumstances and Particularities, and observe how every little thing moved and affected him, and what manner of Impression it made upon his Heart; this done with that Frequency and Carefulness which the Importance of the Duty doth require, would in a short time bring him into a near and intimate Acquaintance with himself."[26]

More immediate to *The Spectator*, Addison's advice would generate a private version of *The Spectator*. The journalist is described as a spectator, merging retirement, observation, and concern for "those we daily converse with" into a single perspective on the world. The journal is a personal miniature of *The Spectator*, a deliberate record of experience, placing "Indifferent Actions" into the patterns that give them meaning. It would represent a temporal plenitude that will resolve the fragments of life into a whole.

Time and Methods of Reading

While *The Spectator* describes a psychology of time and returns advice to the reader about using time, it also creates a psychology of time in its control of our reading. Clearly, a reader may have different impressions of time as he reads the papers. Reading may mimic the movement of time as perception follows perception, and it may mimic the paced continuity of habit. Alternately, reading may freeze time or suspend it, whether through the timelessness of a repeated pattern or the timelessness of a contemplative instant. The essays thus mimic the operations of the mind and initiate a reader into certain attitudes toward time through the form of the essays themselves.

In *Defoe and Fictional Time*, Paul Alkon has argued that the form of a literary work reveals its society's assumptions about the nature of time. "Shared views of time within a culture," he says, "may create expectations about the most desirable ways of dealing with fictional time," and "opinions about the right use of time . . . will influence . . . the pace of reading, the extent to which [books] are thought about after reading and the amount of pressure for rereading."[27] This is surely true of *The Spectator*, yet we need to recognize that there are significant differences between the reading time of *The Spectator* and the forms of narrative time that Alkon has examined. Unlike the reader of a novel, the reader of *The Spectator* is not carried along by the logic of cause and effect or by the teleology of plot. Instead, he is carried along by habit, and this makes for a very different kind of reading than reading fiction.

Like reading a narrative, reading the essays depends on our perceptions of time, as Steele and Addison knew very well. They were keenly attentive to reading time as the papers appeared in the original series and offered several cues as to how the papers ought to be read. Addison in *Spectator* 10 estimated that an essay should take about a quarter of an hour to read, and suggests that the papers become part of a morning ritual for "well regulated Families" and for the "Blanks of Society" who have no ideas of their own but in whom *The Spectator* may "daily instil . . . such sound and wholesome Sentiments, as shall have a good Effect on their Conversation for the ensuing twelve Hours." This view of *The Spectator* as a preparation for the day is recalled several years later in Steele's *Conscious Lovers* when Bevil Junior recommends Addison's "Vision of Mirza," saying, "Such an Author consulted in a Morning, sets the Spirit for the Vicissitudes of the Day, better than the Glass does a Man's Person."[28]

For the original series, *The Spectator*'s reading time would have been determined by two factors: by the time a reader would devote to one essay, and by the interval between one essay and the next. By pacing the essays over a span of years, *The Spectator* becomes a literary analogue of habit; a reader would be initiated into *The Spectator*'s reverence for continuity simply through the act of reading itself.

Reading *The Spectator* in collected volumes does not put these constraints on reading, and thus emphasizes another aspect of time in the essays by collapsing their movement of ideas. Like the reader of a novel, the *Spectator* reader can read anywhere from a few pages to several score at a sitting. But unlike the reader of a novel, he is free to begin reading anywhere that interest or whim or chance may dictate, and he may skip around as he chooses. He may read and reread one essay any number of times, or, conversely, may choose not to read large stretches of *The Spectator* without losing a narrative thread. As a collection, *The Spectator* is inherently protean, since each reader can make up his own version of it by what he chooses to read or not to read.[29] Similarly, the reader has a certain freedom in the degree of cohesiveness he cares to ascribe to the essays. From one point of view, *The Spectator* may be seen as a proto-Shandeanism where the essays do not so much appear with ritual regularity as become a stream of impressions where a faintly comic narrator moves through a series of associations, shuttling between incidents and reflections, referring the reader backwards and forwards to past essays or to projected ones. The essays in this way dramatize Locke's assumptions about the succession of ideas and can transmit them to the reader, who can move just as desultorily through the series itself:[30] the succession of essays can mimic the succesion of ideas, and a reader's impressions of the essays can mimic the changing sensations that make him aware of time.

But a reader's sense of time throws us back onto the paradox of time. A reader can legitimately have two very different impressions of reading time, since *The Spectator* not only suggests a succession of ideas but also suspends time in contemplative moments. Several readers testify to this. One describes how his reading follows a timeless ritual as "I constantly peruse your Paper as I smoke my Morning's Pipe, (tho' I can't forbear reading the Motto before I fill and light)" (No. 134); another explains that without *The Spectator* there would be "nothing to interrupt our Sips in a Morning, and to suspend our Coffee in mid-air, between our Lips and right Ear" (No. 553). Individual essays can also foster this sense of timelessness, as when Mr. Spectator's character disappears into a timeless voice that speaks in aphorisms, or when social scenes are lifted out of time into the timeless present of character sketches, as though certain kinds of behavior were perpetually happening. Even in *The Spectator*'s tales there is seldom a sense of narrative sequence. Instead, the tales may depict tableaux or depict an instantaneous vision, as in Addison's "Vision of Mirza" (No. 159) or his retelling of the Persian fable of a sultan who lives a second life in the instant in which he dips his head in a tub of water (No. 94). In a different way, *The Spectator*'s repetitions (both of its own themes and of "timeless" commonplaces) suggest that the thoughts being recorded are not part of a sequence of ideas at all but have been lifted out of time as part of an endlessly repeated pattern.[31]

At the end of No. 100 (on the subject of man's existence in time), Steele suggests that "it is a Degree towards the Life of Angels, when we enjoy Conversation wherein there is nothing presented but in its Excellence." This can be a striking image, not because it tells us anything about angels, or even much about conversation, but because it suggests that an ideal form of conversation can be elevated into a timeless realm where the vagaries of life are dissolved into a steady contentment and where certain truths are eternally being said. This is precisely the effect that *The Spectator* itself can foster.[32]

Such a cycle of changeless themes is evident again in *Spectator* 554, the penultimate paper in the original series. In No. 554 John Hughes returns to the topic of time and to the imagery of the garden. Here Hughes brings together much of the thematic framework I have traced, probably coincidentally but no less significantly, as a summation of *The Spectator*. He uses Leonardo, Francis Bacon, and Isaac Newton to illustrate the admirable capacity of the mind to hold an inexhaustible variety of ideas in coherent patterns: "It is impossible to attend to such Instances as these without being raised into a Contemplation on the wonderful Nature of an Human Mind, which is capable of such Progressions in Knowledge, and can contain such a Variety of Ideas without Perplexity or Confusion." Common to these men is constant mental activity, occupying themselves in "indefatigable Study." Nevertheless, Hughes observes, inevitably bringing the argument of the paper into a more familiar region of mental experience, "Men of the greatest Application and Acquirements can look back upon many vacant Spaces, and neglected Parts of Time, which have slipped away from them unemployed; and there is hardly any one considering Person in the World, but is apt to fancy with himself, at some time or other, that if his Life were to begin again, he could fill it up better."

The work of *The Spectator* had been to prompt this attention to time and to stimulate a continuing process of thought, not, of course, in the geniuses of the age, but in the "considering Person" who is the *Spectator* reader: "I think I ought not to conclude, without interesting all my Readers in the Subject of this Discourse. I shall therefore lay it down as a Maxim, that tho' all are not capable of shining in Learning or the Politer Arts, yet *every one is capable of excelling in something.* The Soul has in this Respect a certain vegetative Power, which cannot lie wholly idle. If it is not laid out and cultivated into a regular and beautiful Garden, it will of itself shoot up in Weeds or Flowers of a wilder Growth." Hughes's final image points back to Addison's statement of design in *Spectator* 10: "And to the End that their Virtue and Discretion may not be short transient intermitting Starts of Thought, I have resolved to refresh their Memories from Day to Day. . . . The Mind that lies fallow but a single Day, sprouts up in Follies that are only to be killed by a constant and assiduous Culture."

Here Addison looks to the garden not as a completed prospect presented to the eye and imagination, but as an area of growth, cultivated through daily attention. He sees it according to that second version of psychological time mentioned before which sees the mind "still adding Virtue to Virtue, Knowledge to Knowledge"; one intention of *The Spectator* is to present its readers with that "quick and constant Succession of Ideas" which lengthens and enriches experienced time. He sees *The Spectator*, too, as a pattern of repetition. It is a movement which is a stasis. Between No. 10 and No. 554 we have come full circle. Or, rather, both papers are instances of repeated forms throughout *The Spectator.*

The Spectator and Contemporary Representations of Time

The Spectator's analysis of time is an adaptation of larger cultural attitudes. Yet, just as Addison has transformed the imagery of the garden from being a *hortus conclusus* to being a metaphor of consciousness, *The Spectator* has transformed the traditional religious advice about self-examination. Our attention to the minutiae of our lives, which had been the medium of spiritual self-knowledge, is now a medium of social self-knowledge; the materials of spiritual autobiography are now materials for journals that serve as miniature versions of *The Spectator.* We record our gestures in our journals and the scenes in which we participate to assess ourselves in the way that Mr. Spectator would assess us. We have seen its adaptations of traditional religious advice regarding time, yet Locke's account of time, in particular, marks a clear break from the Renaissance obsession with mutability,[33] and his emphasis on personal time stands apart from the cultural time that informs classical allusions, whereby events in the present are mapped onto events from the past.[34] A concern with man's transience and appeals to classical precedent do not disappear from *The Spectator,* but they perform different roles than in, say, Browne's essays or Dryden's poems. Instead of being governing tropes, they are incidental points in a literary structure that affirms psychological continuity and esthetic responsiveness.

Later in the century, Sterne and Hume use Locke's empiricism to question any rigid notions of time sequence, although these more radical assessments of time are very different from Steele's and Addison's efforts to make the succession of ideas coherent and make it a source of gratification or pleasure.[35] *The Spectator*'s sense of time is more closely related to the psychology of sensibility in one respect and to Samuel Johnson's concern with the moral implications of time in another, although its emphasis on continuity distinguishes it from both.

In the broad outlines of his *Studies in Human Time,* Georges Poulet has identified "two distinct forms of interior temporality" in the eighteenth century: "Intensity of sensation ensures the instant; multiplicity of sensation ensures duration."[36] Later in the century this sense of time becomes the psychology of sensibility, "the habit of taking pleasure in rapidly changing emotions,"[37] a self-conscious attention to the movement of feeling which focuses on particular moments of sensation.

These two modes of temporality are amply apparent in *The Spectator*, although Poulet draws implications directly contrary to *The Spectator*'s psychology of time. In those writers he studies—Bayle, Fontenelle, Marivaux, and others—Poulet finds that personal existence for them is ensured only by intense sensations that jolt them from a psychological nothingness into an awareness of their mental states. For *The Spectator*, by contrast, personal experience is not ensured by intensity but by continuity. "It is not perhaps much thought of," Steele writes in No. 222, "but it is certainly a very important Lesson to learn how to enjoy ordinary Life, and to be able to relish your Being without the Transport of some Passion or Gratification of some Appetite." Following this lesson, *The Spectator* constantly resolves itself into considerations of the "Occurrences of common Life" (No. 107), of "the ordinary Commerce and Occurences of Life" (No. 169).

We can draw a similar contrast between *The Spectator*'s account of time and Johnson's. Like Steele and Addison, Johnson insists that our moral life is largely determined by our attitudes toward time, so he, too, explores the subjectivity of time. But these essayists give almost opposite emphases to their analyses of time. While Steele and Addison are well aware of the dangers of indolence or of building castles in the air, *The Spectator* optimistically affirms that it is in the power of everyone to live in consistent contentment with the present moment. Johnson emphasizes that we typically flee from present sensations either through an idleness which will let us pass painlessly through time or through imagination and expectation. The present is too vapid or too painful to bear without fantasy. So, *Rambler* 203, which begins with Johnson's sentence "The time present is seldom able to fill desire or imagination with immediate enjoyment, and we are forced to supply its deficiencies by recollection or anticipation," is a near parody and near attack on Addison's *Spectator* 471, which begins in the same way. Where Addison writes that hope "gives habitual Serenity and good Humour" because it "quickens all the still Parts of Life, and keeps the Mind awake in her most Remiss and Indolent Hours," Johnson writes about the fallaciousness of hope and about men "who, like us, shall be driven awhile, by hope or fear, about the surface of the earth, and then like us be lost in the shades of death."[38]

Johnson's version of time is the more striking and the truer to our own, modern anxieties about time. Still, when Johnson gives an account of a positive perception of time, his essays echo *The Spectator.* He urges his readers to adopt "a habit of being pleased; a constant and perenniel softness of manner, easiness of approach, and suavity of disposition . . . a state between gayety and unconcern; the act or emanation of a mind at leisure to regard the gratification of another" (*Rambler* 72). His comments, too, in *Rambler* 5 start with Addison's premises from *Spectators* 381 and 387 on cheerfulness. "A man," Johnson says, "that has formed this habit of turning every new object to his entertainment, finds in the productions of nature an inexhaustible stock of materials upon which he can employ himself, without any temptations to envy or malevolence; faults, perhaps, seldom totally avoided by those, whose judgement is much exercised upon the works of art. He has always a certain prospect of discovering new reasons for adoring the sovereign author of the universe, and probable hopes of making some discovery of benefit to others, or of profit to himself." We can see the Johnsonian slant in his aside on envy and in the theme of "probable hope," but we can just as clearly see his indebtedness to *The Spectator.*

These comparisons suggest that *The Spectator*'s representations of time provide one point of reference for seeing eighteenth-century attitudes toward it. Still, the importance of time to *The Spectator* is not primarily conceptual but formal. Although Addison's concept of mental activity gives imaginative formulation to the new psychology, and although *The Spectator*'s moralized delight in the commonplace is a serious attempt to understand the continuity of personal identity, we find the most intriguing exploration into time in the medium of the essays themselves. The individual essay is a moment in time, holding social or psychological patterns in an ordered prospect; the series of essays is a succession of such moments. The repetition Addison speaks of in No. 10, therefore, is a pedagogical device: saying the same thing over and over, as *The Spectator* does, will certainly impress its lessons on its readers. But in its transformations of traditional materials, we find that *The Spectator*'s system of themes folds back upon itself: the consciousness of the retired man or of the esthetic observer is a mirror of the spectator's consciousness; the consciousness of time which *The Spectator* recommends for its readers leads us to assess each moment, enlarging on it and judging it in just the way that the spectator does. *The Spectator* alters traditional materials because it transforms them into mirrors of itself and draws them into a closed cycle of themes. The repetition is thus a succession of stances, like the repeated forms of habitual behavior. *The Spectator* is a literary model of the forms of habit and thus participates in the constancy and plenitude of everyday things. It is a literary manifestation of the pleasures of the wise man, a figurative garden, and a circle closing in upon itself.

CHAPTER FOUR

The Family
and Intimate Community

Like cheerfulness, marriage for Addison can be "a perpetual Feast" that "has in it all the Pleasures of Friendship, [and] all the Enjoyments of Sense and Reason" (No. 261). Because it is "the Foundation of Community, and the chief Band of Society," Steele cannot be "too frequent" on this subject that will determine his readers' happiness or misery (No. 522). *The Spectator*'s organizing structures do indeed focus our attention on marriage so that these assertions of its importance are not exaggerations. As we have seen, a gesture can point into a charmed circle of shared emotions and contentment in time, and the family can be such an intimate circle. The essays thus use the same formulas to describe the family as they use to describe other forms of social cohesion. Like the descriptions of gesture, the descriptions of the family redefine our public and private lives so that the family exists as a mediator between the self-display of the public world and the retired isolation of the private. And like the descriptions of time, the descriptions of the family assign a special value to continuity, since the family becomes a source of continual gratification drawn from the satisfactions of daily life. The family is depicted through *The Spectator*'s gestural scenes; it is marked off as a distinctive realm of experience through *The Spectator*'s fabric of evaluative dualisms; and its psychology is defined by *The Spectator*'s psychology of time. As a result, the family becomes a central node in *The Spectator*'s network of themes and a central element in its account of our emotional lives.

Its readers agree about its importance. They regularly write to approve of *The Spectator*'s pronouncements on marriage, or to quarrel with them, or to offer accounts of family life drawn from their own

experience. In this way, *The Spectator,* along with its readers, participates in a reassessment of the family taking place during the late seventeenth and early eighteenth century.

Several scholars have identified remarkable changes in perceptions
of the family during this period. Lawrence Stone in particular has
traced changing concepts of the family from kinship and patriarchal
families to what he calls the companionate family, first evident in the
middle of the seventeenth century. Jean Hagstrum and Randolph
Trombach have reached similar conclusions in investigating literary
works and the papers of aristocratic families.[1] It is important to keep in
mind that, as far as we can tell, the social and economic conditions of
family life changed very little during this period, although there were
changes in domestic life resulting from urbanization and changes in
house architecture. But economics or demographics alone do not determine our perceptions of the family. These are also shaped by conceptual factors that are reflected in and promoted through the language
in which the family comes to be described. In the case of *The Spectator,*
establishing a vocabulary for describing the family becomes a major
contribution to these changing perceptions of the family.

The patriarchal view of the family saw it as headed by the husband or
father with each member obligated to follow definite duties as directed
by him. The rules governing these family relationships had been set out
in a number of religious handbooks such as William Gouge's *Of Domesticall Duties* (1622), Thomas Fuller's *The Holy State* (1642), Jeremy
Taylor's *The Marriage Ring; or, The Mysteriousness and Duties of Marriage*
(1659), and William Fleetwood's *Relative Duties of Parents and Children,
Husbands and Wives, Masters and Servants* (1716).[2] They were also
reflected in more personal advice. Halifax's *Advice to a Daughter* (1688)
explains a woman's subordination to her husband's authority,[3] and in
the Verney letters of the seventeenth century we find Ralph Verney
writing about his daughter's education to ask, "Dear Doctor, teach her
to live under obedience, and whilst she is unmarried, if she would
learne anything, let her aske you, and afterwards her husband, *At
Home.*"[4] A generation later, Edmund Verney writes his children "to
Bee wholly Ruled and Guided by me, and to Bee perfectly obedient to
me in all Things, according to yr Bounden Deuty, and Likewise to
Behave yr selfe always Respectfully towards mee and towards yr
Mother, and to Honor us, That thy Dayes may Bee Long in the Land"
(2:422). One consequence of such paternal authority was a common

acceptance of arranged marriages in which the father would select an appropriate partner and negotiate the conditions of a marriage contract. Because of the expanded obligations of kinship relationships, however, decisions about marriage or about a couple's domestic life would frequently be made not by the father or husband alone but by a large circle of family members and patrons.[5]

The Tatler and *The Spectator* received several letters calling attention to the emotional coldness that could result from such a family arrangement. One correspondent writes about women who complain about children, "always advising their ill treatment rather as slaves than children," and another complains that men's neglect of their wives is "so notorious, that if a man . . . can but prevail with himself to treat her with a little good manners after a few of the first months are over, he is accounted a wonderful good husband."[6] Despite these constraints, the duties that define the patriarchal family could include a wide range of emotional bonds within them.[7] Infant mortality was very high, so that a letter of condolence over the loss of a child became almost a minor genre in the Evelyn family's correspondence.[8] But parents could be very close to their children, even with the constant threat of their deaths. Evelyn lovingly describes his son Richard after the boy's death at the age of six, even though Evelyn's family life otherwise disappears from his *Diary* and seems to have been quite bleak.[9] In 1638, Ralph Verney sent a remembrance to his brother after Ralph's daughter Anna Marie died at the age of four, since "shee was fond of you, and you loved her" (1:219).

In later writers we see the close bond, too, between husband and wife that Stone sees as characteristic of the companionate family, although these descriptions clearly break from the patriarchal patterns of the conduct books. John Dunton, in his *Life and Errors* (1705), records his father's prudent advice about marriage but also the deep and lasting affection between himself and his wife.[10] His wedding was "the beginning of the greatest happiness I have as yet met with in this life" (p. 65). "The piety and good-humour of Iris," he says, "made our lives as it were one continued Courtship"; "those were the golden days. Prosperity and success were the common course of Providence with me then, and I have often thought I was blessed upon the account of Iris" (p. 79). Steele, too, in letters to his wife describes himself and his children, and describes a family idyll, although it was an idyll he was never able to live:

Your Son at the present writing is mighty well employed in Tumbling on the Floor of the room and Sweeping the sand with a Feather. He grows a most delightfull Child, and very full of Play and Spiritt. He is also a very great Scholar. He can read His Primer, and I have brought down my Virgil. He makes most shrewd remarks upon the Pictures. We are very intimate Freinds and Play fellows.[11]

My Wife and my Children are the objects that have wholly taken up my Heart, and as I am not invited or encouraged in any thing which regards the publick, I am easy under that neglect . . . and Chearfully contract that diffusive spirit within the interests of my own family. You are the Head of Us and I stoop to a female reign as being naturally made the Slave of Beauty. . . . [Yet] I would have You, intirely at Leisure to passe Your time with Me in diversions, in Books, in Entertainments, and no manner of Businesse intrude upon Us but at stated times; for . . . a Turn of Care and Huswifry, and I know not what prepossession against conversation pleasures, robbs Me of the Witty and the Handsome Woman to a degree not to be expressed. I will work my brains and fingers to procure us plenty of all things, and demand nothing of you but to take delight in agreeable dresses, Chearfull discourses, and Gay sights attended by Me. (pp. 354–55)

Steele speaks of love as a retirement from the world in a letter he later copies into *Spectator* 142: "I begg pardon that my paper is not Finer but I am forc'd to write from a Coffee-house where I am attending about business. There is a dirty Croud of Busie faces all around me talking of *money*; while all my Ambition, all my wealth is Love!" (p. 198).

This emphasis on an emotional union rather than on duties is a defining characteristic for Stone of the companionate family, and is reflected in two newer perceptions of family relationships. The first is what Phillipe Ariès has called the discovery of childhood; and the second is what might be loosely called a Protestant idea of marriage where marriage is not a sacrament but a spiritual union of husband and wife.[12]

We can see a parent's affection for his children in Steele's letter to Prue; or we can see it in literature in his portrait of Mr. Spectator's friend from No. 192 sitting among his children, or in Fielding's Booth, from *Amelia*, playing on the floor.[13] A discovery of children's distinctive emotional and intellectual needs is marked most prominently in England by Locke's *Some Thoughts Concerning Education*

(1693). Locke recommends that parents concern themselves with their children's health; he recommends that children be disciplined not by beating but by showing or withholding approval; he suggests that small children can learn through games and toys and that the greatest influences in the education of older children are the examples of conduct set by parents, tutors, and visitors.[14] Steele draws from Locke's book in his essays on childrearing and education, and Pamela, in *Pamela*, Part 2, uses Locke's work as a base for developing her own thoughts about education.[15] Apart from the influence of his specific proposals, however, the most significant effect of Locke's attitude was that a greater interest came to be taken in the child as a growing individual and in the household as a nurturing place for the child. The whole world in which the child exists is seen to shape his habits, behavior, experience, and ideas so that attention to the child calls attention to the domestic circle as well. "The Children," Locke says, must be "kept as much as may be *in the Company of their Parents*, and those to whose care they are committed. To this purpose, their being in their presence, should be made easie to them: They should be allowed the liberties and freedom suitable to their Ages, and not be held under unnecessary Restraints, when in their Parent's or Governor's Sight" (p. 164 [sec. 69]).

Protestant descriptions of marriage also focused attention on the affection between husband and wife. An insistence on love had always been part of the conduct books' accounts of marriage. Gouge speaks of "mutual love" and "mutual peace" between husband and wife; for John Dunton, "the mutual happiness of Men and Women" is the second reason for marriage, behind "the glory of God"; for Philogamus, in 1726, one of the reasons for the failure of marriages was "the want of true Love in the young Couple," along with "the want of Religion, and the Decay of Christian Piety."[16] The word "mutual," in fact, becomes a key word in descriptions of marriage. Gouge and Dunton speak of "mutual love," "mutual peace," "mutual affection," and "mutual comfort," and William Haller notes that the 1549 Book of Common Prayer added "the mutual society, help, and comfort, that one ought to have of the other" as the third of three reasons for marriage.[17] But, although there is a unifying tradition here, there are important shifts in emphasis between conduct books such as Gouge's and Steele's or Dunton's account of marriage. The emphasis in the seventeenth-century writings is on the rules of family life as defined

by religious prescriptions; the principal purpose for marriage was religious instruction and the sustained exercise of practical piety. The
cohesion of the family, in this view, was a matter of religious confirmation.[18] Piety remains a consideration in marriage for Dunton or
Steele or Defoe, but their emphasis has shifted away from the religious foundations to the psychological foundations of mutual
peace.[19] The difference can be illustrated by contrasting Dunton's
account of his own marriage with his mother's description of hers,
where her relationships with members of her family were measured
by their degree of religious belief.[20] Thus the bond between husband
and wife, for Dunton and Steele, comes to be examined not so much
as a spiritual bond as a benevolent one. The cohesion of the family
comes to be seen not as a matter of religious confirmation but as a
matter of benevolent feeling.

For this same reason, the nature of the family could be analyzed
according to the psychology of benevolence, in which, according to
Samuel Clarke, "the foundation, preservation, and perfection of [the
agreeing community of all mankind] is *mutual love and benevolence.*"[21]
Clarke describes benevolence as a radiating principle of social order,
giving us, in the language of the moralist, a picture of the family similar to ones given later by Addison or Fielding:

> Next to that natural *self-love,* or care of his own preservation, which
> every one necessarily has in the first place for himself; there is in all
> men a certain natural affection for their children and posterity, who
> have a dependence upon them; and for their near relations and friends,
> who have an intimacy with them. And because the nature of man is
> such, that they cannot live comfortably in independent families, without
> still further society and commerce with each other; therefore they natu-
> rally desire to increase their dependencies, by multiplying affinities.
> (1:210)

The *Spectator*'s essays participate in this redefinition of the family
by helping to establish a set of conventions and formalize a vocabulary
for representing these perceptions of family life. Addison's description of Aurelia and her husband in *Spectator* 15, for example, draws on
the same conventions for describing the family that Fielding uses in
the final paragraph of *Tom Jones* or Richardson uses at the conclusion
of *Pamela,* Part 2. Like Clarke, Addison and Fielding describe the
family as based on "mutual Endearments, and mutual Esteem," and

describe the mutual love of husband and wife as a radiant center of emotional order:

> They both abound [Addison writes] with good Sense, consummate Virtue, and a mutual Esteem; and are a perpetual Entertainment to one another. Their Family is under so regular an Oeconomy . . . that it looks like a little Common-Wealth within it self. . . . By this means they are Happy in each other, beloved by their Children, adored by their Servants, and are become the Envy, or rather the Delight, of all that know them. (No. 15)

> To conclude, as there are not to be found a worthier Man and Woman, than this fond Couple, so neither can any be imagined more happy. They preserve the purest and tenderest Affection for each other, an Affection daily encreased and confirmed by mutual Endearments, and mutual Esteem. Nor is their Conduct towards their Relations and Friends less amiable, than towards one another. And such is their Condescension, their Indulgence, and their Beneficence to those below them, that there is not a Neighbour, a Tenant, or a Servant, who doth not most gratefully bless the Day when Mr. *Jones* was married to his *Sophia.*[22]

Schematic Dualisms, Triangular Perception, and *The Spectator*'s Picture of the Family

Neither Steele's life nor Addison's gives so clear a picture of companionate marriage as Dunton's autobiography. Addison did not marry until age forty-four, only three years before his death, since he had long been in poor health. Although he had known Lady Warwick and perhaps courted her for twelve years, he undertook marriage with the same prudence and discretion that guided all of his decisions, and we have no letters and few records that reflect on their private lives.[23] Steele's life was less governed by rule. He had the romances of a young officer, fathering an illegitimate daughter and managing to marry a widow through whom he soon inherited a plantation in the Barbados. His second marriage, to Prue, was altogether different. His letters suggest an abiding affection and an attachment to domestic life, but Steele badly mismanaged money and his political career and seems to have exasperated his wife, who spent the last years of her life apart from him, living in Wales.[24] The letter I have quoted giving

Steele's ideal of family life was written at long distance and is an imagined scene, not a lived one. As his letters from 1717 show, his actual marriage was closer to that of Fielding's Booth, with Steele unable to manage the competing demands of the family and the world.[25]

This last point is an important one. It is hard to disentangle Steele's marriage from his representation of it, or the reality of his life with Prue from his expectations. But what I am pursuing here are perceptions of the family and conventions for describing it, not the actual conditions of family life nor biography, since the materials we have for biography are inevitably entangled in the conventions. Edmund Verney "naturally" describes his relationship with his children in the language of Ephesians and Dunton "naturally" describes his marriage in the language of mutual support endorsed by the *Book of Common Prayer* since these are the forms of language available to them for shaping their perceptions of the family.

In the case of *The Spectator,* the conventions it establishes for describing the family suggest that the family occupies a distinctive place in *The Spectator*'s imagery of social space. Thus *The Spectator* includes many, many essays on love, courtship, and marriage, on the relationships between parents and children, and on the relationships between masters and servants that integrate descriptions of the family into the larger, more cohesive picture of social relationships that *The Spectator* had begun to establish.[26] These essays use *The Spectator*'s schematic dualisms, its triangular scenes, and its images of continuity in time as techniques for depicting the family; they include letters from readers to enhance the immediacy of these scenes and often include graceful accounts of family relationships, as in Steele's portrait of Pamphilio in No. 137.[27]

In an early essay, Addison uses *The Spectator*'s familiar dichotomies in his portrait of Aurelia. "True Happiness," he writes, "is of a retired Nature, and an Enemy to Pomp and Noise; it arises, in the first place, from the Enjoyment of ones self; and, in the next, from the Friendship and Conversation of a few select Companions. It loves Shade and Solitude, and naturally haunts Groves and Fountains, Fields and Meadows: In short, it feels every thing it wants within it self. . . . On the contrary, false Happiness loves to be in a Crowd, and to draw the Eyes of the World upon her. . . . [She] has no Existence but when she is looked upon." As an exemplar of true happiness, Aurelia "delights in the Privacy of a Country Life, and passes away a great part of her

Time in her own Walks and Gardens." But the pleasures of family life are added to the pleasures of retirement. Aurelia's husband "is her Bosom Friend, and Companion in her Solitudes," and the expanding circle of affection, described earlier, radiates outward from their "mutual Esteem." Aurelia's counterpart, Fulvia, "thinks Life lost in her own Family, and fancies her self out of the World when she is not in the Ring, the Play-House, or the Drawing-Room": she "looks upon Discretion, and good House-Wifery, as little domestick Virtues, unbecoming a Woman of Quality," proper only to "a poor-spirited, unpolished Creature."

The contrast between Aurelia and Fulvia relies on the traditional imagery of retirement, but Addison has significantly modified the tradition by associating the intimacy of the family with the retired life, which had previously been described as contemplative isolation. Maren-Sophie Røstvig has pointed out with regard to this and related passages in *The Spectator* that, while they are indebted to the revered tradition of the *beatus ille*, the use of that tradition has radically changed: "Addison's ideal is practical and social in its implications; his retired rural dwellers form the pattern for a new style of living which combines dignity, urbanity, and good sense with active benevolence towards others."[28] Thus Addison's portrait of Aurelia is obviously related to Joseph Hall's picture of the happy man (derived from Seneca's *De tranquilitate animi*) as one who "lives quietly at home, out of the noise of the world, and loves to enjoy himself always, and sometimes his friend, and hath as full scope to his thoughts as to his eyes."[29] But it is just as obviously related to the final paragraph of *Tom Jones*, where the emphasis in describing happiness is on familial affection. What has happened (and it has happened in *The Spectator*) is that the conditions for personal happiness have become located in the family. The separation of city and country (the emblems of active and retired lives) is accidental to the point Addison intends to make: the crucial division is the separation of family life from the fashionable world. So, we may read Aurelia's portrait against the traditional oppositions, but we have to see that the family is introduced as a new region of social life mediating between the extremes of contemplative retirement and public self-display. Social life and retired life begin to merge in the cohesion of the family.

Modifying the opposition between public and private lives is a first step in identifying the family as a social object. A second step is dramatizing behavior within the family, and here we can see the usefulness of *The Spectator*'s triangular perception. Mr. Spectator intently watches the gestures which define family relationships, while, at the same time, his perspective as an outsider helps to bridge the distance between the public life outside of the family and the intimacy within it.

Consider, for example, a scene from Steele's *Spectator* 479:

> As I visit all Sorts of People, I cannot indeed but smile, when the good Lady tells her Husband what extraordinary things the Child spoke since he went out. No longer than Yesterday I was prevailed with to go home with a fond Husband; and his Wife told him, that his Son, of his own Head, when the Clock in the Parlour struck Two, said Pappa would come home to Dinner presently. While the Father has him in a Rapture in his Arms, and is drowning him with Kisses, the Wife tells me he is but just four Year old. Then they both struggle for him, and bring him up to me, and repeat his Observation of two a Clock. I was called upon by Looks upon the Child, and then at me, to say something; and I told the Father, that this Remark of the Infant of his coming home, and joyning the Time with it, was a certain Indication that he would be a great Historian and Chronologer. They are neither of them Fools, yet received my Compliment with great Acknowledgment of my Prescience. I fared very well at Dinner, and heard many other notable Sayings of their Heir, which would have given very little Entertainment to one less turn'd to Reflection than I was; but it was a pleasing Speculation to remark on the Happiness of a Life, in which Things of no Moment give Occasions of Hope, Self-Satisfaction, and Triumph.

This scene is a conversation piece.[30] We can visualize, as Steele certainly has, the father and mother holding the child, one of them looking at the child, the other at Mr. Spectator, who himself has taken a stance of bemused affection. Steele uses this triangle of postures (child-parent-spectator) to identify the social ground on which the family exists. Central to the description is the ambiguity (a crucial ambiguity for *The Spectator*) between the importance of the public realm and the importance of the private realm. The private world becomes ridiculous when brought into the public: "Men cannot, indeed, make a sillier Figure, than in repeating such Pleasures and Pains to the rest of the World"; the spectator "cannot indeed but smile" when the intimacies of family life are spoken of in company. The parents, then, are placed in this ambiguous region between public and private realms ("They are neither of them Fools, yet received my Compliment with great Acknowledgment of my Prescience"), but it is the spectator who is the pivot between the two. The ambivalence bears most heavily on him. He has carefully established his pose as distanced observer, but as actor he is "prevailed with" to go to dinner and cajoled into making a remark ridiculous even to himself in his capacity as observer. But he is not averse to being ridiculous. Precisely because of his capacity for "Reflection" and "Speculation" he can be entertained by things of "no Moment" and see their value. By making this remark, he participates willingly in the intimate circle presented in the scene.

Time and Commonplace Things in the Family

Steele's scene from No. 479 does not dramatize a precept or rule about family duties but presents the family as a unit of affection. Nevertheless, the scene is part of a schematic analysis of family relationships that makes up the body of the essay. The essay begins, characteristically, by considering the use of a word. Steele reports that he has received several letters from husbands complaining of "Ill-nature" in their wives, yet, "I cannot tell how it is, but I think I see in all their Letters that the Cause of their Uneasiness is in themselves." The word "Ill-nature" reflects less on their wives than on the letter-writers themselves. Steele explains their mistake this way: because they have imagined their wives only as "the Object[s] of Joy" according to their own "half Theatrical, half Romantick" illusions about love, they have not seen them as "subject to Dishumour, Age, Sickness, Impatience, or Sullenness"; "humane Nature it self is often imputed to her as her particular Imperfection or Defect."

The essay's lines of development are already apparent. The details of married life are a constant irritation to the man who does not accept his wife's complicated humanity and who will not accept the trivial affairs of ordinary life. For the husband who does accept such things, each moment is a source of delight: "According as the Husband is disposed in himself, every Circumstance of his Life is to give him Torment or Pleasure."

> The Man who brings his Reason to support his Passion, and beholds what he loves as liable to all the Calamities of humane Life both in Body and Mind, and even at the best, what must bring upon him new

Cares and new Relations; such a Lover, I say, will form himself accordingly, and adapt his Mind to the Nature of his Circumstances. This latter Person will be prepared to be a Father, a Friend, an Advocate, a Steward for People yet unborn, and has proper Affections ready for every Incident in the Marriage-State.

Steele pins down this analysis in two character sketches:

Tom Trusty has told me, that he thinks it doubles his Attention to the most intricate Affair he is about, to hear his Children, for whom all his Cares are applied, make a Noise in the next Room: On the other Side, *Will Sparkish* cannot put on his Perriwig, or adjust his Cravat at the Glass, for the Noise of those damn'd Nurses and squawling Brats; and then ends with a gallant Reflection upon the Comforts of Matrimony, runs out of the Hearing, and drives to the Chocolate-house.

The portraits of Tom Trusty and Will Sparkish entail broad patterns of obligations and illuminate whole ways of living. Will Sparkish, remaining attached to the values of fashion, "is perplexed with every thing around him"; Tom Trusty, nurturing the secure affection of the family, derives pleasure from a world of "indifferent things."

Like Aurelia, Tom Trusty is a version of that type of retirement which *The Spectator* associates with family life. During the summer months of 1711 and 1712, for example, *The Spectator* published several papers on country life, following the conventions of the social season. In one such paper a correspondent observes that "Country-Life is described as the most pleasant of all others," but reminds *The Spectator*'s readers that "the greatest Part of their Time must be spent within themselves," and within "the repeated Occurences in their own Families." Since "an Agreement and kind Correspondence between Friends and Acquaintances is the greatest Pleasure of Life," the letter writer asks *The Spectator* to "now and then give us a lesson of Good-humour, a Family-Piece" (No. 424). By implication, "those who know how to enjoy Leisure and Retirement" are those who know how to enjoy the "repeated Occurences in their own Families." That they are repeated is significant. Like *The Spectator*'s general delight in commonplace things, they are a source of constant satisfaction. Along these same lines, a letter printed in No. 196 urges Mr. Spectator to "speak of the Way of Life which plain Men may pursue, to fill up the Spaces of Time with Satisfaction," suggesting that "domestick Life,

filled with its natural Gratifications" is "an endless Source of Pleasures."

These letters' attitudes toward the family, like the attitudes of
Steele's No. 479, are distinctively spectatorial: the family has a definite place within a metaphorical social space; the satisfactions of family life depend on the inward dispositions of the mind; when seen in
its true character, family life is an endless source of pleasure.

Husband and Wife, Parent and Child, and the Formulas of Social Cohesion

From *The Spectator*'s many essays on the family we can extract a set
of principles about courtship, marriage, and the relationships between
parents and children. At the center of the family is the institution of
marriage. In its many essays on courtship, *The Spectator* adjudicates
among various considerations in marriage, including "a virtuous Disposition, a good Understanding, an agreeable Person, and an easy
Fortune," as Steele puts it in No. 522. But the key advice is to "determine your self" (No. 149); that is, to know your own inclinations and
how they match the inward character of your partner. In a reply to a
woman undecided between two suitors, Steele writes, "You are . . . to
consider which of your Lovers will like you best undress'd, which will
bear with you most when out of Humour; and your Way to this is to
ask of your self, which of them you value most for his own Sake? and
by that judge which gives the greater Instances of his valuing you for
your self only" (No. 149). Similarly, at the end of a paper composed
mostly of one letter from a fashionable lady and a second from a
contented wife, Steele replies to a third letter from a confused suitor,
"Would you marry to please other People, or your self?" (No. 254).
"The happy Marriage, is where two Persons meet and voluntarily
make Choice of each other, without principally regarding or neglect-
ing the Circumstance of Fortune or Beauty. . . . you will find Love
has nothing to do with State. Solitude, with the Person beloved, has a
Pleasure even in a Woman's Mind beyond Show or Pomp" (No. 149).

Steele's tone may be patronizing, but he presents an attractive
ideal. This kind of emotional cohesiveness provides the foundation
for Steele's comprehensive definition of marriage in *Spectator* 490:

Marriage is an Institution calculated for a constant Scene of as much Delight as our Being is capable of. Two Persons who have chosen each other out of all the Species, with Design to be each other's mutual Comfort and Entertainment, have in that Action bound themselves to be good-humour'd, affable, discreet, forgiving, patient, and joyful, with Respect to each other's Frailties and Perfections, to the End of their Lives. . . . When this Union is thus preserv'd (as I have often said) the most indifferent Circumstance administers Delight. Their Condition is an endless Source of new Gratifications.

The internal structure of the marriage determines its outward appearance, just as the carriage of an individual reveals the disposition of his mind. Where there is the balanced correspondence Steele describes in No. 490, the marriage has an unobtrusive grace, beautiful to the observer; but a distortion in the marriage will be reflected in the behavior of its partners. "This Passion towards each other, when once well fixed, enters into the very Constitution, and the Kindness flows as easily and silently as the Blood in the Veins. When this Affection is enjoyed in the most sublime Degree, unskilful Eyes see nothing of it; but when it is subject to be changed, and has an Allay in it that may make it end in Distaste, it is apt to break into Rage, or overflow into Fondness, before the rest of the World" (No. 490). "A good Person," Addison observes, "does not only raise, but continue Love," creating a stable union that "puts the Wife or Husband in Countenance both among Friends and Strangers" (No. 261). John Hughes says of Benevolus in No. 525, "Even those of his Acquaintance, who have never seen him in his Retirement, are Sharers in the Happiness of it; and it is very much owing to his being the best and best beloved of Husbands, that he is the most stedfast of Friends, and the most agreeable of Companions." "There is a sensible Pleasure," Hughes says, "in contemplating such beautiful Instances of domestic Life."

Clearly, marriage has a function in *The Spectator* comparable to that of the retired man, so that the account of the family shares the same descriptive techniques, the same psychology of time, and the same marks of intimacy that we see in other papers. Like the retired man, the happy marriage is a self-contained entity, a "Solitude, with the person beloved," set in contrast to the fragmentation of the public world. It is a source of constant pleasure where "the most indifferent Circumstance administers Delight." It has a harmony within itself that is invisible to "unskilful Eyes" but "a sensible Pleasure" to the sympathetic observer. Like the self-possession of the retired man, too, it becomes the center for an expanding community.

That marriage fits so easily into *The Spectator*'s conventions of social description argues most strongly for its central importance in the series. These same conventions further describe the ideal relationship between parents and children. The bond between them may involve managing or inheriting an estate, but the basis for their relationship is not economics but a mutual good will founded on education and affectionate care. The parent instructs the child in virtue and good-nature, providing the permanent values of character. The child, in turn, perpetuates the best qualities of the parent. Such a union repeats *The Spectator*'s imagery of social cohesion, becoming beautiful in itself and giving delight to trivial things:

> It is the most beautiful Object the Eyes of Man can behold, to see a Man of Worth and his Son live in an entire unreserved Correspondence. The mutual Kindness and Affection between them give an inexpressible Satisfaction to all who know them. It is a sublime Pleasure which encreases by the Participation. It is as sacred as Friendship, as pleasurable as Love, and as joyful as Religion. This State of Mind does not only dissipate Sorrow, which would be extream without it, but enlarges Pleasures which would otherwise be contemptible. The most indifferent thing has its Force and Beauty when it is spoke by a kind Father, and an insignificant Trifle has its Weight when offered by a dutiful Child. (No. 192)

Both in marriage and in the relationship between parents and children this idyll of the family can break into distortions of the family structure. A marriage dissolves either when the family sinks into "Inexistence" through indifference, as have the Tersetts, whose "Life is now at a Stand" (No. 100), or when the family is ruptured by active antagonism, as in the family whose fox-hunting husband has led his sons to look on their mother as no better than she should be and whose fashionable wife has led her daughters to see their father as a clown (No. 128). The bond between parent and child is disrupted either by overbearing parents, such as those who strike a "*Smithfield* Bargain" for their daughter (No. 304), or by a prodigal child, such as the Templar we have seen who ignores his father's expectations (No. 150). Papers tell about a wife abandoned every night by her husband, about a daughter begging her father to accept her new husband, or about a widow whose son is spending away her inheritance.[31]

In Steele's next periodical, *The Guardian*, the family becomes a principle of variation. Papers on politeness, love, education, economy, and the theater begin with conversations in the Lizard family as different members introduce new topics or contribute new perspectives on a topic already considered (as in Nos. 1, 5, 13, 24, 31, 42). *The Guardian* thus condenses into one family a process of variation already established in *The Spectator* through its repeated consideration and reconsideration of questions regarding the family. The fragmentation of the family, then, serves two purposes in *The Spectator*: it shows the internal dynamics of the family and becomes a source of variation from essay to essay. The "as I have said before" (No. 128), "as I have formerly observed" (No. 189), and "as I have often said" (No. 490) that punctuate papers on the family show the essays to be continuing responses to the recurring events of family life; "I do not think I can be too frequent," Steele says, "on Subjects which may give Light to my unmarried Readers, in a Particular which is so essential to their following Happiness or Misery" (No. 522). Thus while Steele proposes at one point "to make a System of Conjugal Morality" (No. 178), that system is presented only in fragments scattered through the series.

Significantly, these accounts are multiplied because of *The Spectator*'s exchange of letters, since its readers contribute constantly shifting views of the family from their own experience: "Among all the Distresses which happen in Families, I do not remember that you have touched upon the Marriage of Children without the Consent of their Parents" (No. 181); "Mr. SPECTATOR having of late descanted upon the Cruelty of Parents to their Children, I have been induced (at the Request of several of Mr. SPECTATOR's Admirers) to enclose this Letter" (No. 189); "When you spoke of the Jilts and Coquets, you then promised to be very impartial . . . which has given me Encouragement to describe a certain Species of Mankind under the Denomination of *Male Jilts*" (No. 288). The exchange of letters expands *The Spectator*'s analysis of the family's dynamics, as I have said, and creates an illusion of community that forms an artificial family. In No. 181 Addison begins with a letter "filled with Touches of Nature" where the writer appeals to a new view of distresses in the family. She is married to a worthy man but has been rejected by her father for marrying without his permission. The conflict is dramatized in tearful scenes involving the father, mother, daughter, and grandchild, and

Addison in response supports the young woman.[32] One week later, however, Addison takes notice of further letters and significantly changes his emphasis. He has exposed the "unnatural Father," but "the Obedience of Children to their Parents is the Basis of all Government." The letters lead Addison through a process of proposal and adjustment in which the second essay does not so much contradict the first as present the issue in a different light, looking at the same relationship from the opposite point of view.

This counterpoint between *The Spectator* and its readers leads to an aspect of Steele's No. 479 I have not yet discussed, its address to its readers. Here, we begin to see how *The Spectator* controls the illusion of community that accompanies its examination of the family. After discussing a husband's acceptance of his wife's human failings, Steele complicates the question: "When I say all this, I cannot deny but there are perverse Jades that fall to Mens Lots, with whom it requires more than common Proficiency in Philosophy to be able to live." His example is Socrates' "philosophic" acceptance of marriage to Xanthippe. This paragraph elicits "a great return of Letters" from sympathetic husbands, as Steele notes in *Spectator* 482. A more interesting response, however,—Mr. Spectator's own—follows this digression at the end of No. 479. The paper had begun as a vindication of marriage and Steele returns to this original purpose at the end of the essay, directly addressing his readers again: "But instead of pursuing my Design of displaying Conjugal Love in its natural Beauties and Attractions, I am got into Tales to the Disadvantage of that State of Life. I must say therefore that I am verily perswaded, that whatever is delightful in humane Life, is to be enjoyed in greater Perfection in the marry'd, than in the single Condition." Steele points up the deliberate selection of material, the intentional artistry that makes *The Spectator* work. He simply cuts short his own contrary example and returns to his intended argument: with seductive candor he points to *The Spectator* as a piece of rhetoric.

The Spectator apparently succeeded as rhetoric. *Spectator* 500 prints a letter from a man declaring, "I am apt to think your Discourses, in which you have drawn so many agreeable Pictures of Marriage, have had a very good Effect in this way in *England*." For Mr. Spectator, "It is my Custom to take frequent Opportunities of enquiring from time to time, what Success my Speculations meet with in the Town. I am glad to find, in particular, that my Discourses on Marriage have been well received" (No. 525, Hughes). As rhetoric, *The Spectator* is a social act. It exists in a context of address where the writer's "I" addresses the reader's "you," and where its consequences are measured by its readers' behavior.

The Family and Friendship, *The Spectator* and Its Readers

This exchange with its readers suggests a second model of community, the union of friendship that serves as an analogue to the family or a surrogate for it. The family and friendship are cognate versions of a single vision of social life. Both are a meeting ground of public and private so that both may be seen equally as ideal societies and as places of retirement from society. For these reasons, *The Spectator*'s imagery of the family extends to include its discussions of friendship. Again, the "location" of friendship is not marked by geographic boundaries but by states of mind so that *The Spectator*'s version of retirement can be translated into the urban world. Steele can speak of even the coffeehouse as a place of retreat, if it is approached in a certain way. "Here," Mr. Spectator explains, "a Man, of my Temper, is in his Element" (No. 49). He enjoys the changing character of the coffeehouse as different elements dominate the scene, but he seeks out men of moderation (presumably also men of the middle state) "who have Business or good Sense in their Faces, and come to the Coffeehouse either to transact Affairs or enjoy Conversation." These are men who "have not Spirits too Active to be happy and well pleased in a private Condition, nor Complexions too warm to make them neglect the Duties and Relations of Life." They are "good Fathers, generous Brothers, sincere Friends, and faithful Subjects," models for the whole spectrum of social life. Common to these men is an acceptance of common life: "The Coffee-house," Steele says, "is the Place of Rendevous to all that live near it, who are thus turned to relish calm and ordinary Life." "You see in their Countenances they are at home, and in quiet Possession of the present Instant, as it passes, without desiring to Quicken it by gratifying any Passion, or prosecuting any new Design. These are the Men formed for Society, and those little Communities which we express by the Word *Neighbourhoods.*"

We have here an idealized version of urban life, just as Aurelia is an idealized version of country life. Formed for society as they are, these men represent what we recognize to be the bases for retirement: the acceptance of ordinary life and the movement into "little Communities." Within these little communities, a figurative geometry of friendship locates personal intimacy in an every narrower sphere. "One would think," Addison observes, "that the larger the Company is . . . the greater Variety of Thoughts and Subjects would be started in Discourse" (No. 68). Just the opposite is true: "In Proportion, as Conversation gets into Clubs and Knots of Friends, it descends into Particulars, and grows more free and communicative: But the most open, instructive, and unreserved Discourse, is that which passes between two Persons who are familiar and intimate Friends. On these Occasions, a Man gives a Loose to every Passion and every Thought that is uppermost, discovers his most retired Opinions of Persons and Things, tries the Beauty and Strength of his Sentiments, and exposes his whole Soul to the Examination of his Friend." The wise man knows how to "pick and cull his Thoughts for Conversation" according to the rules of discretion, except "in private Conversation between intimate Friends . . . for indeed Talking with a Friend is nothing else but *thinking aloud*" (No. 225). Such thinking aloud articulates the "infinite Reveries, numberless Extravagancies, and a perpetual Train of Vanities" that pass through the mind of even a wise man. It is in the circle of Friendship that the constant movement of "retired Opinions" becomes part of social life.

This description of friendship brings us back to *The Spectator*'s description of itself, back to the intimacy of the club (since the club is *The Spectator*'s particular example of the knot of friendship), back to the membership extended to readers through the publication of the papers, and back to Mr. Spectator's description of himself: "I never enter into the Commerce of Discourse with any but my particular Friends, and not in Publick even with them. Such an Habit has perhaps raised in me uncommon Reflections; but this Effect I cannot communicate but by my Writings" (No. 4). The circle of friendship reproduces precisely the "shape" of *The Spectator* itself, extending to include a broad readership while defining at the same time an intimate and closed community where the secret beauties of sentiment are "discovered" in a continuing dialogue. Reading the papers we enjoy, as we would enjoy in the theater, the illusion that we are in a family or that we participate in a circle of friends. *The Spectator* thus fosters an image of society in which its relationship with its readers mimics its own account of social life: it creates conventions of social description that define the rhetorical form of *The Spectator* itself.

CHAPTER FIVE

The Language of *The Spectator*

W e have begun to reconstruct an image of social life that supplants Cowley's view of the city. For Cowley, the self is displaced in the city into a "Creature of the Fancy."[1] For Steele and Addison the spectator becomes a sympathetic observer who views gestures as a language through which he may read the actors' inner lives. He preserves a personal continuity through attention to "things of no moment," even among the distractions of the city. And his essays propose an emotional vocabulary to characterize the intimacy of the family and of friendship.

The preceding chapters have argued that this image of society is not an ad hoc collection of moral exercises but that it is composed of interlocking conventions throughout *The Spectator*'s great variety of topics. Turning to another aspect of the text, this same analysis provides a background for an account of *The Spectator*'s language. For Steele and Addison, the most significant aspect of language is its existence as a social phenomenon; the words we use and the meanings we ascribe to them are created within a fabric of social exchange. Thus when Steele speaks of the "Commerce of Discourse" in No. 4, the phrase is more than a metaphor, since the meanings of words and the values they carry are negotiated as part of a commerce of words and gestures. Exploring *The Spectator*'s language is inevitable, therefore, since social forms condition the authors' language, and their language conditions their account of social forms. This is true not only in the obvious sense that social relationships form the content of the essays; it is also true in the sense that sharing forms of language becomes a vehicle for sharing assumptions about social bonds so that forms of speech become inextricably tied to forms of life.

Because of these qualities, this examination of *The Spectator*'s language works on various levels. These include examining the essays' style (that is, the writers' habits of syntax and vocabulary); examining the essays' rhetorical relationships with their readers; and examining more theoretical views of language that Steele and Addison share with their contemporaries. The central assumption here is that a writer's style—that is, the way he chooses to use words—reflects his conscious or unconscious assumptions about the nature of language. These assumptions will be manifest in the work's rhetoric and may be articulated explicitly in theories of language. The mention of language, therefore, covers a broad range of effects that cannot be readily separated, if they can be separated at all. Many of *The Spectator*'s effects, in particular, are not achieved through the express content of its words but through the assumptions about social allegiance and assumptions about social communication that are transmitted through the forms of language that Addison, Steele, Hughes, and Budgell come to share. Thus the analysis of style is inevitably tied to theories of language in one respect, although in another it never strays far from the analysis of social forms or from *The Spectator*'s dialogue with its readers.

Its connection with social forms returns us to the doubleness of *The Spectator* examined earlier, whereby *The Spectator* is drawn into the world of public exchanges and yet forms a self-contained system of meanings. Considering *The Spectator* in these two lights proves particularly useful in examining both the experiments with language inherent in periodical writing and the experiments with language distinctive to Addison's and Steele's creation of a moral vocabulary. We can approach these points somewhat obliquely by considering, first, *The Spectator*'s use of its reader's letters, since the letters show both the processes of negotiation that assign meanings to words and the processes of appropriation by which its readers assimilate *The Spectator*'s style.

THE SPECTATOR'S LETTERS AND SPEECH COMMUNITIES

The exchange of letters we have seen in *The Spectator*'s account of the family suggests their multiple functions. The letters draw the series in new directions in response to its readers' concerns, and they amplify discussions already under way with new points of view. The basic exchange, of course, takes place between the essayist and the letter writer: Mr. Spectator may reply to a letter, or a letter may reply to an earlier *Spectator*, adding a further opinion or contributing a personal experience. But the exchanges may be very intricate, as in Addison's No. 189 on the unforgiving father. A letter may be prompted by a continuing discussion ("Your Correspondent's Letter relating to Fortune-Hunters, and your subsequent Discourse upon it, have given me Encouragement to send you a State of my Case" [No. 326]); it may be a reply to another letter ("I am Clerk of the Parish from whence Mrs. *Simper* sends her Complaint, in your Yesterday *Spectator*" [No. 284]); it may take another letter as a model ("The SPECTATOR's late letter from *Statira* gave me the Hint to use the same Method of explaining my self to you" [No. 204]); it may use *The Spectator* to communicate with another reader ("When I sat at the Window, and you at the other End of the Room by my Cousin, I saw you catch me looking at you" [No. 204]).

At one extreme, a single letter may make up an entire paper with no other comment from Mr. Spectator than a brief introduction. Or, particularly in some of Steele's papers, several letters may be published together in counterpoint. In No. 268, for example, Steele prints six letters, prefacing them with the comment, "I ought sometimes to lay before the World the plain Letters of my Correspondents in the artless Dress in which they hastily send them, that the Reader may see I am not Accuser and Judge my self." (In No. 158 he says, "Out of a firm Regard to Impartiality I print these Letters, let them make for me or not.") The second letter in No. 268 mirrors *The Spectator*'s own ideas. "Your Discourse of the 29th of *December* on Love and Marriage," this correspondent begins, "is of so useful a kind, that I cannot forbear adding my Thoughts to yours on that Subject." He argues, as *The Spectator* would, that "Virtue, Wisdom, Good-humour, and a Similitude of Manners" are the only foundations of happiness, yet the other letters illustrate an absurd range of behavior surrounding such reasoned speculation. They speak of nose-wringers at the theater, the current fashion in colored hoods, a man bloodying his nose by walking into a post while ogling, and a young man's thwarted adoration of a popular beauty.

One function of the letters is to accumulate new materials for the papers from the correspondents' vantage points. In this respect the letters are part of *The Spectator*'s commerce with the world in negotiating its range of topics and the values to be assigned to them. The letters thus become an extension of the *Spectator* club, and Addison's account of the club in No. 34 illustrates the functions of the letters as well. Because the club is "very luckily compos'd of such Persons as are engag'd in different Ways of Life," Addison assures his readers "that there is always some Body present who will take Care of their respective Interests." Also, "By this Means I am furnish'd with the greatest Variety of Hints and Materials, and know every thing that passes in the different Quarters and Divisions, not only of this great City, but of the whole Kingdom" (No. 34). The letters further incorporate new materials and further guarantee a respect for differing opinions. In a paper soliciting letters, Steele sees such an accumulation of viewpoints as a model of human community, serving to overcome the "Ignorance, and Prejudice" that threaten social order: "I promise my self a great Harvest of new Circumstances, Persons, and Things from this Proposal; and a World, which many think they are well acquainted with, discovered as wholly new. This Sort of Intelligence will give a lively Image of the Chain and mutual Dependance of Humane Society, take off impertinent Prejudices, [and] enlarge the Minds of those, whose Views are confin'd to their own Circumstances" (No. 428). A few weeks later, Steele enlarges this promise into a vision of social plenitude that I am compelled to quote at length for no other reason than its utter comprehensiveness:

> I will invite all manner of Persons, whether Scholars, Citizens, Courtiers, Gentlemen of the Town or Country, and all Beaux, Rakes, Smarts, Prudes, Coquets, Housewives, and all Sorts of Wits, whether Male or Female, and however distinguish'd . . . and Persons of all Sorts of Tempers and Complexions . . . and of what Manners or Dispositions soever . . . and under what Fortune or Circumstance soever . . . and of what Trade, Occupation, Profession, Station, Country, Faction, Party, Perswasion, Quality, Age or Condition soever, who have ever made Thinking a Part of their Business or Diversion, and have any thing worthy to impart . . . according to their several and respective Talents or Genius's, and as the Subject . . . may be made profitable to the Publick by their particular Knowledge or Experience. (No. 442)

"So many Men," Steele says, "so many *Spectators*."

A second purpose in publishing the letters is to establish a common body of shared opinion. William Kinsley has offered a persuasive explanation of how letters work to confirm *The Spectator*'s moral instruction.[2] *The Spectator*, Kinsley notes, insinuates itself into the routines of daily life. Published, as it were, on scraps of paper, *The Spectator* can be found lying around anywhere to be read over almost before the reader is aware he is reading a piece of morality. The publication of the letters contributes to this infiltration, since there is no clear way to differentiate between letters as "outside" and letters as "inside." Kinsley quotes Addison's admission in No. 271 that he receives "a double Advantage from the Letters of my Correspondents": "Sometimes indeed I do not make use of the Letter it self, but form the Hints of it into Plans of my own Invention, sometimes I take the Liberty to change the Language or Thought into my own way of speaking and thinking." As a result, the reader never quite knows whether the paper he is reading is Mr. Spectator's own or is based on the contribution of another reader.

Playing on this uncertainty, the essays can use letters such as that on marriage in No. 268 to suggest that its opinions are already widely shared as a foundation for common sense. *The Spectator* can thus assume that its moral essays will be taken as intended, since it has already assumed—and already demonstrated through the letters it publishes—that it expresses common-sense opinions. Or, it can introduce contrary opinions with understood irony, as when Celimine asks Mr. Spectator in No. 306 to instruct her young kinswoman in the lingo of the eyes, or when a man, railing at *The Spectator* for subverting the wit of the fashionable world, concludes his letter saying, "In short, Sir, you do not write like a Gentleman" (No. 158).

Moving counter to *The Spectator*'s multiplying of perspectives, then, is this second movement toward consistency and closure. At times, the letters exemplify an ideal reciprocity between *Spectator* and reader. When this happens, the letter writer appropriates *The Spectator*'s values and participates in its illusion of community. Thus in No. 134 *The Spectator* publishes a letter that captures its own tone at its best: "I beg leave . . . ," the writer says, to offer "the empty Tribute of an honest Mind, by telling you plainly I love and thank you for your daily Refreshments. I constantly peruse your Paper as I smoke my Morning's Pipe, (tho' I can't forbear reading the Motto before I fill and light) and really it gives a grateful Relish to every Whif, each Paragraph is freight either with useful or delightful Notions, and I never fail of being highly diverted or improv'd." On another occasion, Addison expresses surprise at the "general Reception" his papers have found, even though they are written in a style so different from the accepted wit, vituperation, and scandal of the age that "I did not question but I should be treated as an odd kind of Fellow that had a Mind to appear singular in my Way of Writing" (No. 262). A sympathetic reader can presumably read through the pretended "singularity" of style to grasp the judgment and feeling that lie behind it, just as Mr. Spectator can read through the style of his correspondents' letters to see the character of the writer. This is the reciprocity we see in No. 134, a balance in reading that imitates the spectator's reading of gesture.

In No. 95, Steele introduces a pair of letters that illustrate this balance in more detail:

> Having read the two following Letters with much Pleasure, I cannot but think the good Sense of them will be as agreeable to the Town as any thing I could say either on the Topicks they treat of, or any other. They both allude to former Papers of mine, and I do not question but the first, which is upon inward Mourning, will be thought the Production of a Man, who is well acquainted with the generous Earnings of Distress in a Manly Temper, which is above the Relief of Tears. A Speculation of my own on that Subject I shall defer 'till another Occasion.
>
> The second Letter is from a Lady of a Mind as great as her Understanding. There is, perhaps, something in the beginning of it, which I ought in Modesty to conceal; but I have so much Esteem for this Correspondent, that I will not alter a Tittle of what she writes, tho' I am thus Scrupulous at the Price of being Ridiculous.

What Mr. Spectator "ought in Modesty to conceal" from the second letter is praise of himself, so that Steele, by publishing these praises, puts Mr. Spectator in the awkward position of giving "a sufficient Instance to the World that I did not deserve them" (No. 215). But the second correspondent's praises show him to be participating in an ideal of social order: "As I hope there are but few that have so little Gratitude as not to acknowledge the Usefulness of your Pen, and to esteem it a Publick Benefit, so I am sensible, be that as it will, you must nevertheless find the Secret and Incomparable Pleasure of doing Good, and be a great Sharer in the Entertainment you give." Through the exchange of letters, *The Spectator* is shown to be a meeting ground of public and private, of "Publick Benefit" and "Secret" pleasures. As such, it is a vehicle for a symmetry of feeling. Mr. Spectator is seen to be "a great Sharer in the Entertainment you give." Through his essays, the letter writer may see into his secret pleasures, just as Mr. Spectator, through the letter, may see into the character of the writer to distinguish a man "who is well acquainted with the generous Earnings of Distress" and a woman whose "Mind [is] as great as her Understanding."

This last set of letters conforms to *The Spectator*'s image of intimacy. Just as important, they have absorbed *The Spectator*'s conventions of social representation and its distinctive vocabulary. The use of words in particular is one pivot on which the exchange of letters turns. When a correspondent writes, "I do not know that you have ever touched upon a certain Species of Women, whom we ordinarily call Jilts" (No. 187), he points, however unobtrusively, to a word shared in public discourse, as does the correspondent who asks "your Opinion what in this Age a Woman may call a Lover" (No. 380). The difference between a "Male Jilt" and a "Fribler" in Steele's No. 288 turns on the connotations of the name, and Steele in No. 53 refuses to answer a letter " '*till* Anna Bella *sends a Description of those she calls the Best bred Men in the World.*" Similarly, editing the letters calls attention to *The Spectator*'s ability to dominate the language of the letters, which supposedly represent outside opinions.

We can only rarely see how the *Spectator* essayists edited letters from their readers, since most of the letters were destroyed after being printed. But in two cases we can see how letters have been edited to match *The Spectator*'s conventions and confirm its own language.[3] In the first case, a woman describes her shock when the man who had been courting her for his wife declares he wants her for a mistress. She explains that she ran to a friend and her husband for advice. Steele, from this premise, constructs a scene in which the woman "threw my self on a Couch, and burst into a Passion of Tears. My Friend desired her Husband to leave the Room, but, said he, there is something so extraordinary in this, that I will partake in the Affliction" (No. 402). In the second case, a widower writes about his continued love for his wife. Like many writers he proposes to introduce a new topic, saying, "The just value and esteeme you have alwayes showne for a matrimoniall State, incourages my Address to you for directions to me and others who may be in that sorte of single State I am now in—."[4] Steele, however, completely rewrites the letter, polishing the style, sharpening the contrast between this account and more fashionable views of marriage and interpolating long passages of spectatorial philosophy based on his own language of emotional description: "There might be Rules formed for Men's Behaviour on this great Incident, to bring them from that Misfortune into the Condition I am at present, which is, I think, that my Sorrow has converted all Roughness of Temper into Meekness, Goodnature, and Complacency"; "To those who have not liv'd like Husbands during the Lives of their Spouses, this would be a tasteless Jumble of Words; but to such (of whom there are not a few) who have enjoy'd that State with the Sentiments proper for it, you will have every Line, which hits the Sorrow, attended with a Tear of Pity and Consolation" (No. 520).

This language is not a neutral picture of family life. Instead, it shapes the way the family comes to be seen so that, while *The Spectator* acknowledges its readers' contributions, it assimilates the letters into its own vocabulary and its own conventions of description. As a result they, too, conform to and confirm its picture of social cohesion by endorsing the language that makes this picture visible. This process of marking off a shared vocabulary with its distinctive associations is one effect that comes about through the reference in No. 520 (which is one of Steele's interpolations) to the "Jumble of Words" that will code sentiments so that they can be appreciated by those who know the true value of those words.

In No. 442 Steele offers an explanation for his use of letters that echoes Addison's explanation in No. 271. He says he has rewritten contributions "in my own Stile," adapting them to the "Character and Genius of my Paper" in order that they may "correspond." This "correspondence" works in two ways: it allows different readers whose styles and experience may be peculiar to themselves to communicate with one another; and it draws the published *Spectator* into an integral unit. Through an intriguing rhetorical tactic, the *Spectator*'s letters incorporate an audience's response to the message into the message. Again we see *The Spectator*'s crucial connection between "inside" and "outside," between disposition and gesture. But these letters illustrate another version of "inside" and "outside" that is rendered ambiguous in many ways. Letters from different sources are published together to contribute to a speaking community contained, literally, within the borders of *The Spectator*'s sheets of paper. But in the process of publication, the letters, which supposedly come from "outside," are brought into *The Spectator* and are absorbed into it. The letters, which supposedly represent diverse opinions, originate in *The Spectator*'s own speculations and stand as substitutes for it. They represent an exchange of opinions, yet they are mirrors of *The Spectator* that reflect its ideas and its vocabulary as transposed into other hands. The unresolved ambiguity that this causes, with the letters being both message and response to a message, allows the letters to be read in different ways according to the two types of correspondence. The published *Spectator* may be seen as an actual dialectic of opinions, a medium of communication between reader and reader. Or it may be seen as a fabrication, where all responses to *The Spectator* are *The Spectator*. Throughout the series we can shift from one such view of the letters to the other, in the way that our eyes shift between interpretations of an optical illusion.

THE SPECTATOR'S LANGUAGE: GESTURE AND FIELD

I have dealt in such detail with *The Spectator*'s letters because they provide a framework for seeing two facets of *The Spectator*'s language. Briefly, these are its operational and its structural dimensions. Seen from the first point of view, the meaning of a word is discovered through the behavior that accompanies its use; the word is a physical, public object used in the context of public behavior and forming part of a complex system of public actions. Seen from the second point of view, the meaning of a word is discovered in its relationship to other words in a linguistic system; its semantic connections imply a system of ideas that divides the world into identifiable parts.[5] These two qualities of language shape *The Spectator*'s style, its rhetoric, and its implied theories of language: they bring it on one side into a behavioral context where meanings are tied to social habits and to processes of negotiation, and bring it on the other side into a verbal context controlled by *The Spectator*'s patterned syntax and moral vocabulary. The difference between the behavioral and verbal context is the difference between *The Spectator* as a piece of rhetoric (a public act) and *The Spectator* as a literary system; the connection between the two explains how *The Spectator*'s words participate in the world of gestures that surrounds them.

Like the letters, the *Spectator* essays frequently focus on a word. This is most obvious in naming character types, such as an Idler, a Demurrer, or an Idol, where the use of the word identifies what is relevant and important in behavior. But the essays also show a concern with words as used in ordinary language. In No. 85, for example, Addison examines "what the World calls Zeal"; in No. 169 he speaks of "a kind of artificial Humanity, which is what we express by the Word *Good-Breeding*," and proposes to "examine thoroughly the Idea of what we call so." Steele in No. 143 considers "that part of Life which we ordinarily understand by the Word Conversation" and considers "this Vicissitude of Motion and Rest, which we call Life" in order to redefine the word: "There is no real Life, but chearful Life." Or:

> It is a very common Expression, That such a one is very good-natur'd, but very passionate. The Expression indeed is very good-natur'd, to allow passionate People so much Quarter. (No. 438)

> I would most earnestly advise them to observe a quite different Conduct in their Behaviour; and to avoid as much as possible what Religion calls *Temptations*, and the World *Opportunities*. (No. 198)

> I know no one Character that gives Reason a greater Shock, at the same Time that it presents a good ridiculous Image to the Imagination, than that of a Man of Wit and Pleasure about the Town. This Description of a Man of Fashion, spoken by some with a Mixture of Scorn and Ridicule, by others with great Gravity as a laudable Distinction, is in every Body's Mouth that spends any Time in Conversation. (No. 151)

> It is here in *England* come into our very Language, as a Propriety of Distinction, to say, when we would speak of Persons to their Advantage, they are People of Condition. (No. 294)

> It is owing to the forbidding and unlovely Constraint with which Men of low Conceptions act when they think they conform themselves to Religion . . . that the Word Christian does not carry with it at first View all that is Great, Worthy, Friendly, Generous, and Heroick. (No. 356)

The use of words enters into social behavior in two ways. First, the objects that words identify are selected, or created, through behavioral habits: we focus our attention on something like "good-nature" because it is important to a certain way of life. Second, words are learned through social contact: "one gets Phrases naturally," Steele observes, "from those with whom one converses" (No. 206). If words

are tied to behavioral habits, as this series of examples suggests, then
the meanings of words may change from speaker to speaker, and the
meanings given to words may delicately discriminate between different social groups. For this reason each of the *Spectator* essayists is
concerned with giving the proper definitions to moral words, and with
giving them their true moral weight; in weighing words *The Spectator*
weighs social attitudes.

The exchange of letters illustrates such negotiations over the
meanings of words in a series of papers following Steele's essays on
prostitution. Explaining his blunt words, Steele says that he has been
severe with keepers, pimps, and whores by naming them as such, but
that differing circumstances require that not all unfortunate women
"be huddled in the common Word due to the worst of Women":
"Calling Names does no Good; to speak worse of any thing than it
deserves, does only take off from the Credit of the Accuser, and has
implicitly the Force of an Apology in the Behalf of the Person ac-
cused. We shall therefore, according as the Circumstances differ, vary
our Appellations of these Criminals" (No. 274). In spite of this justification, *The Spectator* prints a letter two days later from Mr. Courtly,
who is offended: "Your Papers which regard the fallen Part of the fair
Sex, are, I think, written with an Indelicacy which makes them unworthy to be inserted in the Writings of a Moralist who knows the
World." The last phrase, "who knows the World," places Mr.
Courtly's opinions about words within a view of polite society counter
to that of *The Spectator*. Mr. Courtly is particularly offended that *The
Spectator* speaks of the indiscretions of fashionable ladies in the same
way that it speaks of the sins of the lower class: "A Man of Breeding
speaks of even Misfortune among Ladies, without giving it the most
terrible Aspect it can bear; and this Tenderness towards them, is
much more to be preserved when you speak of Vices." (This same
paper includes letters from a woman taken aback by a gentleman
"who took Liberty to name the Words Lusty Fellow in my Presence,"
and from a girl in keeping concerned that she might be called "by one
very rude Name which I do not care to repeat.")

A week later a second correspondent defends *The Spectator*: "True
delicacy, as I take it [and notice that he defines "delicacy" even in this
phrasing], consists in Exactness of Judgment and Dignity of Sentiment" (No. 286). Such exactness of judgment must be brought to the

use of words. The meaning of a word (that is, the values which it conveys) must correspond to the meaning of the act it identifies:

> I know not any thing more pernicious to good Manners, than the giving fair Names to foul Actions; for this confounds Vice and Virtue, and takes off that natural Horrour we have to Evil. . . . Who knows not that the Difference between obscene and modest Words expressing the same Action, consists only in the accessary Idea, for there is nothing immodest in Letters and Syllables. Fornication and Adultery are modest Words, because they express an evil Action as criminal, and so as to excite Horrour and Aversion.[6]

Mr. Courtly's ill-considered euphemisms bring with them an "accessary Idea" which utterly confuses the moral issue, and the second correspondent corrects him by making that accessory idea explicit:

> The most free Person of Quality, in Mr. *Courtly*'s Phrase, that is to speak properly, a Woman of Figure who has forgot her Birth and Breeding, dishonour'd her Relations and her self, abandon'd her Virtue and Reputation, together with the natural Modesty of her Sex, and risqued her very Soul, is so far from deserving to be treated with no worse Character than that of a kind Woman, (which is doubtless Mr. *Courtly*'s Meaning if he has any) that one can scarce be too severe on her, in as much as she sins against greater Restraints, is less expos'd, and liable to fewer Temptations, than Beauty in Poverty and Distress.

This sequence of papers is a dramatic illustration of a continual assessment of a moral vocabulary. In a context which makes it clear he is speaking of a social semantics, John Hughes says, "It has been my Ambition, in the Course of my Writings, to restore, as well as I was able, the proper Ideas of Things" (No. 525). Steele had made a similar, although more particular, observation in No. 490: "I have very long entertained an Ambition to make the Word *Wife* the most agreeable and delightful Name in Nature." Both these statements of purpose reflect a supposition about how words obtain meaning. Like the correspondent in No. 286, Steele and Hughes apparently understand the meaning of a word to reside in an "accessary Idea." This is, roughly, a set of associative connotations that are not only verbal connotations but also behavioral connotations: if a person uses a word in a certain way, he will *act* in a certain way, because words and actions are equally parts of behavioral habits. Meaning, then, is not a matter of reference but of a word's place within a cluster of values. That cluster of values will become apparent in the way a speaker uses the word, and it will become apparent in a pattern of behavior.

This is the background for Hughes's ambition to "restore . . . the proper Ideas of Things," and the background for the character of Benevolus, whom we saw earlier to be the best of friends because he is "the best and best beloved of Husbands." The Restoration wits who had lampooned marriage had defined words in a way which must be corrected: "It was determined among those airy Criticks, that the Appellation of *a Sober Man* shou'd signify *a Spiritless Fellow.* And I am apt to think it was about the same time, that *Good-nature,* a Word so peculiarly elegant in our Language that some have affirmed it cannot well be expressed in any other, came first to be rendered Suspicious, and in danger of being transferred from its original Sense, to so distant and Idea as that of *Folly.*" The use of words shades into the usages of style. The conceited billets-doux written by wits to their mistresses "would make any one Sick in the reading." "But in how different a Stile must the wise *Benevolus,* who converses with that good Sense and Good-humour among all his Friends, write to a Wife who is the worthy Object of his utmost Affection?"

There is an intimate connection between the meanings attributed to words and modes of behavior, as Hughes shows in the modalities of style. A similar analogy had been drawn in No. 350 with respect to "true Courage": "There is a Propriety in all things; and I believe what you Scholars call just and sublime, in Opposition to Turgid and bombast Expression, may give you an Idea of what I mean, when I say Modesty is the certain Indication of a great Spirit, and Impudence the Affectation of it. He that writes with Judgment, and never rises into improper Warmths, manifests the true Force of Genius; in like Manner, he who is Quiet and Equal in all his Behaviour, is supported in that Deportment by what we may call true Courage." In No. 354 a correspondent, well skilled in "the Language of the Eyes," explains that he can see in the impudence of young men "a general Affectation of Smartness, Wit and Courage." In *The Spectator* as social criticism, the contextual determinants which constitute "style" include a broad range of extralinguistic actions, actions that embody the values of a group.

The Problem of Definition: *The Tatler*

Words, particularly moral words, which John Locke had found to be especially susceptible to subtle shifts of value, can provide access to the social structures that give them meaning. I can further illustrate such shifts in meaning with two examples from *The Tatler* that bring the interdependence of language and behavior into clear relief.

In *Tatler* 56 Steele presents a discussion of words notably reminiscent of one argument Locke makes concerning language, an argument I will comment on later. Isaac Bickerstaff explains that a young man has been visiting him from a foreign country:

> He has but very little of our Language, and therefore I am mightily at a Loss to express to him Things, for which they have no Word in that Tongue to which he was born. It has been often my Answer upon his asking, Who such a fine Gentleman is? That he is what we call a *Sharper*, and he wants my Explication. I thought it would be very unjust to tell him, he is the same the *French* call *Coquin*; the *Latins, Nebulo*; or the *Greeks*, Ράσκαλ: For as Custom is the most powerful of all Laws, and that the Order of Men we call Sharpers are receiv'd amongst us, not only with Permission, but Favour, I thought it unjust to use 'em like Persons upon no Establishment. Besides that, it would be an unpardonable Dishonour to our Country, to let him leave us with an Opinion, that our Nobility and Gentry kept Company with common Thiefs and Cheats.

After Bickerstaff's deliberations, his friend Sophronius explains that the acceptance of sharpers has, "by Custom," "crept into the Conversation-Part of our Lives," and that "it must be corrected where it began . . . by bringing Raillery and Derision upon the Persons who are guilty, or those who converse with 'em." "For the *Sharpers* (continued he) at present are not as formerly, under the Acceptation of Pick-pockets; but are by Custom erected into a real and venerable Body of Men, and have subdu'd us to so very particular a Deference to them, that tho' they are known to be Men without Honour or Conscience, no Demand is call'd a Debt of Honour so indisputably as theirs." This acceptance of sharpers is part of a mode of behavior that has infiltrated certain segments of English society, and that is also reflected, Sophronius says, in a false understanding of the word "Honour." Thus the "Raillery and Derision" that Sophronius advocates as a remedy for sharpers penetrate the whole system of social activity which makes a sharper possible by bantering on the false sense of a word.

The second example involves a more delicate discrimination of meanings. Earlier in *The Tatler* Bickerstaff had received a letter which "A Gentleman has writ to me out of the Country": "There are many Terms in my Narratives which he complains want explaining, and has therefore desir'd, that, for the Benefit of my Country Readers, I would let him know what I mean by a *Gentleman,* a *Pretty Fellow,* a *Toast,* a *Coquet,* a *Critick,* a *Wit,* and all other Appellations of those now in the gayer World who are in present Possession of these several Characters" (*Tatler* 21). Steele, as Bickerstaff, begins with "him we usually call a *Gentleman,* or Man of Conversation": "It is generally thought, That Warmth of Imagination, quick Relish of Pleasure, and a Manner of becoming it, are the most essential Qualities for forming this Sort of Man. But any one that is much in Company will observe, That the Height of good Breeding is shown rather in never giving Offence, than in doing obliging Things. Thus, he that never shocks you, tho' he is seldom entertaining, is more likely to keep your Favour, than he who often entertains, and sometimes displeases you."

It is clear that Steele is doing more here than enlightening his country readers. He uses the meanings of the word to discriminate different perspectives on the world. He defines a true gentleman in contrast to what is "generally thought," and defines him in terms of an attitude toward society which stands apart from conventional behavior.

Stephen Ullman uses the English word *gentleman* to demonstrate how the meaning of a word can depend upon a pattern of cultural associations: "To foreigners, this concept seems so typically British that in most cases no attempt is made to translate the word. The ideal norm of moral qualities and social attitudes which the term represented for generations of Englishmen is well brought out . . . in Steele's famous formula: 'The Appellation of *Gentleman* is never to be affixed to a Man's Circumstances, but to his Behaviour in them.' "[7] (For Augustan moralists "good-nature" would have been the most profound example of a distinctive and untranslatable English word.) Steele would presumably have agreed with Ullman's broader argument that a moral word gets its meaning through the moral qualities and social attitudes of a nation, but he would not have been altogether content with Ullman's handling of "gentleman." Like Ullman, Locke

in the *Essay Concerning Human Understanding* points out that there can
be insurmountable problems in translation, since the cultural values
assigned to words vary from nation to nation, but Steele and Addison
have taken Locke's observations a step farther to suggest that variations in the uses of words not only distinguish different nations but
can distinguish different speech communities within any one nation.
Moreover, these differences in the uses of words imply differences in
behavior, since the values assigned to words are part of a complex of
behavioral habits: different speech communities are different behavioral communities. A proper understanding of the word *gentleman* will
be integrated into a whole mode of action. But a proper understanding can be achieved only by someone who appreciates a sphere of
values limited even within the fashionable world in England. Thus by
redefining *gentleman* Steele has shifted from what "is generally
thought" into a more intimate and more cohesive sphere of values.
Just such a shift of value occurs in *Spectator* 2, for example, when
Steele describes Sir Roger de Coverley as "a Gentleman that is very
singular in his Behaviour": the phrase marks the shift from the values
of the world to the values of the club.

Consciousness of Words and Theories of Language

An interest in what I have called the operational dimension of language is part of a general Augustan fascination with words,[8] with
words as indices of national character (as in No. 137), with words as
empty formalities (as in No. 371), with words as elements in social
dialects. One correspondent, for example, writes to *The Spectator*
about fashionable idioms ("among Men of Dress it is a common
Phrase to say *Mr.* Such an one *has struck a bold Stroke*" [No. 319]), and
another writes about the misleading language of "the Trading World"
("let none of your Correspondents impose on the World, by putting
forth base Methods in a good Light, and glazing them over with improper Terms. . . . Let not Noise be call'd Industry, nor Impudence
Courage. Let not good Fortune be imposed on the World for good
Management, nor Poverty be call'd Folly" [No. 443]).

One of *The Spectator*'s most extended discussions of social dialect
includes a quotation from Tillotson:

> The World is grown so full of Dissimulation and Compliment, that
> Mens Words are hardly any Signification of their Thoughts. . . . The

Dialect of Conversation is now-a-days so swell'd with Vanity and Compliment, and so surfeited (as I may say) of Expressions of Kindness and Respect, that if a Man that lived an Age or two ago shou'd return into the World again, he would really want a Dictionary to help him to understand his own Language, and to know the true intrinsick Value of the Phrase in Fashion. (*Spectator* 103)

A quarter of a century later, Fielding returned to these same topics in his periodicals with a discussion of compliments, swearing, and jargon (*Champion,* January 17, 1739/40), a definition of good nature (*Champion,* March 27, 1740), a glossary of modern usage (*Covent-Garden Journal,* No. 4, January 14, 1752), and a disquisition on verbal parochialism (*True Patriot,* No. 23, April 8, 1746): "Now, when the divine, the free-thinker, the citizen, the whig, the tory, &c., pronounce such an individual to be a good man, it is plain that they have all so many different meanings; and he may be a very good man in the opinion of one of the company, who would be a very bad one in that of all the others."[9]

A concern with words as reflections of social ethics is of ancient origin. Thucydides, for one, had found a changing value in words to be symptomatic of ethical change: "The received value of names imposed for signification of things was changed into arbitrary. For inconsiderate boldness was counted true-hearted manliness: provident deliberation, a handsome fear: modesty, the cloak of cowardice: to be wise in every thing, to be lazy in every thing."[10] But an interest in verbal precision, and a corresponding awareness of verbal ambiguities, were given new impetus, above all, by Locke's discussions of the abuse of words in book 3 of the *Essay.* Justifying his extended discussion of words, Locke explained:

Men would often see what a small pittance of reason and truth, or possibly none at all, is mixed with those huffing opinions they are swelled with; if they would but look beyond fashionable sounds, and observe what *ideas* are or are not comprehended under those words with which they are so armed at all points, and with which they so confidently lay about them. I shall imagine I have done some service to truth, peace, and learning, if, by any enlargement on this subject, I can make men reflect on their own use of language.[11]

Eustace Budgell quotes this argument as a preface to his own essay on the abuse of words (*Spectator* 373) and writes: "I know no two

Words that have been more abused by the different and wrong Interpretations which are put upon them, than those two, *Modesty* and *Assurance*"—Thucydides' moral emphasis and his vocabulary have been retained, but Budgell's corrections appeal to newer authority. (These efforts at redefinition apparently succeeded, since a correspondent in No. 461 writes to say that "Modesty is become fashionable, and Impudence stands in need of some Wit, since you have put them both in their proper Lights"—although twenty-eight years later, Fielding cites the same passage from Locke to introduce his own discussions of jargon.)

Locke's main line of argument in book 3 emphasizes the need for precision in the use of words: in order to use a word accurately, a speaker must have a clear and distinct idea of what that word means.[12] As a secondary argument, Locke also explains how variations in meaning come about, by calling attention to the behavioral circumstances that influence meaning. He offers "an argument that appears to me new and a little out of the way" (3.5.16). He describes languages as social creations, arguing that semantic inequality between languages is the result of different experiences within cultural groups.

> A moderate skill in different languages will easily satisfy one of the truth of this, it being so obvious to observe great store of words in one language which have not any that answer them in another. Which plainly shows that those of one country, by their customs and manner of life, have found occasion to make several complex ideas, and given names to them, which others never collected into specific ideas. . . . Nay, if we look a little more nearly into this matter, and exactly compare different languages, we shall find that, though they have words which in translations and dictionaries are supposed to answer one another, yet there is scarce one of ten amongst the names of complex ideas, especially of mixed modes, that stands for the same precise idea which the word does that in dictionaries it is rendered by. (3.5.8)

As emphasized in this last sentence, Locke is particularly concerned with those words that designate "mixed modes," that is, ideas compounded from other ideas. Foremost among these are ideas of moral qualities.

Locke is a thorough empiricist in his writings on language. Words, he argues, are assigned to ideas that exist in the mind of the individual speaker. Because there is no inherent connection between words and ideas, the meanings of words and the structures of language are arbitrary (3.2.1, 8; 3.5.6). Man, however, has been given language for the purpose of social communication, and a common use of words is established through conventions created within a society (3.1.1, 5; 3.2.1, 2, 8). Each society assigns words to ideas or compounds of ideas that are especially important to that society or common in its everyday life (3.5.6, 7, 13). The use of a word, then, can vary from language to language, because in each language a word will be associated with a combination of actions particular to one nation. Furthermore, words attain connotative value through habitual associations, that is, through repeated usage, and these associations too are determined by cultural patterns of a particular way of life (3.2.6).[13] The problem in communication still remains that words correspond only to ideas held by the individual speaker, so that two interlocutors may have different ideas connected with the same words, but the thrust of Locke's argument is that languages are social. A core of common experience shapes the resources of language and for the most part overcomes discrepancies in individual meanings.

To the importance of social conventions, Locke adds a further condition to the origins of language: language originates in sensible things, in objects or actions which one person can show another. The social conventions that define words are created through public behavior, through physical gesture. Words for physical objects can be defined by an ostensive gesture, by pointing or showing. Assigning words to mental phenomena is more complicated. Locke reasons that our words for mental objects are derived from physical things or physical actions (he gives as examples *imagine, apprehend, comprehend, adhere,* and so forth) because physical actions can be publicly observed (3.1.5). Physical gestures are held in common; they are mental acts brought into the public world. Once words have been agreed upon, then they themselves become "external sensible signs, whereof those invisible ideas, which [the speaker's] thoughts are made up of, might be made known to others" (3.2.1).[14]

Although we cannot read a twentieth-century semantics back into the eighteenth century, we can use a twentieth-century semantics to reveal implications of an eighteenth-century concept of words. For this reason, I want to turn to Ludwig Wittgenstein's discussion of meaning in the *Philosophical Investigations.* Here Wittgenstein concisely sets out the principles of an operational view of language: "For a *large* class of cases—though not for all—in which we employ the word 'meaning' it can be defined thus: the meaning of a word is its use in the language,"[15] a gnomic phrase that Stephen Ullman explains further: "The full significance of a word can be grasped only in the light of the context in which it occurs, with reference to the situation in which it is spoken, and, ultimately, within the framework of the whole culture of which it forms part."[16] Wittgenstein particularly emphasizes the importance of physical gestures that accompany the use of words: the "rules" that govern linguistic forms are, for Wittgenstein, learned through experience of public behavior. But if the meaning of a word for Wittgenstein is to be found in the behavior that surrounds its use, the word itself becomes a kind of gesture: "In order to get clear about aesthetic words," Wittgenstein argues, "you have to describe ways of living. We think we have to talk about aesthetic judgments like 'This is beautiful', but we find that if we have to talk about aesthetic judgements we don't find these words at all, but a word used something like a gesture, accompanying a complicated activity"; "The judgment is a gesture accompanying a vast structure of actions not expressed by one judgment."[17] If the word itself can be seen as a gesture, then we find that the word in *The Spectator* is only one gesture among many gestures, and that words are only one language among many languages. That "vast structure of actions" that Wittgenstein speaks of shades into the histrionics of cursing and making love, of masquerade and affectation that make up a second language of posture, gesture, and deportment.

Any society (and the *Spectator* essayists were, in practice, well aware of this) is composed of interlocking languages that condition and define one another. One of these is the language of words; another is the language of deportment and gesture: words become behavior; behavior becomes a code accompanying words. So, to understand the meanings given a word, we need to interpret it according to the "circumstances" in which it is used, just as we must interpret a gesture according to the circumstances in which it appears. By looking at the use of words as the *Spectator* essayists do, we are brought into the world of gestures that surrounds the word, the world of manners and courtesy, of coffeehouses and street scenes that *The Spectator* is famous for portraying.

By looking at the use of words, too, the *Spectator* essayists bring into collision different experiences of social behavior. Out of these collisions they intend to create a common language, to create a community of values where words can be understood with a common acceptation. A word, then, would be a sign that would call out the same response in both speaker and listener because it is part of a "mechanism of conduct" common to both.[18] At this point, however, we come to the second dimension of *The Spectator*'s language, the creation of a system of words through the verbal system of the text. In this respect, the vocabulary of *The Spectator* does not participate in behavioral habits but forms a self-enclosed system.

The Background of *The Spectator*'s Style

In the most famous description of Addison's style, Samuel Johnson called it a "model of the middle style" in prose. It is "pure without scrupulosity, and exact without apparent elaboration; always equable, and always easy, without glowing words or pointed phrases."[19] The tradition Addison followed encouraged these effects. *The Spectator* had followed the lines of the gentlemanly essay of Cowley, Temple, and Halifax, but its style is not the loose Senecanism of the late seventeenth century. Instead, it is Ciceronian, not because it is oratorical or because of any sustained hypotaxis but because of the careful logic of subordinate clauses and attention to prose rhythms in Addison's essays, in particular.

Jan Lannering has provided an analysis of these effects in a persuasive account of how Addison's "middle style" succeeds.[20] Lannering describes Addison's reliance on parallelism and contrast, which may mean a duplication of elements within a construction or a pairing of constructions, and describes his reliance on a modified hypotaxis, where the main clause is placed at the beginning and the sentence extended through a succession of relative clauses. Such reliance on a formal syntactic skeleton, for Lannering, "may be briefly described as an extensive delegation of sense-content from main statement to subordinate elements. The latter are thus syntactically subordinated, while being from a stylistic point of view the most important parts of the sentence in that they carry the bulk [of the meaning]" (p. 97). One effect of this delegation of meaning is a stylistic *copia* that allows for balance, cadence, and euphony. A second effect is a high degree of structural redundancy. A reader can readily pick up on the pattern of the sentence and anticipate its line of thought.

The most striking feature of Addison's style is the doubling or trip-

ling of constructions through pleonasm, antithesis, or chiasmus: "Delightful scenes," Addison writes, "whether in nature, painting, or poetry, have a kindly influence on the body, as well as the mind, and not
only serve to clear and brighten the imagination, but are able to dis-
perse grief and melancholy, and to set the animal spirits in pleasing
and agreeable motions" (No. 441). Lannering's analysis suggests that
Addison deliberately strives for cadence and cursus in a sentence like
this and that many of its amplifications are intended to improve the
sentence's rhythm. The effect, as Lannering identifies it, is a controlled conversational tone and stylistic elegance (p. 132). Cicero and
Quintilian had given detailed consideration to prose rhythms, including the rhythms of the familiar style, and, like Lannering, Hugh Blair
has noticed the combination of *copia* and rhythm in Addison's style:
"In . . . these instances, little or nothing is added by the second
member of the Sentence to what was already expressed in the first:
. . . though the free and flowing manner of such an author as Mr.
Addison, and the graceful harmony of his period, may palliate such
negligences."[21]

Clearly, the rhythmic effects were a principal motivation for Addison's multiplying of constructions, and they have a rhetorical impact
we will examine later. However, both Blair and Lannering also point
to semantic implications that are just as closely allied to *The Spectator*'s
rhetorical purpose. According to rhetorical tradition, pleonasm and
synonymy can be used to teach new or unfamiliar words by pairing
new words with words the hearers will already know.[22] Blair disap-
proves but describes the semantic implications of such redundancy in
the "diffusive" styles earlier in the century: "Few authors . . . are
more clear and perspicuous, on the whole, than Archbishop Tillotson, and Sir William Temple; yet neither of them are remarkable for
Precision. They are loose and diffuse; and accustomed to express
their meaning by several words, which show you fully whereabouts it
lies, rather than to single out those expressions, which would convey
clearly the idea which they have in view, and no more. Neither, indeed, is Precision the prevailing character of Mr. Addison's Style;
although he is not so deficient in this respect as the other two authors" (1:192). *The Spectator*, decidedly, has a style which may "show
you fully whereabouts" its meaning lies. It also has a more positive use
for synonymy. Words will be synonymous for Blair "because they
agree in expressing one principal idea; but, for the most part, if not

always, they express it with some diversity in the circumstances. They are varied by some accessory idea which every word introduces, and which forms the distinction between them" (1:195). A careful writer, Blair says, will pair words to "suppl[y] by one, what was wanting in the other" (1:195), and in his analysis of *Spectator* 411 he points to just such a pairing. In this case, Addison's own analysis deals with the ability to "fix" and "determine" the differences between "fancy" and "imagination."

> Though *fix* and *determine* [for Blair] may appear synonymous words, yet a difference between them may be remarked, and they may be viewed, as applied here, with peculiar delicacy. The author had just said, that the words of which he is speaking were *loose* and *uncircumscribed*. . . . We *fix* what is *loose*; that is, we confine the word to its proper place, that it may not fluctuate in our imagination, and pass from one idea to another; and we *determine* what is *uncircumscribed*, that is, we ascertain its *termini* or limits, we draw the circle round it, that we may see its boundaries. For we cannot conceive the meaning of a word, nor indeed of any other thing clearly, till we see its limits, and know how far it extends. These two words, therefore, have grace and beauty as they are here applied. (1:418)

In attempting to fix or circumscribe the meaning of *The Spectator*'s own terms we come to a central feature of *The Spectator*'s style, both because its style tends to diffuse meaning over a broad range of words and because its doubling and tripling of phrases mark discriminations among words that will teach its readers how to use moral terms. Like Addison, Steele uses parallelism and antithesis, but he does so without Addison's attention to rhythm. Seeing such duplications as a feature of Steele's style reminds us that the motivation behind them is not "grace and beauty" alone but also semantic reinforcement of a moral argument. Like Addison's rhythmic patterning, the semantics of repetition are part of *The Spectator*'s persuasive strategy.

Ronald Paulson has suggested that "*The Spectator*'s satire exploits the balanced syntax of parallel and antithesis in two ways: to infer the absent ideal of behavior by stating opposite extremes, as when we are told of the Tersetts that 'their Fortune has placed them above Care, and their Loss of Taste reduced them below Diversion' (No. 100); or to qualify censure through concession, as when Mr. Spectator says that Sir Roger 'left me at a Loss whether I was more delighted with my Friend's Wisdom or Simplicity' (No. 109)."[23] Beyond these ironic effects, however, the dominant impression of *The Spectator*'s style is a semantic alignment. Speaking of Restoration prose, Robert Adolph has said, "One has the feeling . . . that ordinary nouns, such as Envy, Benevolence, and Hatred actually stand for fixed, technical concepts, of which everyone has a clear and distinct idea, and which have already been defined."[24] One has the same feeling in reading *The Spectator*: words tend to become semantic counters, corpuscles, or atoms aligned according to formal patterns or syntax. Words or phrases in equivalent positions tend to take on semantic equivalence so that, as a passage repeats a syntactic construction through parallel or antithesis, it generates an array of associated words that share meaning within a carefully constructed system of rhetorical valuation.

Consider a sentence from Steele's *Spectator* 422, on raillery: "It is, methinks, below the Character of Men of Humanity and Good-manners, to be capable of Mirth while there is any one of the Company in Pain and Disorder." This sentence contains an operational definition of "Humanity and Good-manners"—by describing people's behavior it establishes criteria for using these words—and it establishes a pattern of logical relationships. The first two words are simply an expletive opening; the parenthetic "methinks" marks a transition within the paragraph and reminds us of Mr. Spectator's presence as an interpreter of behavior. This leaves the rest of the sentence to set up relationships among nominalized moral qualities. It establishes a system of oppositions between above and below, humanity and mockery, mirth and pain in which "Humanity and Good-manners" may be found. The two terms perform the same function within this system, and, since they are functionally equivalent, each may be defined in terms of the other. "Good-manners" is "Humanity," and "Humanity" is "Good-manners." This is a second type of definition, not based on contexts of behavior but on structures created within the essay and within the language itself.

The importance of verbal alignment is further apparent in the paragraph in which this sentence appears:

> It is really monstrous to see how unaccountably it prevails among Men, to take the Liberty of displeasing each other. One would think sometimes that the Contention is, who shall be most disagreeable. Allusions to past Follies, Hints which revive what a Man has a Mind to forget for ever, and deserves that all the rest of the World should, are commonly brought forth even in Company of Men of Distinction. They do not

thrust with the Skill of Fencers, but cut up with the Barbarity of Butchers. . . . They who have the true Taste of Conversation, enjoy themselves in a Communication of each others Excellencies, and not in a Triumph over their Imperfections. *Fortius* would have been reckoned a Wit, if there had never been a Fool in the World: He wants not Foils to be a Beauty, but has that natural Pleasure in observing Perfection in others, that his own Faults are overlooked out of Gratitude by all his Acquaintance.

Such a paragraph obviously draws from an observed world. Steele gives special weight to showing and seeing—"to shew you are well inclined," "to shew a Man you do not care." Even the innocuous sentence opener "It is really monstrous to see" suggests observed behavior. But this observed behavior is absorbed into a rhetorical alignment that has its own, self-generating logic. The paragraph reflects the conflict Augustan moralists saw between a Hobbesian state of war (preserved in Steele's metaphor of the duel) and a benevolent harmony. The individual is set against the social, revelation against communication, imperfections against excellencies. These oppositions are exceedingly simple, yet they are complete, complete in the sense that each sentence logically implies every other, and in the sense that each valuative word implies every other. The paragraph thus aligns words on one side or the other of a central division, generating two spheres of words that are related because each, in some way, entails the others:

> displeasing, disagreeable, Contention, Allusions, Follies, Hints, what a Man has a Mind to forget, Pain, Disorder, Triumph, Imperfections

> Humanity, Good-manners, the true Taste of Conversation, enjoy, Communication, Excellencies, Beauty, natural Pleasure, Perfection, Gratitude.

Even the character sketch of Fortius is absorbed into a double chiasmus: wit-fool-foil-beauty, observing-perfections-faults-overlooked.

An earlier sentence also draws from an observed scene, yet analyzes it according to a strict symmetry of ideas: "He [*Acetus*] can be pleased to see his best Friend out of Countenance, while the Laugh is loud in his own Applause: His Raillery always puts the Company into little Divisions and separate Interests, while that of *Callisthenes* cements it, and makes every Man not only better pleased with himself, but also with all the rest in the Conversation." The sentence starts with an explosion of laughter following Acetus's jokes, but it formulates the scene by setting "his best Friend out of Countenance" against "every Man . . . better pleased with himself," actions "in his own Applause" against actions to please "all the rest in the Conversation," the separation of "little Divisions and spearate Interests" against the cementing of society.

If we search for definitions of "Humanity" and "Good-manners" in this essay we find that their definitions reside in this system of alignments, and that the meaning of these words is shared by every other term in the same sphere of associated words. We find the same result if we search for a definition of *raillery*. Steele proposed to correct "the false Notion some People have of Raillery," or ("as the Term is") "biting." He assumes (and this is a strategic, not a negligent assumption) that once raillery is correctly defined, proper behavior will accompany the use of the word: all that is needed is to correct a misunderstanding, to align social values in such a way that the true meaning of raillery will become apparent. But this realignment means that Steele must control the semantic field that surrounds the word *raillery*. To do this, he repeatedly applies a moral bifurcation to generate an array of words that have equivalent roles and a common semantic value within this dominant structural scheme. The true meaning of raillery is found within the field of words.

A similar semantic diffusion is found in Addison's *Spectator* 169, although it shows still more clearly how the definition of a word does not depend on an external reality but on the patterns of *The Spectator* itself.

In No. 169 Addison points to the word "Good-nature" as an element in our language: "Half the Misery of Human Life might be extinguished, would Men alleviate the general Curse they lye under, by mutual Offices of Compassion, Benevolence and Humanity. There is nothing therefore which we ought more to encourage in our selves and others, than that Disposition of Mind which in our Language goes under the Title of Good-nature, and which I shall chuse for the Subject of this Day's Speculation."

I looked earlier at the moral argument of this paragraph, suggesting that good-nature mediates between the dispositions of the mind and the "mutual Offices" of public behavior, making possible *The Spectator*'s ideal symmetry of social responses. Good-nature, therefore, has a definite place in Addison's model of social relationships. If we look at good-nature, however, as a word "in our Language," we find something far more elusive. Insofar as it can be defined at all, good-nature can only be defined in terms of behavior: a good-natured man is one who behaves in a certain way. Indeed, Addison goes on in a companion essay to say that we recognize good-nature in ourselves not through introspection, but by looking at our behavior "at all Times, and in every Place," much as we would observe the behavior of another (No. 177). (He offers, here, an example of the good-natured man that recalls *The Spectator*'s recurring motifs: Eugenius, on his way to the playhouse, gives the money for admission to "an Object of Charity," "and afterwards pass[es] his Evening in a Coffee-house, or at a Friend's Fireside, with much greater Satisfaction to himself than he could have receiv'd from the most exquisite Entertainments of the Theatre" [No. 177].)

Good-nature is never given an analytic definition in these essays, but is "defined" within a cluster of synonyms. Good-nature serves the same function as do "Compassion, Benevolence and Humanity." All may be defined in terms of the others and may be substituted for one another. If we wished, we could, without changing the "meaning" of the paragraph, make up a phrase such as "the mutual Offices of Compassion, Good-nature and Humanity . . . which in our Language goes under the Title of Benevolence," and the substitution could be made throughout the essay. Two paragraphs later Addison speaks of "Good-nature, or in other Terms, Affability, Complaisance, and Easiness of Temper." Again, this growing cluster of words does not indicate different qualities of mind. Taken together, all of these terms indicate, simply, that one "Disposition of Mind" which is "the Subject of this Day's Speculation."

No. 169 creates an expanding cluster of words centered around good-nature because various words share the same contexts with good-nature. Then, through the course of the essay, good-nature itself is used in a succession of contexts, each one revealing new semantic connections:

Good-nature is more agreeable in Conversation than Wit, and gives a certain Air to the Countenance which is more amiable than Beauty.

There is no Society or Conversation to be kept up in the World without Good-nature.

Good-nature is generally born with us.

Xenophon in the Life of his Imaginary Prince . . . is always celebrating the *(Philanthropy)* or Good-nature of his Hero, which he tells us he brought into the World with him.

In that celebrated Passage of *Salust*, where *Caesar* and *Cato* are placed in such beautiful, but opposite Lights; *Caesar's* Character is chiefly made up of Good-nature.

This part of Good-nature, however, which consists in the pardoning and over-looking of Faults, is to be exercised only in doing our selves Justice, and that too in the ordinary Commerce and Occurences of Life.

It is grown almost into a Maxim, that Good-natured Men are not always Men of the most Wit.

As is typical in Addison's essays, each paragraph grows from the one before, like links in a chain. Through this series of linked topics, Addison brings good-nature into various semantic fields: it is part of a circle of words dealing with society or conversation, where it serves the same function as do wit and beauty; it is an innate disposition, in contrast to being acquired behavior; it is related to government and to the exercise of judgment in daily life; it is included in conventional maxims about wit. Each of these shifts in context reveals new alignments in the semantics of good-nature, or new connections possible within an expanding array of contexts. In No. 177 Addison explains that since "I treated of Good-nature, as it is the effect of Constitution, I shall now speak of it as it is a Moral Virtue," opening out a new range of possible connections.

Certain words in *The Spectator*, such as "Good-nature," are nodes or knots in a semantic network. These words become centers for a process of verbal accretion that brings more and more words into alignment with them. And they become focal points for *The Spectator's* concern with correct definition. In No. 177, for example, we learn that "Good-nature" makes "a Man easie in himself, and agreeable to others"; it provides "secret Satisfaction and Contentment of Mind," and "the kind Reception it procures us in the World." The vocabulary of *The Spectator's* moral analysis casually clusters around this one word. Good-nature, however, that arises only from bodily constitution "implies no Merit in him that is possessed of it"; it "must not assume the Name of a Moral Virtue"—that name is reserved for the good-nature which arises from the mind.

The word *virtue* is another node in the network, and it illustrates again how the processes of semantic alignment and accumulation operate in *The Spectator.* At the beginning of No. 243, on the beauty and loveliness of virtue, Addison focuses on the meaning of the word: "I understand by the word Virtue such a general Notion as is affixed to it by the Writers of Morality, and which by Devout Men generally goes under the Name of Religion, and by Men of the World under the Name of Honour." Being a "general Notion" is an inseparable feature of *The Spectator*'s vocabulary. This is what allows a word to enter into a multitude of semantic contexts. Virtue is "amiable"; it is associated with "a secret Fondness and Benevolence"; it is associated with "Beauty and Loveliness." Through these associations, Addison makes the crucial connection I have mentioned before: "The two great Ornaments of Virtue, which shew her in the most advantageous Views, and make her altogether lovely, are Chearfulness and Good-nature."

If we look back on this essay—No. 243—from this present point of view, the connection between cheerfulness and good-nature may be seen not so much as a juncture in *The Spectator*'s moral system as a juncture in a fabric of words. If we look closely at even such key terms in *The Spectator* as good-nature, cheerfulness, pleasure, or beauty, we do not find their meanings becoming more precise. Instead, we find their meanings spread over an array of associated words either by creating synonyms or by putting words into repeated collocations. Either the same context can accommodate several different words or the same word can be used in several different contexts; that is, different words may be substituted, paradigmatically, within the same syntagmatic chain so that they become functional synonyms, or the same word may be used in different syntagmatic chains bringing it into new collocations that absorb further words into its network of synonyms. We have seen this first type of semantic diffusion in No. 422 and have seen both in No. 169. We have seen them, too, in No. 306, which begins with Parthenissa's letter on smallpox. Here, a remarkably small number of words is used repeatedly to form a network where charm = cheerfulness = good-humor = good-nature = agreeability = an easy behavior.

This principle of synonymy has been mentioned in passing by A. R. Humphreys ("*The Tatler* insists . . . on the equivalence among the three terms. The true gentleman, liberally educated, is to be the true

Christian; equally, the true Christian, liberally educated, is to be the true gentleman"), and by Edward and Lillian Bloom ("Following the principle of reason, concepts like 'religion,' 'philosophical learning,' and 'morality' become virtually synonymous for Addison").[25] But Steele himself in *The Tatler* gives the most emphatic statement of this principle: "And the Words, Truth, Law, Reason, Equity, and Religion would be but Synonymous Terms, for that only Guide which makes us pass our Days in our own Favour and Approbation" (*Tatler* 48). In this way *The Spectator*, too, creates a field of related words, and teaches its readers how words are to be used within it.

Rhetoric as System and Exchange

In any rhetorical use of language the speaker creates or endorses a system of correspondences. He creates a system of identifications in which one thing stands for another, or where two things are equivalent to one another, or where two things are seen to be variations of one another. The speaker manipulates the contexts of words so that these identifications may become apparent: he creates a system of synonyms. Such identifications may be complex, and the speaker's manipulation of context may mean a realignment of cultural values; rhetoric may go to the heart of our cognitive taxonomies and may demand that we reevaluate our verbal divisions of the world. For my purposes here, however, it will be sufficient to recognize two types of identification that Kenneth Burke has found implicit in the classical notion of persuasion: identification of the speaker with his audience, and identification of one verbal form with another. The speaker projects a world of discourse (a speech community) where "men have common sensations, concepts, images, ideas, attitudes"; and he creates a vocabulary in which these common attitudes may be expressed.[26]

Both forms of identification are forms of repetition. The attitudes of the audience repeat those of the speaker, just as the letters submitted to *The Spectator* become mirrors of *The Spectator*. The arguments of rhetoric succeed because the audience to some degree participates in them. And this participation is insured because the audience participates in the formal repetition of the text. Burke explains:

> We know that many purely formal patterns can readily awaken an attitude of collaborative expectancy in us. For instance, imagine a passage

built about a set of oppositions ('*we* do *this*, but *they* on the other hand do *that*; *we* stay *here*, but *they* go *there*; *we* look *up*, but *they* look *down*,' etc.). Once you grasp the trend of the form, it invites participation regardless of the subject matter. Formally, you will find yourself swinging along with the succession of antitheses, even though you may not agree with the proposition that is expressed in this form. (p. 58)

Lannering explains the rhythmic effect of this style and its effect on reading time. The pairing of terms distributes rhythmic stresses, and as the intervals between the stresses are lengthened the sentence's semantic cues follow each other at a greater distance. This enables the reader to follow the sentence easily and quickly, even though the sentence will be longer than a compressed form that avoids the structural clues (p. 56). The redundancy inherent in pleonasm and antithesis drives the momentum of reading.

Moreover, we can compare these effects with Wittgenstein's explanation of how we learn a language game. Using as an example the game of reading, Wittgenstein explains that the forms of the game will be repeated until the learner is able to say "I can go on," and continues to generate new forms of the same type (*Philosophical Investigations*, sections 150–55). This is why the didactic repetition of *The Spectator* is as important as it is: *The Spectator*'s syntactic redundancy, its repeated use of a few key words, its periodic publication that will "refresh [readers'] memories from Day to Day" (No. 10) all serve to teach a moral language to the point that the reader can "go on" using that language.

Wittgenstein would deny that an ability to use words accurately is a "state" or "disposition" of mind. It is, instead, the ability to behave in an appropriate way in "*particular circumstances*": "The application," Wittgenstein says, "is still a criterion of understanding" (sections 149, 154, 146) (a formula we can compare with one of Steele's—"The Application of Wit in the Theatre has as strong an Effect upon the Manners of our Gentlemen, as the Taste of it has upon the Writings of our Authors" [No. 65]). Again, those activities that accompany the use of a word and that show how it is to be used include a pattern of extralinguistic behavior. The ability to use words or to read them correctly is part of a pattern of behavior that we learn by seeing how words are used (sections 150–51). So, while *The Spectator* redefines a social vocabulary it effectively alters the behavior that accompanies it.

In this respect, *The Spectator* enters the social world less because it speaks *about* behavior than because speaking *is* behavior.

Still, the structural dimension of language does imply a "state" or "disposition" where any word in *The Spectator*'s moral vocabulary has its place within a field of associated words—a field which implies a distinctive model of social relationships. The central term in this field of words is *pleasure*, together with such synonyms as *gratification* and *satisfaction*. Pleasure has a private or personal dimension, expressed in *cheerfulness*, and a social dimension expressed in *good-nature*, along with its variants—*amiability, good-humor, complaisance, humanity, benevolence*, and so on. (The social dimension of *The Spectator*'s calculus of pleasure is manifested in *society, conversation, wit, beauty*, and in an ideal of social presence expressed in *modesty, moderation, consistency, order, decorum, sincerity*, and the like.) This system of words creates a tautologous moral logic. Each word has value within this verbal system, but none of them can be defined except in terms of the others: if we look at any one of these words, we find its definition spreading out to incorporate all of the other words in the field.

This idea of tautology is more nearly Burke's emphasis when he analyzes the effects of repetition, of "going on." Any terminology, Burke points out, is suasive, since it shapes our perception of the world in a particular way; any vocabulary implies what Burke calls a "terministic screen." Moreover, "*many of the 'observations'* [which a writer records] *are but implications of the particular terminology in terms of which the observations are made.* In brief, much that we take as observations about 'reality' may be but the spinning out of possibilities implicit in our particular choice of terms."[27] Any terminology is a tautology, since the conclusions drawn from it are already implicit in it. *The Spectator* is such a tautology, and such a spinning out.

Linguistic Dualism and the Form of *The Spectator*: An Overview and Extended Analogy

The Spectator succeeds because of this doubleness in language. Many features of the papers contribute to their success as rhetoric: the essays give entertaining sketches of contemporary life (and informative ones to those of us studying that era 275 years later); the character of Mr. Spectator is carefully balanced between participant and observer, comedian and savant; *The Spectator*'s whole program embraces an expanding readership while it creates the illusion of an intimate community. But at the heart of *The Spectator*'s balance of public and private communication is the duality of language: words can modify behavior because they participate in behavior, and they control behavior because they have a structure of their own. *The Spectator,* because it is so deliberately a piece of rhetoric, illuminates the doubleness of whatever we read: it draws from and returns to its society; and it forms a self-enclosed, self-contained, self-reflecting world within itself.

The doubleness of language as transaction and as system also illuminates the form of *The Spectator.* To explain this, I need to trace out certain lines of analogy.

If we look at a word as being spoken by an individual, we can see that word as a social act, as a gesture caught up in a world of gestures, both verbal and nonverbal, which surrounds it. In this way, we look outside of the word to assess its meaning, toward its circumstances.[28] Alternately, we can look at the word as a manifestation of the speaker's conscious or unconscious mind. In this way, we try to penetrate into a core of meaning which lies somehow behind the word, since the speaker's psychology, even if disguised, is (presumably) revealed in or embodied in the word or in the way it is spoken. More abstractly (setting aside the matter of the speaker), we can see the word as part of an operation, where the meaning of the word is to be found in the context in which it is used, or as part of a linguistic system, where the meaning of the word is its function in the system. In the first case, an analysis of the word again leads outside it to its context. In the second case, an analysis of the word again leads inside in an attempt to find a core, an invariant heart to the structure—"that invariant of which everything in a work is a variation."[29]

The next step in this series of comparisons leads me to consider how a word may be used: it may be used to explain a phenomenon or to name a phenomenon. If we attempt to explain a phenomenon, that is, if we attempt to describe its causes and implications, we are led to consider multiple facets of the situation in which it occurs. Explanation, interpretation, commentary all look at an event against the context in which it occurs (all look at a gesture against its circumstances), and all proliferate, expand, enlarge, expound, adding words on words. If we name a phenomenon, or designate, or demark it, we fit the name into a system of names and tend to assume that there is an essence within the phenomenon which can be named (a gesture manifests an inward disposition, which is one of various types of dispositions). Explanation leads outward to show the phenomenon as part of a plenitude; naming leads inward to show the phenomenon as part of a system. These two impulses in using words, which correspond to the two sides of words themselves, illuminate two movements in *The Spectator*. The first is its drive toward plenitude, by which the series absorbs more and more topics, letters, and comments from readers in an expanding dialectic of perspectives. The second movement is a corresponding movement toward the wholeness of a system that will contain this plenitude within the careful patterning of *The Spectator*'s syntax and vocabulary, and that will thus give the illusion of wholeness within a carefully defined sphere of attention.

Through this line of thought we can see how *The Spectator*'s mode of publication takes advantage of the doubleness of language as transaction and as system. In concluding this meditation on form, however, I want to examine a second set of parallels that leads in a somewhat different direction: these are the parallels I have noted between the processes of reading and *The Spectator*'s accounts of social perception. We have seen these parallels at various points. They are first suggested in *The Spectator*'s opening sentence with its parallel between "observing" and "perusing," and they are suggested in *The Spectator*'s account of reading gestures, since, as in reading words, we can "read" gestures according to the context in which they occur or according to the inward character that may become apparent in them. The processes of reading and the processes of social observation also share *The Spectator*'s dimensions of time and space. Ideally, for Steele and Addison, reading and social behavior share a constancy or permanence in time, where the continuity of habit and the continuity of the papers' publication preserve an integrated self on the one hand or an integrated verbal system on the other. Most important, though, reading and social action share the same metaphoric "space," so that through this reading of *The Spectator* essays I have traced the transformations of spatial metaphors at various levels of structure.

At the heart of *The Spectator*'s representation of social life is its system of spatial metaphors opposing the inside and the outside, the private and the public dimensions of the self. Mr. Spectator exists as comedian and savant, and actors in *The Spectator*'s scenes are analyzed according to affectation or sincerity because *The Spectator*'s model of social life defines behavior according to outside and inside, gesture and disposition. This is the "shape" of *The Spectator*'s "stage," and the roles its actors can perform must conform to the roles that the stage makes possible. Given the polarity between public and private, outside and inside, *The Spectator*'s ideal form of community mediates between the poles: *The Spectator*'s modified version of retirement carries within it an immediate gracefulness observable to others; good-nature joins the dispositions of the mind with mutual agreeableness; and the ideal community is based on a symmetry of responses where an observer can feel in himself the same sentiments that inspire an actor. The family, especially, takes on a particular prominence in *The Spectator* because it has a definite place within this social geometry. It, too, mediates between public and private and can be seen, therefore, as a little society within itself. It combines the dramatized gestures and diversity of responses that characterize the public world with the intimacy of feeling that characterizes the private.

Mediating between the public and private sides of the self is central to the world represented within *The Spectator*. On another level of structure, we find that these processes of mediation also define the relationship between *The Spectator* and its readers. A gesture in the social world mediates between the public and the private: it is a public act, yet for the attentive observer it reveals the inward character of the actor. The printed word (at least this is the presupposition) also mediates between public and private: it is part of a transaction between writer and reader, and it is a revelation of an inward self. *The Spectator* re-enacts this doubleness at most levels of discourse: the essays are published, Mr. Spectator says, for the good of the public, yet they are revelations of a secret self; the published papers are distributed to a large public, yet they turn inward to create the illusion of an intimate community; *The Spectator*'s words participate in a commerce of words and gestures, yet fold back upon themselves to form a self-defining vocabulary. *The Spectator* itself exists within the dialectic of inside and outside: it is an historical, rhetorical document, and it is an esthetic entity.

At a further level of structure, though, this dialectic of inside and outside is itself absorbed into *The Spectator*. We have seen nested levels of structure in *The Spectator*. The processes of "reading" character, as represented within *The Spectator*, are duplicated between *The*

Spectator and its readers. At this level, the verbal conventions formed within *The Spectator* are set over against the world of its readers, which exists outside of *The Spectator.* But the world of *The Spectator*'s readers, which surrounds *The Spectator,* is brought into it. The context becomes part of the text whenever *The Spectator* comments on its own rhetorical transactions. The actions which prompt the writing of the text and the actions which result from reading the text are all written into the text. A reader's comments, or his new forms of behavior, or his snorts of indifference, which are effects of *The Spectator,* are written into *The Spectator* where they become part of the papers' fictional universe. If a reader wants to describe his reactions to these papers, or if he wants to comment on another reader's comments, this becomes part of *The Spectator,* too, in a later issue. So I have come again, from a different direction, to how language operates in periodical writing: we see the transactions which make up the social dimension of language, but these transactions, as we see them, have been assimilated into the conventions that are dictated by the internal patterns of the text. The commerce of words and gestures existing between reader and text becomes part of the text's own system. In the end, from this point of view, *The Spectator* is an isolated monad, a self-contained sphere or bubble. When we read *The Spectator* we are brought into a self-contained world where time is suspended by the forms of repetition which link essay to essay, just as a reader's coffee cup may be suspended in the air between his cheek and right ear. We are brought into a circle of words which grows out of itself and which is absorbed back into itself, where momentary gestures are frozen in momentary pieces of writing, to be placed before the reader at an hour set aside for tea.

CHAPTER SIX

The Spectator and Its Times

The preceding chapters have described how *The Spectator* exploits the doubleness of discourse. The essays emphasize the processes of negotiation that take place between a writer and reader, while, at the same time, they share conceptual formulas that draw *The Spectator* into an imaginative unit and create, in it, a self-contained verbal universe. The preceding chapters, too, have shown how traditional metaphors and images have been transformed because of their role in *The Spectator*'s own field of conceptual relationships. Thus Cowley's image of retirement is transformed into a "public sort of Obscurity"; commonplaces regarding physiognomy are transformed into a basis for sentimental response; and the traditional imagery of the garden is transformed into a metaphor for esthetic response.

These investigations into *The Spectator* have been a response to one set of questions I posed in the introduction. In this conclusion I want to address a second set of questions regarding *The Spectator*'s relationship to other images of social man in the early eighteenth century. To do this, I need to turn back to the two senses of "framing" I outlined in chapter 1. In one sense, the printed sheets of paper become a "frame" in which the writer (or persona) presents himself to his readers; in the second sense, the social world becomes a "frame" in which he presents himself as an actor, in the way that the stage becomes a frame enclosing the gestures of a stage actor. This distinction allows me to discuss, on the one hand, the essays' conventions for representing a writer's consciousness, and, on the other hand, *The Spectator*'s assumptions about the structures of social life, each of these becoming a frame for a particular type of self-presentation.

The Conventions of the Periodical Essay

The Spectator's most obvious impact on eighteenth-century literature was to formalize the conventions of the periodical essay. Like any other genre, the periodical essay implies a particular rhetoric and a particular epistemology, because it carries certain assumptions about what we can know and about how we can best record what we know, and because it carries assumptions about the nature of communication and, therefore, about the nature of social cohesion.

The rhetoric of *The Spectator* is Horatian. Like the Horatian epistle, the essay simultaneously presupposes and creates a world of discourse, addressing its readers as though they shared common assumptions while at the same time formulating those assumptions through its own careful tutelage. Of the circle of Maecenas, Steele remarks that "a certain Unanimity of Taste and Judgment . . . was the Band of this Society" (No. 280), and it is precisely such a "band" that *The Spectator* intends to create between itself and its readers. Similarly, the periodical's persona is Horatian. In each of his various manifestations (as Isaac Bickerstaff, as Mr. Spectator, as Mr. Censor, as Hercules Vinegar, as Mr. Rambler) the essays' persona is a keen observer of the world, but one who is not involved in it. As a result, he can afford a degree of self-mockery and a degree of tolerance toward men of differing opinions. *The Spectator*'s rhetoric, then, is a rhetoric of assimilation, in contrast to the rhetoric of exclusion of the Tory satirists. This is how Addison characterizes his practice in *The Free-Holder*, by contrast to Swift's *Examiner.* "The *Examiner* would not allow such as were of a contrary Opinion to him, to be either Christians or Fellow Subjects. With him they are all Atheists, Deists, or Apostates, and a separate Common-Wealth among themselves, that ought either to be extirpated, or, when he was in a better Humour, only to be banished out of their Native Country" (*Free-Holder* 19). Like the *Free-Holder* persona, Mr. Spectator does not heighten the antagonism between himself and his adversaries but, through a rhetorical sleight of hand, assimilates them into his own "Community" and "make[s] them happy in the same Government with [himself]." The aim of both periodicals is to draw men together into a cohesive community.[1] This potential for toleration allows for the eighteenth century's characteristic comedy of perspectives, built up by compounding different characters' points of view. The main plot here involves a metamorphosis whereby the underlying bonds of attachment are revealed from beneath characters' humors in the way that Addison's fox-hunting Tory squire is metamorphosed into a Whig (*Free-Holder* 45) or in the way that the affection between Sir Roger de Coverley and Sir Andrew Freeport is revealed near the end of *The Spectator* in spite of their political disagreements (*Spectator* 517).

In addition to serving as a vehicle for social cohesion, the periodical essay suggests a particular epistemology. It suggests that we process knowledge according to corpuscular moments of experience, according to moments of sensation or momentary glimpses of peoples' characters: the medium of publication mimics the medium of cognition. The periodical essay in this way dramatizes Locke's succession of ideas, although the flux of experience is also paired with the continuity of reflection. *The Spectator* shows a great confidence in language and in the essay as ways of ordering experience. This is still the flush of confidence that accompanies a new medium of representation. And the periodical essay *is,* for 1711, a new medium: it is a momentary piece of writing, the product of momentary experiences, which can be read in a quarter of an hour; yet it brings together a comprehensive vision of a moral universe. Each detail in our lives becomes a window onto the whole, and through the ordering power of language (the ordered garden, the methodized essay) the whole can be made coherent. This confidence about the ordered essay is clearly a corollary, too, to Locke's confidence that the mind can order experience through reflection: the mind can achieve clear and distinct ideas, and it can array propositions in coherent sequences, even from the flux of sensations.

Finally, *The Spectator* fosters a double sense of the self where we may be aware of ourselves as actors in social scenes and also aware of ourselves as observers, watching our own performances from the point of view of a distanced second self. In recording dramatized scenes and fostering this kind of double consciousness, the periodical moves away from formal discourse toward other genres, such as letters and diaries, that capture momentary perceptions and put forward an amused reflection on the performing self. As a commentary on social behavior and a medium of self-reflection, *The Spectator* can be said to be a public analogue to personal letters or to that more private periodical, the diary. And letters and diaries, in turn, become private analogues to *The Spectator.* Boswell, for example, in the *London Jour-*

nal (1761–62) often identifies himself as a spectator: "But a person of imagination and feeling, such as the Spectator finely describes, can have the most lively enjoyment from the sight of external objects without regard to property at all. London is undoubtedly a place where men and manners may be seen to the greatest advantage." And Horace Walpole also likens himself to a *Spectator* figure: "Well! I have made out half a letter with a history very like the journal in the *Spectator*, of the man, the chief incidents of whose life were stroking his cat, and walking to Hampstead." In his own Introduction to the *London Journal* Boswell takes a characteristically spectatorial attitude toward himself: "A man cannot know himself better than by attending to the feelings of his heart and to his external actions, from which he may with tolerable certainty judge 'what manner of person he is.' "[2]

As we shall see shortly, the impossibility of Boswell's attempt to know "what manner of person he is," along with Sterne's exploded explanations of gesture, lead by the 1760s to the collapse of *The Spectator*'s conceptual synthesis. But *The Spectator*, in its portrayal of daily life as a succession of gestures, had promoted a particular way of looking at one's self. And it had brought a new view of society into literary prominence by redefining regions of social experience, by marking out a region of intimacy. This redefinition of social space constitutes the second sense of "framing" which helps explain *The Spectator*'s impact on the eighteenth century.

The Spectator's Paradigm of Social Life

Michel Foucault in *The Order of Things* has said that he has investigated "an epistemological space specific to a particular period" in order to outline the various kinds of relationships that can be articulated in the discourse of different eras.[3] With something of the same purpose, I have been investigating a concept of social space specific to a particular period by reconstructing an implicit model of the social world from *The Spectator*'s metaphors and semantic fields. One of the most important features of *The Spectator* is its redefinition of the public and private dimensions of social man. In redefining these relationships the *Spectator* essays provided an image of society that influenced representations of social life for fifty years.

The dominant model of society for seventeenth-century writers had been based on a polarity between the public world and the private world, the *vita activa* and the *vita contemplativa.* The public world is a realm of power, of social encounters and social manipulation; it is the world of the courtier. The private world is a realm of individual retirement. This is a division reflected in Cowley's essays, in Temple's essay "Upon the Gardens of Epicurus," or in Marvell's poem "Upon Appleton House." Or, it is reflected in the pamphlet debate between George Mackenzie and John Evelyn, where Mackenzie wrote a *Moral Essay on Solitude, Preferring it to Publick Employment* (1665) and Evelyn replied by inverting the terms—*Publick Employment and an Active Life Prefer'd to Solitude* (1667). After the publication of his pamphlet, Evelyn allied himself to the other side and wrote to Cowley to say that "I conjure you to believe y^t I am still of the same mind, & that there is no person alive who dos more honor and breathe after the life and repose you so happily cultivate."[4] For Cowley, as he explains in a letter to Evelyn, the subject "is one of the noblest controversies both modern and ancient."[5]

Evelyn's ambivalent allegiances are significant not so much because of the choice itself as because of the alternatives that define the choice. An individual can either participate in the mechanisms of power (whether this is the political power of the court or the social power at the heart of seventeenth-century comedy), or he can separate himself from them in retirement. There is simply no place for something like the family in this model of social life. Or rather, the family is relegated to a shadowy realm outside of the principal focus of people's attention. There are rules for demeanor in the family (these are laid out in various conduct books or books of religious advice, or in pieces of personal advice such as Halifax's "Advice to a Daughter"), but the affections and tensions of family life have no assigned value within this model. To move into the family is to disappear from people's conscious attention. Early in the century, for example, Bacon had written that "He that hath *Wife* and *Children*, hath given Hostages to Fortune; for they are Impediments, to great Enterprises. . . . Certainly, the best workes, and of greatest Merit for the Publike, have proceeded from the *unmarried* or *Childlesse Men*; which, both in Affection, and Meanes, have married and endowed the Publike."[6] This perception of the family had not much changed when Halifax wrote for his daughter near the end of the century: the public realm is the realm of the husband; the wife will receive no recognition for keeping the household, but only contempt if she fails—"I say, when a *Husband*, whose Province is without Doors, and to whom the Oeconomy of the House would be in some degree Indecent, findeth no *Order* nor *Quiet* in his *Family* . . . The *Mistaken Lady*, who thinketh to make *amends* for all this, by having a well-chosen *Petty-Coat*, will at last be convinced of her *Errors* and with grief be forced to undergo the Penalties that belong to those who are willfully *Insignificant*."[7]

One conceptual shift taking place during the eighteenth century was to modify this traditional separation of public and private lives. The distinction between public and private became blurred, or came to be replaced by a distinction between coherent communities (an "inside") and the chaos of the public world (an "outside"), so that the family came to be described as an intimate community with its own drama and its own adjustments.[8] I can illustrate this shift with two examples, one drawn from political theory and the second from Restoration comedy. Both examples illustrate a changing emphasis away from a concern with an exercise of power in a public realm toward a concern with a process of negotiation within the newly defined realm of the family.

In political theory, there are crucial differences between Hobbes's image of the family (which is structurally similar to Filmer's) and Locke's. For Hobbes, "He that hath the dominion over the child hath dominion also over the children of the child, and over their children's children. For he that hath dominion over the person of a man hath dominion over all that is his" (*Leviathan*, chap. 20). For Locke, the social order is a system of contracts made between equal individuals. Men and women, he reasons, unite "by a voluntary Compact" for procreation and also for "mutual Support and Assistance." Within the commonwealth of the family " 'tis plain . . . That the *Master of the Family* has a very distinct and differently limited *Power* both as to time and extent, over those several Persons that are in it. . . . And he certainly can have no absolute power over the whole *Family* who has but a very limited one over every individual in it" (*Concerning Civil Government*, 2.7.78,86): decisions within the family have to be adjusted for the different interests and needs of the members of the family.[9]

In drama, Congreve's *Way of the World* contains the magnificent proviso scene in which Mirabell and Millamont set the conditions for their marriage, and in doing so go through the rituals of courtship by which they fall in love. Such social comedy (generically) is made up of a system of tests which distinguish true from false, polite from affected, powerful from weak. Those characters who pass these tests enjoy a social power, a manipulative control over others. By turning toward the personal accommodation they have themselves attained, Mirabell and Millamont separate themselves from this world of manipulative power—although they, of course, enjoy its benefits.

In the subsequent "drama" of narrative fiction the world of manipulation fades into the background until it ceases to form a cohesive plot, while the proviso scene comes into the foreground to become the plot of the novel. The plot of the eighteenth-century family novel (generically) is the adjustment of individuals in a family, set against a background of social manipulation. So, while the intimacy of family life had had no defined place in the traditional distinction between public action and private retirement, a conflict between the public and the private becomes a recurring theme in the mid-century novel as a way of defining the nature of family life, in Fielding's *Amelia* as well as in Richardson's novels. Although they may be drawn into a closed world through the power of passion, men in Richardson's novels typically exist in a public world where they enjoy the clarity provided by different viewpoints and where they cannot be imposed upon, while women try to establish security within the household, often with only themselves as witnesses. One source of tension, therefore, is an attempt to define acceptable relationships between these two realms of action. Clarissa calls attention to their competing demands when she writes that if she were to escape her family for London "the rashness [would be] *public*, the motives, were they escuseable, *private*"; and one issue after Pamela's marriage is Mr. B's respect for her privacy and his conduct when they are alone.[10] *Amelia* has a similar source of conflict, although the drama here lies less in the separation of the family from the world than in their interpenetration. Both Booth and Amelia attempt to establish a secure life within the family, but the novel is driven by an ironic logic whereby each attempt to preserve the family leads it into a destructive encounter with the venality of the world. The secure inside is subverted by the disordered outside so that the relationship between public and private has become a framework in which to locate the family and examine the dynamics of family relationships.[11]

Of course, I see *The Spectator* as a major factor in promoting this newer perception of social life because it provides a vocabulary and popularizes a form of social description, both of which are based on a new sense of the public and private. We see this in *The Spectator*'s analysis of gesture and its scenes of family life, such as Steele's picture of a family in No. 479. But *The Spectator* is only one representative of a shift taking place over a wider spectrum of thought, in political theory, in concepts of manners, in concepts of commerce, as well as in these pictures of family life. So we can see *The Spectator*'s overall concept of social bonds against a larger context of social description.

As John Pocock has argued, the more conservative political theorists of the late seventeenth and early eighteenth centuries saw the English freeholder to be a version of the Roman citizen, whose political independence was guaranteed by the economic independence of a self-sufficient estate or freehold. The economy of the estate and the mechanisms of government were understood to be separate areas of activity, a division made all the sharper by the back-benchers' distaste for the favoritism and corruption which they saw to be the moving forces behind government policy.[12] In a commercial economy, by contrast, property does not depend upon holding a place, but upon liquid capital and traded goods whose value depends upon a system of exchange guaranteed by a system of credit.[13] It became an article of faith for the Whig propagandists, Steele and Addison prominent among them, that English liberty can be equated with freedom of trade and that trade "is absolutely necessary and essential to the Safety, Strength, and Prosperity of our own Nation" (*Free-Holder* 42). Because commercial wealth is based on exchange, Addison in his panegyric on the Royal Exchange in *Spectator* 69 can conflate the public and private aspects of property: "For this Reason I am wonderfully delighted to see such a Body of Men thriving in their own private Fortunes, and at the same time promoting the Publick Stock; or in other Words, raising Estates for their own Families, by bringing into their Country whatever is wanting, and carrying out of it whatever is superfluous"—"They knit Mankind together," he says, "in a mutual Intercourse of good Offices." Or, the merchant "communicates his Profit with Mankind," as Steele has Sir Andrew Freeport say in *Spectator* 174.

While it would be impossible to specify any kind of causal connections, there are several suggestive analogies in changing concepts of manners to the blurring of "the old border line between private and political"[14] in economic thought. To begin with, there was the changing image of retirement we have already seen. Related to this was a changing understanding of the behavior of a gentleman. The renaissance ideal of the gentleman had been modeled after Aristotle's magnanimous man; the accomplishments of a courtier were meant to distinguish him and to advertise the degree to which he excelled other men. But this ideal came to be changed in two ways. For Steele, manners are, explicitly, a medium of equality. The true graces are those which can be achieved by anyone, and are those which facilitate an easy communication among equals. Second, by the late seventeenth century the disinterestedness of the courtier began to be displaced by the ideal of a gentleman who would actively practice charity and whose social presence was determined by emotions of the heart.[15] La Chetardie in his *Instructions for a Young Nobleman* remarks that "happy is he who has such [a heart] to be sensible to the Pleasure there is in doing good to others"; sentiment is attributed to *l'honnête homme*.[16] Tillotson casually translates the central teaching of the New Testament into the medium of courtesy in terms of inward and outward, emotional and social: "*I say unto you, love your enemies*; here the inward affection is requir'd. *Bless them that curse you*; here outward Civility and Affability are requir'd."[17]

Finally, these concepts of manners based on sensibility and on a notion of interdependence can combine into an image of social cohesion. For the benevolist thinkers of the late seventeenth and early eighteenth centuries, a classical emphasis on civic duties is transformed into an emphasis on social behavior motivated by feeling. Cicero's ladder of human association from *De officiis* (1.4.17)—moving from self-love, to love of family, to love of mankind—takes on a new importance in the passage from Samuel Clarke's *Discourse of Natural Religion* that I quoted in chapter 4. "Because the nature of man is such," Clarke says, "that they cannot live comfortably in independent families, without still further society and commerce with each other; therefore they naturally desire to increase their dependencies, by multiplying affinities." Two corollaries follow from this network of multiplied affinities. First, all men are equal in their dependence on the social bond, and second, "there is no duty whatsoever, the performance whereof affords a man so ample pleasure and satisfaction . . . as the performance of this one duty, of universal love and benevolence, naturally affords."[18] To summarize this social commerce, Clarke uses the same phrases Addison uses later, in *The Spectator*, to characterize economic commerce: men "enlarge their friendships, by mutual good offices"; "The foundation, preservation, and perfection of [the agreeing community of mankind] is *mutual love and benevolence.*"

It should be clear that Steele and Addison in *The Spectator* are redefining forms of social behavior, including the behavior of the gentleman, according to a new model of social bonds. And the redefined idea of the gentleman incorporates the behavior of the citizen. Admitting that "the unhappy Distinctions among us in *England* are so great, that to celebrate the Intercourse of commercial Friendships (with which I am daily made acquainted) would be to raise the virtuous Man so many Enemies of the contrary Party," Steele nevertheless equates charity with commerce, combines commerce with a spectrum of virtues, and celebrates the citizen: "He conceals under a rough Air and distant Behaviour a bleeding Compassion and womanish Tenderness" (No. 346). A "Citizen who is frank in his Kindnesses, and abhors Severity in his Demands; he who in buying, selling, lending, doing acts of good Neighbourhood, is just and easy; he who appears naturally averse to Disputes, and above the Sense of little Sufferings, bears a nobler Character, and does much more Good to Mankind than any other Man's Fortune without Commerce can possibly support."

A description such as this is not a picture of a certain social class; instead, it binds together a particular model of social life which includes a notion of economics, a notion of manners, and a notion of social bonds. If an individual's (economic) value does not rest on a private freehold but in a commercial exchange, then, as Pocock points out, "the individual could exist, even in his own sight, only at the fluctuating value imposed upon him by his fellows."[19] This is precisely what happens, too, in manners. If an individual's social value is not fixed according to a certain place or status, then his social value, too, fluctuates according to the value imposed on him by others. Manners, in this case, are not a display of one's status, but a medium of exchange; they are part of a transaction.

This notion of social commerce as taking place in a social region somewhere between public and private realms has certain implications for how social life can be depicted. First of all, social experience, as in *The Spectator*'s attention to momentary behavior, will be in flux: an observer cannot univocally fix a person's status in a character sketch; instead, he will find that status fluctuating according to different encounters. Thus social roles are inevitably caught up in the flow of experience through time, captured in momentary scenes. In contrast to this sense of fluidity, though, there will be attempts to stabilize social experience rather than leave a person's value undetermined. Since a person's "value" can be "imposed upon him by his fellows," we can try to preserve cohesive communities, such as families or circles of friends, where other people will consistently see our true worth. Or, we can seek to define an "intrinsic" value in a person separate from the "nominal" value which he may have in public life: we can seek to find an inner core which anchors his true worth.

The importance of *The Spectator* is that it creates a language that can articulate this model of society. It creates a vocabulary and a set of conventions which are vehicles for this model; it formalizes a particular perception of society through the shaping power of language, through the power of discourse to shape what we see in the world. I can illustrate this idea by modifying an earlier observation about *The Spectator.* In his 1913 article on Steele and Addison for the *Cambridge History of English Literature,* R. V. Routh gave a suggestive description of how urban life shaped a new social consciousness, especially in the institution of the coffeehouse. According to Routh, "Men who gathered day after day in these resorts were not only interested in their companions' ideas and demeanour; they cultivated an eye for trivial actions and utterances, a gift for investigating other people's prejudices and partialities, and they realized the pleasure of winning their way into the intricacies of another man's mind."[20] Routh has apparently read an idealized sensitivity, represented in *The Spectator,* as an attribute of actual social habits. But it is a mistake to take *The Spectator*'s scenes as transcriptions of actual behavior: the pleasure men may take in seeing into the characters of others has a definite place in the highly artificial system of social representations in *The Spectator;* it is the system of conventions created in *The Spectator* that allows us to see the coffeehouse as a region of intimacy in just this way. The process is familiar in any art: referentiality is subsumed under the work's own schemata; the conventions of art create the objects that we are able to see in the world.

What I mean to suggest by this analysis is that the social world enters literature not through a transcription of social behavior nor through commitments to any sociological group, but through a set of metaphors and conventions that vary historically and that are part of a more comprehensive model of society. *The Spectator* can synthesize perceptions drawn from etiquette, economics, and esthetics, for example, because it articulates a model of society that can subsume these various dimensions of thought under a single schema. During the seventeenth century the dominant model of society entailed a polarity separating public and private lives. During the eighteenth century this separation came to be blurred or redefined. The newer model, as *The Spectator* expresses it, entails a search for a cohesive order within an intimate group, secure against the self-interest and disorder of the outside world. In this, *The Spectator* expresses a vision of life and of the human self that, to the minds of Addison and Steele and to the eyes of their many readers, was meaningful, secure, and substantive. The epistemological center and unified vision of the papers give form to a conceptual realignment that made the family, for instance, and the impulses of sentiment visible in a new way as foundations for manners and behavior.

This kind of discovery does not mean that the object was always there but never noticed; it is not like finding a penny on the sidewalk. Instead, it entails a shift in peoples' perceptions of their world. A new set of perceptions becomes a filter through which new objects become visible,[21] and *The Spectator*'s vocabulary and persona became such a filter for social thought of the eighteenth century.

The Collapse of *The Spectator*'s Synthesis

We can argue, as I have, for *The Spectator*'s impact as a synthesis of opinions in its time. It establishes conventions absorbed by later periodicals and by other genres later in the century, and its own thinking and language have absorbed, integrated, and transmitted lines of thought from many disciplines. In this *The Spectator* conveyed a harmonious and integrated understanding of man in a social, moral, and esthetic context: the individual papers as a whole body of work become an image of that integration, of the harmonizing of disparate qualities and dimensions of human character and experience.

At the same time, however, we need to account for two other features of *The Spectator*'s history. The first is the dissolution of its synthesis later in the century; the second is the dissatisfaction that many readers have felt with the series. In a famous antithesis, Samuel Johnson says of Addison that "he thinks justly; but he thinks faintly."[22]

Many twentieth-century critics have been less kind. Bonamy Dobrée finds aspects of Addison's work "puerile," and Lee Andrew Elioseff has described *The Spectator*'s social program as a program of complacency and self-deception, masking any true moral analysis.[23] Clearly, I don't agree with such assessments, but *The Spectator*'s weaknesses are intimately tied to its greatest strengths. *The Spectator*'s descriptive formulas and its array of essentially synonymous psychological terms give the series great cohesion and synthesizing power, but they also leave it open to assertions that its authors have not enough examined the foundations of their thought. In another respect, *The Spectator* fosters a psychology of sensibility that values individual moments of sensation. For Steele and Addison, this capacity for sensation is part of an analysis of pleasure; yet for later writers such moments of sensation become fragmenting rather than integrating. Like its descriptive conventions and its creation of a moral framework, such fragmentation becomes part of *The Spectator*'s legacy, too.

Several features of *The Spectator*'s observer are carried into the later eighteenth century. Thomas Lockwood has pointed out that Fielding repeats many of the spectator's techniques for breaking a narrative frame in his addresses to the reader and self-reflexive interchapters.[24] In a different way, *The Spectator* anticipates Richardson's domestic dramas in its attention to the family and in its attention to countenances and to the physical arrangement of characters. Pamela describes the play of gestures at her meeting Mr. B's mistress, noting that "one is apt to form people's countenances by what one judges of their hearts," and Clarissa observes that "the air and manner in which things are spoken . . . often express more than the accompanying words."[25] A. D. McKillop has called this a "Richardsonian treatment of mannerism, approaching Sterne."[26]

Such attention to gesture is carried into the sentimental novel and the novel of manners, where successive scenes teach us to indulge in the pleasures of feeling or to distinguish polite from affected behavior. Burney's Evelina, for example, on first coming to London retails a spectatorial commonplace about the theater: "We sat in the pit, where every body was dressed in so high a style, that, if I had been less delighted with the performance, my eyes could have found me sufficient entertainment from looking at the ladies."[27] Her whole education proceeds by an attention to minute changes in behavior that allow her to make careful discriminations among alternative forms of conduct.

Along different lines of development, we see hints of *The Spectator*'s silent communication in a scene from Mackenzie's *Man of Feeling*:

> The boy heard his grandfather's voice, and, with that silent joy which his present finery inspired, ran to the door to meet him: putting one hand in his, with the other pointing to his sister, "See," said he, "what Miss Walton has brought us?"—Edwards gazed on them. Harley fixed his eyes on Miss Walton; hers were turned to the ground;—in Edwards' was a beamy moisture.—He folded his hands together—"I cannot speak, young lady," said he, "to thank you." Neither could Harley. There were a thousand sentiments; but they gushed so impetuously on his heart that he could not utter a syllable.[28]

The novel's attention to gesture had reached its greatest expression, of course, some years before the *Man of Feeling*, in Sterne's *Tristram Shandy*. Sterne's novel is punctuated with gestures of ineffable meaning: Trim dropping his hat, Uncle Toby flourishing his cane, Walter Shandy stretching his arm across his chest to reach a handkerchief in the opposite pocket. In many ways, *Tristram Shandy* represents an apex of the spectatorial psychology. For Sterne, preeminently, gesture is a "psycho-physical crossroads of life."[29] Moreover, Tristram exhibits the engaging comedy of the persona who can mock his own seriousness and exhibits a "journalistic" consciousness that ranges from topic to topic according to whatever comes to his attention. Tristram looks intently at the family as a unit of human intimacy and looks intently at trivial gestures in daily life. Gestures and trivial objects near at hand become a microcosm for Tristram whose interrelationships, if they could be traced fully, would reveal the outlines of the macrocosm. But while *Tristram Shandy* may be some kind of crazy analogue to *The Spectator*, it also reveals the collapse of *The Spectator*'s Lockean epistemology with its confidence that the external scene is made coherent by the perceiving mind. Whereas each detail of a person's look or dress, for *The Spectator*, has its place in an interpretative system, the system for Tristram is impossibly elusive. He cannot, however hard he tries, explain the patterns that give meaning to the detail.

If *The Spectator*'s sense of social space is one of its most enduring features, its confidence that man can know himself as observer and actor is one of its most transient. When Johnson takes up the periodical essay in *The Rambler* he turns his attention to the difficulty of interpreting our motives and true character. Like Fielding's compounded perspectives and Richardson's evocations of the divided mind, Johnson's account of man's immense capability for self-deception presents a more complex version of the self than the *Spectator* essays can present. All of these are modes of discourse that call into question *The Spectator*'s confidence that reflections on human nature and reflections on our own actions will let us "into the Knowledge of ones-self" (No. 10).

We can recognize two features of self-awareness that dissipate, for later writers, the confidence in self-knowledge that we find in Steele's and Addison's psychology. Earlier, I pursued an analogy between gestures and verbal signs. Both point outward toward the circumstances in which they are used and also inward toward some core of meaning or toward some secret self hidden within the gesture. In interpreting the gesture or sign we may turn centrifugally outward to look at the surrounding context, or we may turn centripetally inward to try to penetrate to that core of meaning. Steele and Addison assume that these processes of interpretation can reach a conclusion, that with attentive observation and the right frame of mind we can reach a secure knowledge of the characters of others or (what is best) a knowledge of ourselves. However, if we pursue an intuitive sense of a natural self, we may find that the inward self is impossibly elusive, or, if we search for the meaning of a gesture in its accompanying circumstances, we may be led outward from layer to layer of context with no stopping place to show us that this, finally, is what the gesture means. We find these two forms of uncertainty in later writers, and they are uncertainties that we share.

These possibilities are realized in Boswell's *London Journal* and in Sterne's various experiments with the narrating self. The techniques Sterne and Boswell apply in trying to understand the self are the same as those *The Spectator* suggests: beginning with a momentary gesture, the "investigator" can interpret that gesture according to the context of actions that surround it (for Sterne in *Tristram Shandy*) or according to a core of meaning that lies immanent within the gesture (for Boswell). The crucial difference is that the meaning of the gesture for Sterne or Boswell can never be determined.

For his part, Boswell assiduously records the scenes in which he plays a part, trying to find out though those scenes "what manner of person he is." But the various roles Boswell conscientiously records never converge on one image of himself. Instead, Boswell finds himself playing at a series of roles while an "intrinsic" self disappears. This fragmentation of the self has come about for two reasons. First, from Mr. Spectator's play with his two selves to Boswell's attempt to know who he is, there is an increasing distance between man as a public actor and man as a private sentient. Through the self-consciousness which *The Spectator* inevitably fosters, the self becomes objectified to itself so that any possibility for a unified intuition of the self is lost. Moreover, the man who watches his own performances sees himself as an actor, and sees his roles constituted outside of himself. Then, second, for Boswell the private self does not offer any basis for continuity because its sensations change with the fluctuations of day-to-day affairs (this being one of Boswell's favorite pastimes). *The Spectator* advocates uniformity, continuity, and habit to ensure the preservation of the self, but this advocacy is belied by the form of the essay itself. Like a writer's attention in his diary, *The Spectator*'s interests, moods, and tone fluctuate from day to day: this is inherent in *The Spectator*'s implied epistemology. So, when they are projected onto a work such as Boswell's journal, *The Spectator*'s strategies of self-consciousness become a vehicle for an evanescent self. The attempt to find an inward self within the play of gestures is bound to fail.

A similar disjunction between actor and observer is evident in Sterne's famous self-description in the *Journal to Eliza*: "When Molly spread the Table Cloath, my heart fainted within me—one solitary plate—one knife—one fork—one Glass!—O Eliza! twas painfully distressing,—I gave a thousand pensive penetrating Looks at the Arm chair thou so often graced on these quiet, sentimental Repasts—& sighed & laid down my knife and fork,—& took out my handkerchief, clap'd it across my face & wept like a child."[30] Sterne (or Yorick, or the Brahmin, or Tristram, all of them different roles that Sterne takes on) had earlier warned Eliza about a couple who entertained her: "*They* love thee! What proof? Is it their actions that say so? or their zeal for those attachments, which do thee honour, and make thee happy? or their tenderness for thy fame? No—But they *weep*, and say *tender things.*—Adieu to all such for ever" (p. 23). It seems clear that Sterne dramatizes his own tears and tender words to somehow turn them into an "action" that will prove his love to Eliza, and perhaps to himself as well. It is also clear that Sterne is aware of the tactic: he is outside his tears, seeing what they show him about himself at this moment.

As with Boswell, this self-consciousness marks the elusiveness of the inward self, and such elusiveness is one difficulty undermining *The Spectator*'s program of self-knowledge. The second complication is the dissolution of the self as it is absorbed into its external context. Sterne dramatizes this complication, too, in *Tristram Shandy.* Like the *Spectator* essays, Sterne starts his anecdotes again and again with a momentary scene. But when Tristram describes one of his family member's postures, he tries to explain that posture by describing an ever-widening, ever more digressive circle of contexts to try to locate the meaning of the gesture. He can leave his father's foot suspended between one stair and the next or leave his mother bending at a key-hole for several chapters while the ramifications of the gesture (and the ramifications of recording the gesture) spin out for page on page.

Sterne can never find the meaning of a gesture because that meaning includes the whole past of the gesture and all of the reactions of everyone present when the gesture is performed. And Boswell can never find the meanings of his gestures because the secret self hidden behind his actions always eludes him. The processes of reading a gesture according to its surrounding gestures (as in the postures of a history painting), or according to the performing self (as in the actor's gestures in the theater) no longer lead to any stopping place that can be identified as "knowledge." Fifty years after it was first published, the assumptions on which *The Spectator* was based could no longer situate man in the world.

The Spectator's psychology of sensation is one feature of the series that begins to erode its assumptions about the nature of social man later in the century. A second source for the dissolution of *The Spectator*'s synthesis lies in the form of the series itself and in its forms of language. Again, the potential for dissolution is tied to the essays' greatest strengths. Addison and Steele in *The Spectator* have created a set of conventions which for the early eighteenth century became a vehicle for a literary and conceptual synthesis. They have created a genre and by doing so have expressed an implicit metaphysics. For this reason, the essential question to ask in reading *The Spectator* is not, How does the text question or undermine conventions? but, How does it establish conventions that construct and confirm an image of the world and that confirm the integrity of the *Spectator* series itself?

As we have seen, the integrity of *The Spectator* is ensured by the perceptual coordinates in space and time that the essays endorse. In space, a phenomenon can be located along an axis connecting the "inside" and "outside" dimensions of social experience. Thus *The Spectator* writes about the outward and inward man, about external appearances and internal reality, about those outside and those inside a social group. In time, phenomena may be continuous or discontinuous. The disinterested spectator finds constant pleasure in all things about him, while the affected person halts jerkily between gesture and self-approbation. *The Spectator* series guarantees its own integrity within these coordinates by creating the illusion of an inward community containing itself and its readers: it pulls its readers' impressions, behavior, and language into itself through its control of their styles of speech, and it establishes its own continuity through its self-references and through the essays' cycle of themes that bring the last issues back to the metaphors of the first issues.

Within its verbal universe, *The Spectator* shapes one myth of the modern age. I have quoted Lionel Gossman's comment regarding "the modern, 'bourgeois,' dream of intimate and inward communication." *The Spectator* gives us this dream. It gives us an image of social man not as a courtier displaying himself but as an observer who is at once sensitive, tolerant, and critical in such a way that he can penetrate our social impostures to discover our secret selves. *The Spectator* gives us a mythology of sincerity and intimate social communion that makes the family, for one thing, visible in literature for almost the first time. It gives us the mythology of the present age.

Although they give *The Spectator* its cohesion and rhetorical power, these conventions also embody assumptions about our integrity and continuity in life that have made many readers uneasy in the eighteenth century and in our own. The centripetal movement from outward to inward implies that there *is* a substantial self hidden within us, a natural and authentic self that only needs to be discovered. To preserve that substantial self, *The Spectator*'s search for continuity implies that repetition *is* repetition, that an action we perform today or a state of mind we enjoy today is congruent with the "same" action we performed or the "same" state of mind we felt yesterday. Yet these assumptions are not immediately acceptable, and *The Spectator*'s own analysis of social forms helps to formulate some reservations.

The movement toward the center that *The Spectator* endorses has a corresponding eccentricity that we see in Johnson, in Sterne, or in Boswell's journals, as he moves in and out of alternate views of himself, and forward and backward in time. We may see such eccentricity in Mr. Spectator as well if we see him not as the essays' integrating force but as the idiosyncratic actor whose speculations commonly lead from topic to topic in long chains of divergent associations. This eccentricity takes the two forms we have seen in *The Spectator*'s psychology: it may be a centrifugal pull away from the center, or it may be an attempt to approach the center only to find that the center is inconstant.

Although the essays postulate an inward self, they also demonstrate the extent to which our selves are constituted outside of ourselves, by the social gestures that surround us, and suggest the elusiveness of introspection. When we seek to discover an inward self, we often find we are pulled outward instead, toward surrounding circumstances where we interpret our actions according to the dozens of languages of posture, gesture, or deportment that surround them and invest them with meaning. The elusiveness of an inward self is a second form of eccentricity. We also know ourselves, we may say, through introspection: we know ourselves because we know the movements of our sentiments, and we may cultivate these sentiments to ensure both the intensity and continuity of experiences in time. Still, this promise of permanence assumes that our sentiments are constant, that we do not subtly or radically shift our sentiments from moment to moment in a way that changes our identities through time without our being aware of our own discontinuities. If our sentiments of the self change in the way that our perceptions change, moving from idea to idea along chains of association, then, when we turn to seek the self through introspection, we find only its eccentricities as its essence continually slips away from us.

The Spectator shares something of this uncertainty. Although the papers postulate an inner self, they show, too, the degree to which we constitute ourselves through a play of surfaces. In the same way, they show the eccentricities of our words and gestures, since the forms of language share the centrifugal pull into circumstances and the centripetal search for an inward nature. If we try to define a sign, either we are pulled outward toward the externals that circumscribe it (as with the negotiations that establish the meanings of words), or we try to approach the "essence" of its meaning only to find that the essence always eludes us. In this second case we come to the uncertainty Blair feels about the synonymy of the diffusive style. *The Spectator* creates a rhetorical fabric of great cohesive power, but its network of synonyms points only to "whereabouts" its meaning lies.

Such synonymy may—and has—given the impression of commonplace and complacency, but it is also a fact about the essays' structure that is inevitable in their forms of expression. As we read *The Spectator*, we follow the papers' graceful movement from word to word along the surface of a pellucid crystal. But we cannot penetrate the surface. If we try to find the meaning of "Good-nature," instead of finding a semantic core or essence of the word, we slip from one word to another, from one synonym to another so that we know "whereabouts" the meaning lies, in affirming a community of speakers, without being quite able to say "here." "I am resolved," Mr. Spectator says in the first issue, "to communicate the Fulness of Heart . . . and to Print my self out, if possible, before I Die." Here is *The Spectator*'s whole program *in ovo*, its version of social intimacy and its play of surfaces, since the fullness of his heart exists, of course, only in print, as one word leads into another.

Notes

INTRODUCTION

1. Abraham Cowley, *The Essays and Other Prose Works*, ed. Alfred B. Gough (Oxford: Clarendon Press, 1915), pp. 108, 115.

2. *The Prose Works of Jonathan Swift*, ed. Herbert Davis (Oxford: Basil Blackwell, 1948), 3:5.

3. Cowley, *Essays*, p. 117. Michael O'Loughlin, in *The Garlands of Repose, A Literary Celebration of Retired Leisure: The Traditions of Homer and Vergil, Horace and Montaigne* (Chicago: University of Chicago Press, 1978), discusses Cowley's indebtedness to Montaigne, who deals with these same themes. See pp. 235–42, 252–57.

4. Donald F. Bond's introduction to his edition of *The Spectator* (Oxford: Oxford University Press, 1965) includes invaluable information about the authorship, publication, and reception of the series; see esp. pp. xx–xxix on the distribution of the papers. Richmond P. Bond in *"The Tatler": The Making of a Literary Journal* (Cambridge, Mass.: Harvard University Press, 1971), pp. 24–30, also provides information about the format of Steele's and Addison's periodicals. For Blair, see Hugh Blair, *Lectures on Rhetoric and Belles Lettres*, ed. Harold F. Harding (1783; rpt. ed., Carbondale: Southern Illinois University Press, 1965), 1:408 (Lecture 20).

5. One of the most useful descriptions of *The Spectator* is D. F. Bond's introduction, where Bond gives a concise description of characters, topics, and essay types. With similar thoroughness, R. P. Bond has described *The Tatler* in *"The Tatler": The Making of a Literary Journal*. A. R. Humphreys's *Steele, Addison, and Their Periodical Essays* (London: Longmans, Green, 1959) is an overview of all the periodicals. Samuel Johnson's descriptions of Addison's contributions to the periodicals in the "Life of Addison" (1779) is still a valuable statement of cardinal points in *Spectator* criticism. In addition to these general studies, I have been able to distinguish five principal approaches to *The Spectator* in recent criticism: (1) Attempts to categorize the

essays, as represented by Bond's introduction and by Donald Kay, *Short Fiction in "The Spectator"* (University: University of Alabama Press, 1975). (2) Attempts to correlate *The Spectator*'s success with changes in the English reading public: Bonamy Dobree, in "Steele" and "Addison," in *English Literature in the Early Eighteenth Century, 1700–1740*, vol. 7 of *The Oxford History of English Literature* (Oxford: Clarendon Press, 1959), pp. 73–84, 102–20. (3) Reconstructions of *The Spectator*'s moral system: R. P. Bond, *"The Tatler": The Making of a Literary Journal*; A. R. Humphreys, *Steele, Addison*; Wallace Jackson, "Addison: Empiricist of Moral Consciousness," *Philological Quarterly* 45 (1966): 455–59; Edward Bloom and Lillian Bloom, "Addison on 'Moral Habits of the Mind,'" *Journal of the History of Ideas* 21 (1960): 409–27, and *Joseph Addison's Sociable Animal: In the Marketplace, on the Hustings, in the Pulpit* (Providence, R.I.: Brown University Press, 1971). (4) Analyses of rhetorical tactics: C. S. Lewis, "Addison," in *Essays on the Eighteenth Century, Presented to David Nichol Smith* (Oxford: Clarendon Press, 1945), pp. 1–14; Philip Stevick, "Familiarity in the Addisonian Familiar Essay," *College Composition and Communication* 16 (1965): 169–73; Ronald Paulson, *The Fictions of Satire* (Baltimore: Johns Hopkins University Press, 1967), pp. 210–20; William Kinsley, "Meaning and Format: Mr. Spectator and His Folio Half-Sheets," *ELH* 34 (1967): 482–94; and Albert Furtwangler, "The Making of Mr. Spectator," *Modern Language Quarterly* 38 (1977): 21–39. (5) Descriptions of prose style: Jan Lannering, *Studies in the Prose Style of Joseph Addison* (Uppsala: A.-B. Lundequistska Bokhandeln, 1951). Various studies have assessed *The Spectator*'s adequacy as a vehicle for moral philosophy, among them: J. H. Plumb, "Addison's *Spectator*," *Spectator* 7178 (January 21, 1966): 76–77; Peter Gay, "The Spectator as Actor: Addison in Perspective," *Encounter* 29, no. 6 (1967): 27–32; and Lee Andrew Elioseff, "Joseph Addison's Political Animal: Middle-Class Idealism in Crisis," *Eighteenth-Century Studies* 6 (1973): 372–81.

6. Lannering, *Prose Style of Addison*, pp. 19–70.

7. Two other features contribute to the impression of syntactic control. First, Addison commonly constructs sentences based on a series of qualifications, where succeeding clauses qualify or place constraints on an assertion made in the first clause. Second, he commonly uses a full clausal phrasing in a sentence, instead of shortening the sentence by using infinitive or participial phrases or by using elliptical phrases. Rather than writing "this natural Curiosity," he writes, "this Curiosity, which is so natural to a Reader"; rather than "presaged any future Dignity," he writes, "presaged any Dignity that I should arrive at in my future Life" (*Spectator* 1). When he does use parenthetical phrases, the parenthesis usually comes near the head of the sentence and is usually a short phrase indicating time or the source of information.

8. See Murray Krieger, *A Window to Criticism: Shakespeare's Sonnets and Modern Poetics* (Princeton, N.J.: Princeton University Press, 1964), pp. 17–18 and 53–66, and "The Theoretical Contributions of Eliseo Vivas," in *Poetic Presence and Illusion: Essays in Critical History and Theory* (Baltimore: Johns Hopkins University Press, 1979), pp. 115–28. For Frye see *Anatomy of Criticism: Four Essays* (Princeton, N.J.: Princeton University Press, 1957), p. 349; see also p. 73 for Frye's distinction between centrifugal and centripetal aspects of the text. It is important to clarify that when I speak of "centrifugal" aspects of the text I do not mean that the work points to an external referent but that the work's language depends on public conventions and on the shared meanings of words that exist because those words are used in various kinds of public exchanges. This aspect of language is explained further in chapter 5. The esthetic dualism is also discussed, within different critical traditions, in Eliseo Vivas, *Creation and Discovery: Essays in Criticism and Aesthetics* (New York: Noonday Press, 1955), pp. 137–41, and F. W. Galen, "Literary System and Systematic Change: The Prague School Theory of Literary History, 1928–48," *PMLA* 94 (1979): 275–85.

9. Gossman, "Literature and Society in the Early Enlightenment: The Case of Marivaux," *Modern Language Notes* 82 (1967): p. 323.

CHAPTER ONE

1. "A Friend of mine the other Night applauding what a graceful Exit Mr. *Wilks* made, one of those Nose-wringers overhearing him, pinch'd him by the Nose. I was in the Pit the other Night, (when it was very much crowded) a Gentleman leaning upon me, and very heavily, I very civilly requested him to remove his Hand; for which he pulled me by the Nose" (No. 268). "Not long ago I was relating that I had read such a Passage in *Tacitus*, up starts my young Gentleman in a full Company, and pulling out his Purse offered to lay me ten Guineas, to be staked immediately in that Gentleman's Hands, (pointing to one smoking at another Table) that I was utterly mistaken. I was Dumb for want of ten Guineas; he went on unmercifully to Triumph over my Ignorance how to take him up, and told the whole Room he had read *Tacitus* twenty times over, and such a remarkable Incident as that could not escape him" (No. 145).

2. One of *The Spectator*'s most extravagant encounters is a scene Addison fabricates outside a stage door: "As I was walking in the Streets about a Fortnight ago, I saw an ordinary Fellow carrying a Cage full of little Birds upon his Shoulder." The birds are sparrows to be released, accompanied by appropriate music, to sing in a queen's bower, notwithstanding the possibility that "they may make their Entrance in very wrong and improper Scenes, . . .

besides the Inconveniencies which the Heads of the Audience may sometimes suffer from them" (No. 5).

3. The translation is provided by D. F. Bond, in *The Spectator*, ed. D. F.
Bond, 1:1.

4. Jonathan Swift, *Journal to Stella*, ed. Harold Williams (Oxford: Clarendon Press, 1948), 1:36 (Letter 5, October 1, 1710).

5. Morris Golden, *The Self Observed: Swift, Johnson, Wordsworth* (Baltimore: Johns Hopkins University Press, 1972), p. 5.

6. Steele can later invert the tenuous balance of singularity and good
nature and describe Sir Roger as "a great Lover of Mankind; but there is
such a mirthful Cast in his Behaviour, that he is rather beloved than es-
teemed": Mr. Spectator places no great confidence in Sir Roger's practical
judgment, especially in the administration of government.

7. Stevick, "Familiarity." Ian Watt, in "The Ironic Tradition in Augustan
Prose from Swift to Johnson," Clark Library Seminar, no. 3 (Berkeley and
Los Angeles: University of California Press, 1956), has suggested that Augustan irony divides readers into the indiscriminate "mob" that sees only a
surface meaning and a select group that understands the veiled satire. But
The Spectator seems deliberately to blur the boundary between the larger and
smaller audiences. Similarly, it plays with the notion of common sense which
"sometimes implies no more than that Faculty which is common to all Men,
but sometimes signifies right Reason" (No. 259). In this last meaning, "there
are fewer, who against common Rules and Fashions dare obey its Dictates."
As exponents of common sense, the *Spectator* essayists on the one hand offer
an "easy Philosophy" that anyone can follow while, on the other hand, they
suggest that such common sense distinguishes a small nucleus of reasonable
men.

8. In *Spectator* 618 Ambrose Philips gives a description of Horace's epistles ("such Epistles in Verse, as may properly be called Familiar, Critical, and
Moral") that is clearly also a description of *The Spectator*: "He that would
excel in this kind must have a good Fund of strong Masculine Sense: To this
there must be joined a thorough Knowledge of Mankind, together with an
Insight into the Business, and the prevailing Humours of the Age. Our Author must have his Mind well seasoned with the finest Precepts of Morality,
and be filled with nice Reflections upon the bright and the dark sides of
human Life: He must be a Master of refined Raillery, and understand the
Delicacies, as well as the Absurdities of Conversation."

9. Irene Simon, *Three Restoration Divines: Barrow, South, Tillotson*, Bibli-
othèque de la Faculté de philosophie et lettres de l'Université de Liege, fasc.
181 (Paris: Société d'édition "Les Belles Lettres," 1967), p. 282.

10. See Robert Adolph's discussion of this tradition in *The Rise of Modern
Prose Style* (Cambridge, Mass.: MIT Press, 1968), pp. 133–36.

11. Quintilian, *The Institutio Oratoria of Quintilian*, trans. H. E. Butler (Cambridge, Mass.: Harvard University Press, 1926), 3:365. See Cicero, *De oratore*, 3.53, and see 2.67 on Socrates' forms of speech.

12. Anthony [Ashley Cooper, Third] Earl of Shaftesbury, *Characteristics of Men, Manners, Opinions, Times*, ed. John M. Robertson (1900; rpt. ed., New York: Bobbs-Merrill, 1964), 1:128 ("Advice to an Author," 1.3). See also Norman Knox, *The Word Irony and Its Context, 1500–1755* (Durham, N.C.: Duke University Press, 1961), pp. 51–53, for a discussion of Socratic irony.

13. Shaftesbury, *Characteristics*, 1:128–29. See also Stephen Cox's discussion of "the spectator whom we imagine observing us" in Adam Smith's *Theory of Moral Sentiments* (1757), in *"The Stranger Within Thee": Concepts of the Self in Late-Eighteenth-Century Literature* (Pittsburgh: University of Pittsburgh Press, 1980), p. 31.

14. See Locke's description of psychological processes in *An Essay Concerning Human Understanding*, 3.1. Page references in the text are to Alexander Campbell Fraser's edition (Oxford, 1894).

15. Rosalie Colie, "John Locke and the Publication of the Private," *Philological Quarterly* 45 (1966): 24–45.

16. Shaftesbury, *Characteristics*, 2:168 ("Miscellaneous Reflections," 1.3).

17. Johan Huizinga, *Homo Ludens: A Study of the Play-Element in Culture*, trans. R. F. C. Hull (London: Hunt, Barnard, 1949), p. 10.

18. See George Herbert Mead, *Mind, Self, and Society*, ed. Charles W. Morris (Chicago: University of Chicago Press, 1934), pp. 149–64.

19. Huizinga, *Homo Ludens*, p. 12.

CHAPTER TWO

1. Cowley, *Essays*, pp. 109, 136, 129 ("Of Liberty," "Of Obscurity," "Of Solitude").

2. John Evelyn, *Numismata: A Discourse on Medals, Antient and Modern . . . to Which is Appended a Digression Concerning Physiognomy* (London, 1697). See also Henry Fielding's "An Essay on the Knowledge of the Characters of Men," in *Miscellanies by Henry Fielding, Esq.*, ed. Henry Knight Miller (Middletown, Conn.: Wesleyan University Press, 1972), pp. 153–78, and William Hogarth's *The Analysis of Beauty*, ed. Joseph Burke (Oxford: Clarendon Press, 1955), pp. 134–45 (chap. 15), as later, more skeptical discussions of physiognomy. John Graham, "The Development of the Use of Physiognomy in the Novel" (Ph.D. diss., Johns Hopkins University, 1960), gives a history of physiognomic theory through the eighteenth century.

3. E. H. Gombrich, *Art and Illusion: A Study in the Psychology of Pictorial Representation* (Princeton, N.J.: Princeton University Press, Bollingen Books,

1969), p. 334. See also Gombrich's article "The Mask and the Face: The Perception of Physiognomic Likeness in Life and in Art," in *Art, Perception, and Reality,* ed. Maurice Mandelbaum (Baltimore: Johns Hopkins University Press, 1972).

4. Fielding, "Characters of Men," p. 157.

5. John Graham, "Physiognomy in the Novel," p. 71.

6. Marcus Tullius Cicero, *Tully's Three Books of Offices in English,* trans. [Thomas Cockman] (London, 1699), p. 123 (1.36). All quotations will be from this edition.

7. Cicero, *Offices,* p. 137 (1.41).

8. René Descartes, *The Passions of the Soul,* in *The Philosophical Works of Descartes,* trans. Elizabeth S. Haldane and G. R. T. Ross (1911; rpt. ed., Cambridge: Cambridge University Press, 1968), 1:331–427.

9. Gombrich, *Art and Illusion,* p. 348.

10. "Orator" Henley's letter similarly assumes that there are signatures of character which are the properties of physiognomic analysis: the eyes are windows to the soul; the nose conforms to the size of the intellect; one prominent ear signifies reprobation; "a contracted Brow, a lumpish downcast Look, a sober sedate Pace, with both Hands dangling quiet and steddy in Lines exactly parallel . . . is Logic . . . in Perfection. So likewise the *Belles Lettres* are typified by a Saunter in the Gate, a Fall of one Wing of the Peruke backward, an Insertion of one Hand in the Fobb, and a negligent swing of the other, with a Pinch of right and fine *Barcelona* between Finger and Thumb" (No. 518).

11. See Rensselaer Lee, *"Ut Pictura Poesis*: Humanistic Theory of Painting," *Art Bulletin* 22 (1940): 217–26, and Brewster Rogerson, "The Art of Painting the Passions," *Journal of the History of Ideas* 14 (1953): 68–94. Discussions of gesture in academic painting are included in Gombrich, *Art and Illusion,* pp. 358–60, and in several works by Ronald Paulson: "The Pictorian Circuit and Related Structures in Eighteenth Century England," in *The Varied Pattern: Studies in the Eighteenth Century,* ed. Peter Hughes and David Williams (Toronto: A. M. Hakkert, 1971), pp. 165–87, *Hogarth: His Life, Art, and Times* (New Haven, Conn.: Yale University Press, 1971), 1:262–65, and *Emblem and Expression: Meaning in English Art of the Eighteenth Century* (Cambridge, Mass.: Harvard University Press, 1975), pp. 128–29. Steele's phrasing in his description of the cartoons is typical of descriptions of academic paintings. The Abbé du Bos, for instance, in his *Critical Reflections on Poetry and Painting,* uses this picture by Raphael as one example supporting his contention that "there is no one passion of the mind, that is not at the same time a passion of the body" (trans. Thomas Nugent, from the 5th ed., 3 vols. [London, 1748], 1:70; originally published in French in 1719).

12. Stephen Cox, in *"The Stranger Within Thee": Concepts of the Self in*

Late-Eighteenth-Century Literature (Pittsburgh: University of Pittsburgh Press, 1980), points out that a literature of sensibility "may easily turn into a literature of situations rather than a literature that is really concerned with exploring the individual self and its 'feelings'"; it "places its emphasis on situations as they impinge on the delicate web of sensibility and are internalized by the self" (p. 52).

13. Adam Smith, *The Theory of Moral Sentiments* (London, 1759), pp. 6, 8. See also Walter Jackson Bate's discussion of the epistemological and esthetic implications of moral sentiment in *From Classic to Romantic: Premises of Taste in Eighteenth-Century England* (Cambridge, Mass.: Harvard University Press, 1949), pp. 127–44. Du Bos draws similar implication from his studies of gesture and natural responsiveness: "We are moved by the tears of a stranger, even before we are apprized of the subject of his weeping. The cries of a man, to whom we have no other relation than the common one of humanity, make us fly instantly to his assistance, by a mechanical movement previous to all deliberation. A person that accosts us with joy painted on his countenance, excites in us a like sentiment of joy, even before we know the subject of his contentment" (*Critical Reflections*, pp. 32–33).

14. Norman Holland, in *The First Modern Comedies: The Significance of Etherege, Wycherley, and Congreve* (Cambridge, Mass.: Harvard University Press, 1959), describes the moral universe of Restoration comedy in terms similar to those I use to describe *The Spectator.* He takes the dominant theme of Restoration comedy to be a contrast between "appearance" and "nature," and argues that this division governs both form and theme in the drama. See, for example, p. 58.

15. Alan S. Downer in "Nature to Advantage Dressed," *PMLA* 57 (1943):1002–35, discusses the importance of gesture in eighteenth-century acting; and E. R. Wasserman in "The Sympathetic Imagination in Eighteenth-Century Theories of Acting," *Journal of English and Germanic Philology* 46 (1947): 264–72, discusses the emphasis on emotional identification in theories of acting. See also Rogerson, "Painting the Passions."

16. [William Oldys], *The History of the English Stage . . . by Mr. Thomas Betterton* (London, 1741), p. 54. Oldys also reports Betterton's comparison between acting and academic painting: both arts depend on intimate understanding of the correlations between emotions and actions. According to Betterton, "If they [actors] made Playing their Study, . . . as it is their Business, they . . . would, like *Le Brun*, observe Nature wherever they found her offer any thing that could contribute to their Perfection. For this great Master was often seen to observe a Quarrel in the Street betwixt various People, and therein not only to regard the several Degrees of the Passions of Anger rising in the Fray, and their different Recess, but the distinct Expressions of it in every Face that was concerned" (p. 51). Le Brun's attention to gestures

and expressions (according to Betterton's characterization) is very much like Mr. Spectator's.

17. Roscommon's translation, quoted in Oldys, *History of the English Stage*, p. 53.

18. René Rapin, *Reflexions on Aristotle's Treatise of Poesie* (London, 1674), pp. 125–26.

19. Betterton discusses similar occurrences: "The Ladies just mentioned always entered into their Parts. How often have I heard Mrs. *Barry* say, that she never spoke these Words in the *Orphan,—Ah! poor CASTALIO!—*without weeping. Nay, I have frequently observed her to change her Countenance several Times as the Discourse of *others* on the *Stage* have affected her in the Part she acted. This is being thoroughly concerned, this is to know one's Part, this is to express the Passions in the Countenance and Gesture" (p. 53).

20. Steele appeals to this same movement of sensibility in *The Conscious Lovers*: "If Pleasure be worth purchasing, how great a Pleasure is it to him who has a true Taste of Life, to ease an Aking Heart, to see the humane Countenance lighted up into Smiles of Joy" (*The Plays of Richard Steele*, ed. Shirley Strum Kenny [Oxford: Clarendon Press, 1971], p. 337 [II.iii]).

21. Jean Baptiste Morvan de Bellegarde, *Reflexions upon Ridicule, and the Means to Avoid It* and *Reflexions upon the Politeness of Manners; with Maxims for Civil Society*, 2 vols. in 1 (London, 1717), p. 40, originally published in French in 1696 and 1698. These ideas were, of course, commonplace. See, for example, La Bruyère's *Characters*, trans. Jean Stewart (London: Penguin, 1970), p. 51: "There is no action so slight, so simple, so inconspicuous but our way of doing it betrays us. A fool does not come in, or go out, or sit down, or rise, or hold his tongue, or stand on his feet as a man of sense does" (2.37); or see Courtin's *The Rules of Civility* (London, 1676), esp. p. 2. While continental in origin, these ideas were also commonplace in England, as may be illustrated by Halifax's description of "Vanity" in his "The Lady's New-Year's-Gift; or, Advice to a Daughter," in *The Complete Works of George Savile, First Marquess of Halifax*, ed. Walter Raleigh (Oxford: Clarendon, 1912), pp. 38–42 ("She cometh into a Room as if her Limbs were set on with ill-made Screws, which maketh the Company fear the pretty thing should leave some of its artificial Person upon the Floor" [p. 40]). With typical trenchancy, John Locke surveys the entire conduct tradition in two paragraphs of his *Some Thoughts Concerning Education*, in *The Educational Writings of John Locke*, ed. James L. Axtell (Cambridge: Cambridge University Press, 1968), p. 160 (sec. 66): "He that will examine, wherein that Gracefulness lies, which always pleases, will find it arises from that Natural Coherence, which appears between the Thing done, and such a Temper of Mind, as cannot but be approved of, as suitable to the Occasion. . . . The Actions, which naturally flow

from such a well-formed Mind, please us also, as the genuine Marks of it; and being as it were natural Emanations from the Spirit and Disposition within, cannot but be easy and unconstrain'd. . . . On the other side, *Affectation* is an awkward and forced Imitation of what should be Genuine and Easie, wanting the Beauty that Accompanies what is Natural; because there is always a Disagreement between the outward Action, and the Mind within."

22. Cicero, *Offices*, p. 123 (1.36).

23. "On ne peut nier que *Damon* n'ait beaucoup d'esprit & de belles qualitez, mais il le sait trop bien; il en parle à tout propos, & se conne mille louanges, quand les autres ne prennent pas le soin de le louer: Il a un talent mermeilleux pour la Poesie, mais il étourdit tout le monde par le récit de ses Vers; il les savoure en les lisant; chaque mot le fait extasier; mais le plaisir qu'il trouve, empêche celui des autres, & les applaudissemens qu'il se donne, les dispensent de le peine d'y applaudir. Ce qui le devoroit fair rechercher, s'il en faisoit un bon usage, est cause qu'on le fuit comme un importun" (*Reflexions sur la politesse des moeurs*, 6th ed. [Paris, 1728], pp. 53–54).

24. See Steele's contrast between a Gentleman and a Pretty Fellow in *Tatler* 21: "In Imitation of this agreeable Being, is made that Animal we call a *Pretty Fellow*; who being just able to find out, That what makes *Sophronius* acceptable is a Natural Behaviour; in order to the same Reputation, makes his own an Artificial one. *Jack Dimple* is his perfect Mimick, whereby he is of Course the most unlike him of all Men living. *Sophronius* just now pass'd into the inner Room directly forward: *Jack* comes as fast after as he can for the Right and Left Looking-glass, in which he had but just approv'd himself by a Nod at each Glass, and march'd on. He will meditate within for Half an Hour, 'till he thinks he is not careless enough in his Air, and will come back to the Mirrour to recollect his Forgetfulness."

25. The close link between these gestures and the theater can be seen by comparing Steele's scene with the mock courtship between Harriet and Young Bellair in Etherege's *Man of Mode*, where we have actors playing at playacting as Young Bellair instructs Harriet in "a look and gestures that may persuade 'em I am saying all the passionate things imaginable": "Clap your fan then in both your hands, snatch it to your Mouth, smile, and with a lively motion fling your body a little forwards. So! . . . Admirably well acted!" (*The Man of Mode*, ed. W. B. Carnochan [Lincoln: University of Nebraska Press, 1966], pp. 55–56).

26. A jet is "an affected movement or jerk of the body; a swagger." The *OED* cites this passage from *The Spectator* as an illustration.

27. Compare Deane Bartlett's discussion of mechanism in *Guardian* 130. According to his division between "gentlemen" and "mechanics," "all Men

and Women, by what Title soever distinguished, whose Occupation is either
to ogle with the Eye, flirt with the Fan, dress, cringe, adjust the Muscles of
the Face, or other Parts of the Body, are degraded from the Rank of Gentry."
Freethinkers, in particular, are to be considered as *"Automata . . .* as destitute of Thought and Reason, as those little Machines which the Author
from whom I take the Motto of this Paper has so elegantly described." The
epigraph is from Addison's Latin poem *Musae Anglicanae*: "Vacuum sine
mente popellum."

28. Another example of the same rhetoric is Steele's *Spectator* 153, with
the same schematic dualisms, valuative words, and correlation between extravagant gesture and distortions of the mind: "Of all the impertinent
Wishes which we hear expressed in Conversation, there is not one more
unworthy a Gentleman or a Man of liberal Education, than that of wishing
one's self Younger. I have observed this Wish is usually made upon Sight of
some Object which gives the Idea of a past Action, that it is no dishonour to
us that we cannot now repeat, or else on what was in it's self shamefull when
we performed it." A perceptual context is kept constantly before us ("when
we hear expressed," "I have observed," "upon Sight of some Object"), but it
is absorbed into a moral framework. A series of valuative words moves
through these sentences and through the following paragraph ("impertinent," "unworthy," "dishonour," "shamefull," "foolish," "dissolute," "absurd") to be set in contrast to the substantial virtues of Nature, Justice, Law,
and Reason. Like the reply to Celimene, the argument in No. 153 is based
on schematic oppositions and on a psychophysical parallelism. Qualities of
mind are apparent in public behavior so that Steele can describe false judgment as a mental confusion and make it clear that this mental confusion is
part of our public experience.

29. This principle of symmetry is also illustrated in Steele's sketch of
Sophronius in *Tatler* 21: "His Judgment is so good and unerring, and that
accompanied with so chearful a Spirit, that his Conversation is a continual
Feast, at which he helps some, and is help'd by others, in such a Manner,
that the Equality of Society is perfectly Kept up, and every Man obliges as
much as he is oblig'd."

30. Discussions of Addison's esthetics include: Clarence D. Thorpe,
"Addison's Theory of the Imagination as 'Perceptive Response,'" *Papers of
the Michigan Academy of Science, Arts, and Letters* 21 (1936): 509–30, and
Thorpe, "Addison's Contribution to Criticism," in *The Seventeenth Century:
Studies in the History of English Thought and Literature from Bacon to Pope, by
Richard Foster Jones and Others Writing in His Honor* (Stanford, Calif.: Stan-
ford University Press, 1951), pp. 316–29; Martin Kallich, "The Association
of Ideas and Critical Theory: Hobbes, Locke, and Addison," *ELH* 12

(1945): 290–315; Lee Andrew Elioseff, *The Cultural Milieu of Addison's Literary Criticism* (Austin: University of Texas Press, 1963); Ernest Lee Tuveson, *The Imagination as a Means of Grace: Locke and the Aesthetics of Romanticism* (Berkeley and Los Angeles: University of California Press, 1968); and Leopold Damrosch, Jr., "The Significance of Addison's Criticism," *Studies in English Literature* 19 (1979): 421–30.

31. A parallel between art and behavior is one important theme running through *The Spectator*, since critical taste and social discernment are cognate expressions of a single faculty of judgment. Expanding the papers on wit, Steele tells us that it would be pointless to explain wit without "considering the Application of it" (No. 65): "The Seat of Wit, when one speaks as a Man of the Town and the World, is the Play-house," and "The Application of Wit in the Theatre has as strong an Effect upon the Manners of our Gentlemen, as the Taste of it has upon the Writings of our Authors." In No. 6, Steele's argument shifts ambiguously between art and manners, and his vocabulary of taste applies equally to both, since "such false Impressions are owing to the abandon'd Writings of Men of Wit, and the awkard Imitation of the rest of Mankind"; "but this false Beauty will not pass upon Men of honest Minds and true Taste." Similarly, a correspondent in No. 244 draws an analogy between styles in manners and styles in painting: " 'Tis for want of this that Men mistake in this Case and in common Life, a wild extravagant Pencil for one that is truly bold and great, an impudent Fellow for a Man of true Courage and Bravery, hasty and unreasonable Actions for Enterprizes of Spirit and Resolution, gaudy Colouring for that which is truly beautiful, a false and insinuating Discourse for simple Truth elegantly recommended."

32. George Williamson, *The Senecan Amble: A Study in Prose Form from Bacon to Collier* (Chicago: University of Chicago Press, 1951), p. 333.

33. Elioseff, *Cultural Milieu*, pp. 185–86.

34. See Jerome Stolnitz, "Beauty: Some Stages in the History of an Idea," *Journal of the History of Ideas* 22 (1961): 185–204; and Tuveson, *Imagination*, p. 102. Tuveson describes Addison's contribution to esthetics according to a contrast between spontaneous apprehension and reasoned assent. Before Addison's description of the esthetic stance, the perceiver had been seen as looking at an esthetic object and then figuratively turning his back on it to reflect on its meaning. "He realizes that the universe exhibits a great moral lesson, but he must reason to derive that lesson. Addison's innovation consists in the omission of turning one's back, of conscious reflection. The effect as Addison describes it is indeed not finally a lesson at all, for it is a state of mind. The analogy is with those powerful impressions which, as Locke observed, influence our moods and actions even though they lie outside conscious awareness."

CHAPTER THREE

1. Locke, *An Essay Concerning Human Understanding,* ed. Fraser, 1:245, 239–40 (2.14.16, 4).

2. Ibid., 1:194 (2.10.2).

3. Locke compares the movement of ideas to "the images in the inside of a lantern, turned round by the heat of a candle"—static panels which give the illusion of movement (ibid., 1:243 [2.14.9]).

4. Maximillian Novak describes the suspension of time in the novel in "The Extended Moment: Time, Drama, History, and Perspective in Eighteenth-Century Fiction," in *Probability, Time, and Space in Eighteenth-Century Literature,* ed. Paula Backscheider (New York: AMS Press, 1979), pp. 141–66; see also Dorothy Van Ghent's discussion of suspended time in *Tristram Shandy* in *The English Novel: Form and Function,* 2d ed. (New York: Holt, Rinehart, and Winston, 1961), pp. 84–93. Robert Morris describes the effect of the garden in *Lectures on Architecture* (London, 1734), quoted in Paulson, *Emblem and Expression,* p. 21: "Care should be taken so to lay out and dispose the several Parts, that the Neighbouring *Hills,* the *Rivulets,* the *Woods* and little *Buildings* interspers'd in various Avenues, . . . should render the Spot a kind of agreeable *Disorder,* or *artful Confusion*; so that by shifting from Scene to Scene, and by serpentine or winding Paths, one should, as it were, accidentally fall upon some remarkable beautiful Prospect, or other pleasing Object."

5. William James, *The Principles of Psychology* (New York, 1890), 1:609.

6. Locke, *An Essay Concerning Human Understanding,* 1:241, 245 (2.14.6, 15).

7. For example: "Take a Fine Lady who is of a Delicate Frame, and you may observe from the Hour she rises a certain Weariness of all that passes about her. I know more than one who is much too nice to be quite alive. They are sick of such strange frightful People that they meet, one is so awkward and another so disagreeable, that it looks like a Penance to breath the same Air with them" (*Spectator* 143).

8. These comments on the consciousness of time set aside other aspects of the eighteenth century's concept of time, such as Newton's speculations about absolute time, the fascination with new clock mechanisms, and the relatively new sense of historical eras. See Lewis White Beck, "World Enough, and Time," in *Probability, Time, and Space,* ed. Backscheider, pp. 113–39; Samuel L. Macey, *Clocks and the Cosmos: Time in Western Life and Thought* (Hamden, Conn.: Archon Books, 1980); Earl Miner, "Time, Sequence, and Plot in Restoration Literature," in *Studies in Eighteenth-Century Culture,* ed. Ronald C. Rosbottom (Madison: University of Wisconsin Press, 1976), 5:67–85; Ernst Cassirer, *The Philosophy of the Enlightenment,* trans.

Fritz C. A. Koebln and James P. Pettegrove (Princeton, N.J.: Princeton University Press, 1951), pp. 197–233.

9. On the associative psychology of the garden see H. F. Clark, "Eighteenth-Century Elysiums: The Role of 'Association' in the Landscape Movement," in *England and the Mediterranean Tradition: Studies in Art, History, and Literature*, Publications of the Warburg and Courtauld Institutes (London: Oxford University Press, 1945), pp. 154–78; Ronald Paulson's chapter "The Poetic Garden" in *Emblem and Expression*, pp. 19–34; and John Dixon Hunt, *The Figure in the Landscape: Poetry, Painting, and Gardening During the Eighteenth Century* (Baltimore: Johns Hopkins University Press, 1976), esp. pp. 58–104, 196–99, and 218–24. See also the anthology of statements on gardens edited by John Dixon Hunt and Peter Willis, *The Genius of the Place: The English Landscape Garden, 1620–1820* (New York: Harper and Row, 1975). For the history of garden designs see Derek Clifford, *A History of Garden Design*, rev. ed. (New York: Praeger, 1966), and Christopher Hussey, *English Gardens and Landscapes, 1700–1750* (London: Country Life, 1967). S. Lang, in "The Genesis of the English Garden," in *The Picturesque Garden and Its Influence Outside the British Isles*, ed. Nikolaus Pevsner (Washington, D.C.: Dumbarton Oaks, Trustees for Harvard University, 1974), pp. 1–29, argues that Addison's descriptions of gardens were part of an established literary tradition but that they did not have much effect on actual garden design; the selections in Hunt and Willis, *The Genius of the Place*, though, show Addison's great influence on how gardens came to be described in the eighteenth century.

10. On traditional images of the garden see Hunt, *The Figure in the Landscape*, pp. 1–12; and Terry Comito, *The Idea of the Garden in the Renaissance* (New Brunswick, N.J.: Rutgers University Press, 1978), pp. 25–50.

11. Sir William Temple, in "Upon the Gardens of Epicurus; or, Of Gardening, in the Year 1685" had given what came to be a standard (although inaccurate) account of Chinese gardens, noting the same sudden effect on the imagination: "their greatest reach of imagination is employed in contriving figures, where the beauty shall be great, and strike the eye, but without any order or disposition of parts that shall be commonly or easily observed . . . and where they find it hit their eye at first sight, they say the *sharawadgi* is fine or is admirable, or any such expression of esteem" (*Five Miscellaneous Essays by Sir William Temple*, ed. Samuel Holt Monk [Ann Arbor: University of Michigan Press, 1963], p. 30).

12. The causes of actual changes in garden design are hard to establish. Scholars have suggested influences from painting, stage design, and Italian gardens as models for British garden styles, as well as esthetic pronouncements such as Addison's or Pope's. Hunt notes that "though with hindsight we may see that the English landscape garden did not spring fully armed

from the head of, say, Addison or Pope, the contemporary pride in its *invention* by the British was pervasive" (*The Figure in the Landscape*, p. 246).

13. Hilbert H. Campbell, "Addison's 'Cartesian' Passage and Nicholas Malebranche," *Philological Quarterly* 46 (1967): 408–12, has shown that this passage is derived from Malebranche's *De la recherche de la verite* (1674).

14. Cowley, *Essays*, pp. 132, 133.

15. Locke, *An Essay Concerning Human Understanding*, 2.14.3–4. See also Campbell, "Addison's 'Cartesian' Passage."

16. *The Works of the Most Reverend Dr. John Tillotson, Late Lord Archbishop of Canterbury: Containing Fifty Four Sermons and Discourses on Several Occasions . . . Being All that Were Published by His Grace Himself*, 7th ed. (London, 1714), p. 155 (Sermon 14, "The Folly and Danger of Irresolution and Delaying"). This is a commonplace of seventeenth-century religious handbooks. Compare Thomas Fuller, *The Holy State* (London, 1642), p. 202, "*He is a good Time-server that improves the present for Gods glory, and his own salvation. Of all the extent of time, onely the instant is that which we can call ours*"; and Jeremy Taylor, *The Rule and Exercises of Holy Living*, 6th ed. (London, 1660), pp. 4–5 (chap. 1, sec. 1), "God hath given to man a short time here upon earth, and yet upon this short time eternity depends: but so, that for every hour of our life . . . we must give account to the great Judge of Men and Angels." See also G. A. Starr, *Defoe and Spiritual Autobiography* (Princeton, N.J.: Princeton University Press, 1965), pp. 4–9, for a discussion of seventeenth- and eighteenth-century concepts of the moral use of time.

17. Tillotson, *Works*, p. 445 (Sermon 38, "A Conscience Void of Offence towards God and Man"). See also John Wilkins's sermon preached at Whitehall, quoted by William Fraser Mitchell in *English Pulpit Oratory* (London: Macmillan, 1932), p. 333: "As he that is upon a Journey, doth so order all his *Particular* Motions, as may be most conducible to his *General* End: so should men *habitually*, though they cannot *actually*, in every affair have respect to their chief End."

18. See particularly the *Nichomachean Ethics*, 2.1. Aristotle points out the etymological connection between ethics (*ethike*) and habit (*ethos*) and argues that moral virtue can be acquired only through the exercise of good actions. Moral character is tied to moral habit since character itself is determined by habitually chosen actions: "It makes no small difference, then, whether we form habits of one kind or of another from our very youth; it makes a very great difference, or rather *all* the difference" (trans. W. D. Ross, in *The Basic Works of Aristotle*, ed. Richard McKeon [New York: Random House, 1941], p. 953). See also Cicero's *De inventione*, 1.24.36, where he discusses habit as one means of characterization. Tillotson discusses the nature of habit in several sermons (Sermon 10, "Of the Deceitfulness of Sin," pp. 111–12, and Sermon 29, "On the Difficulty of Reforming Vicious Habits," pp. 340–

48), as does Locke in his psychology (*Essay*, 1.33.6) and in his theories of education (*Of the Conduct of the Understanding*, sec. 4), where Locke adds a psychological explanation to the commonplace observations. H. K. Miller in his *Essays on Fielding's Miscellanies: A Commentary on Volume One* (Princeton, N.J.: Princeton University Press, 1961), p. 219, discusses the importance of habit to Fielding's moral psychology. Miller quotes from *Covent Garden Journal*, No. 66: "Habit hath often been called a second Nature, the former may indeed be said to govern and direct the latter. I am much deceived, (and so was Mr. Lock too) if from our earliest Habits we do not in a great Measure derive those Dispositions, which are commonly called our Nature, and which afterwards constitute our Characters."

19. Steele immediately takes up Addison's discussion of habit in No. 447 at the beginning of No. 448 and offers some standard advice regarding habits: "The first Steps towards Ill are very carefully to be avoided, for Men insensibly go on when they are once entered"; "We should not make any thing we our selves disapprove habitual to us, if we would be sure of our Integrity." Henry Grove in *Spectator* 601 discusses habit in the context of benevolism. Our natural benevolence is constrained by the desires of the body and by the customs of the world, "However, a great deal may be done [to restore the heart to its 'native Freedom of Exercise'] by a Course of Beneficence obstinately persisted in; this, if any thing, being a likely way of establishing a moral Habit, which shall be somewhat of a Counterpoise to the Force of Mechanism." See also Steele's No. 76 (inconstancy "proceeds from the Want of forming some Law of Life to our selves, or fixing some Notion of things in general, which may affect us in such Manner, as to create proper Habits both in our Minds and Bodies") and Addison's No. 162.

20. Torgny T. Segerstedt, "Groups and Values," in *Proceedings of the Sixth International Congress of Aesthetics*, ed. Rudolf Zeitler, *Figura: Uppsala Studies in the History of Art*, n.s., 2 (Uppsala, 1972), p. 3.

21. Steele also uses the theater as a vehicle for discussing the full use of time in *Spectator* 153: "If Hours, Days, Months, and Years pass away, it is no Matter what Hour, what Day, what Month, or what Year we dye. The Applause of a good Actor is due to him at whatever Scene of the Play he makes his Exit: It is thus in the Life of a Man of Sense, a short Life is sufficient to manifest himself a Man of Honour and Virtue."

22. The device of the journal is picked up two weeks later in No. 323 when Addison fabricates a journal from Clarinda, who spends her time at the theater and admiring the wit of Mr. Froth (most of it lifted from *The Spectator*). Clarinda confesses she "never thought of Considering" how she passed her time "before I perused your Speculation upon that Subject," and resolves to do better. Still, her letter concludes in bewildered vacillation: "I am at a loss to know whether I pass my Time well or ill."

23. In *Guardian* 131 Steele vividly depicts the anguished self-deceptions of an idle man.

24. See Starr, *Defoe and Spiritual Autobiography*, and William Haller, *The Rise of Puritanism* (1938; rpt. ed., New York: Harper Torchbooks, 1957), pp. 95–98, for discussions of the role of diaries in self-examination.

25. Tillotson, *Works*, p. 141 (Sermon 13, "Of the Nature and Benefit of Consideration").

26. *The Prose Works of Jonathan Swift*, ed. Davis, 9:355.

27. Paul Kent Alkon, *Defoe and Fictional Time* (Athens: University of Georgia Press, 1980), p. 81. Alkon notes the importance of discussions of reading time in A. A. Mendilow, *Time and the Novel* (London: Peter Nevill, 1952).

28. Sir Richard Steele, *Plays*, ed. Shirley S. Kenny (Oxford: Oxford University Press, 1971), p. 317 (I.ii).

29. This freedom to recreate the series is largely lost for modern readers, for whom essays have already been selected and arranged in anthologies.

30. Whatever version of *The Spectator* a reader may construct for himself, it is important to notice that his reading decisions are not governed by any rules of sequence; there is little sense in *The Spectator* that one essay must precede or follow another or that one event must follow another according to a temporal rule of antecedence or consequence. Similarly, Locke argues that our awareness of time does not depend on the movements of external things, movements which may be governed by the rules of a process or by the laws of cause and effect. Our consciousness of time is not keyed to the movement of objects outside of the mind (which, for a reader, would imply that his impressions of a book are not necessarily keyed to the sequence of events on the page). Instead, it is created out of the much more random flow of ideas. We are aware of time because one perception follows another, but these perceptions do not necessarily follow in any particular sequence. See the *Essay*, 2.14.6–8, 16.

31. D. F. Bond points out such repetitions in his notes to *Spectator* 143 and 144. For No. 143 he notes that "much of this opening paragraph repeats ideas and phrases which Steele had already used in No. 100" (*The Spectator*, ed. Bond, 2:64), and for No. 144 he notes that Steele introduces commonplaces on beauty "from Aristotle, Plato, Socrates, Theophrastus, and Carneades . . . [which] are frequently quoted together" (2:68).

32. Frank Kermode, in *The Sense of an Ending: Studies in the Theory of Fiction* (London: Oxford University Press, 1966), pp. 70–74, speaks of the *aevum*, a term drawn from angelology, which he uses to characterize that dimension of time in which people act out timeless patterns.

33. See Ricardo J. Quinones, *The Renaissance Discovery of Time* (Cambridge, Mass.: Harvard University Press, 1972) for a discussion of Renais-

sance attitudes toward time. Mutability is a governing trope in many works, including *The Faerie Queene* and Shakespeare's sonnets; Browne's *Hydriotaphia or Urne Buriall* (1658) becomes a veritable glossary of time terms. The sense of mutability and decline continues through Rochester's poems and finds extravagant expression in *The Dunciad.*

34. See for example Reuben A. Brower's chapter "An Allusion to Europe: Dryden and Poetic Tradition," in *Alexander Pope: The Poetry of Allusion* (London: Oxford University Press, 1959), pp. 1–14.

35. Hume's explanation of personal identity shows the subversive potential of Locke's account of the succession of ideas: "But setting aside some metaphysicians of this kind, I may venture to affirm of the rest of mankind, that they are nothing but a bundle or collection of different perceptions, which succeed each other with an inconceivable rapidity, and are in a perpetual flux and movement. . . . The mind is a kind of theatre, where several perceptions successively make their appearance; pass, repass, glide away, and mingle in an infinite variety of postures and situations. There is properly no *simplicity* in it at one time, nor *identity* in different, whatever natural propension we may have to imagine that simplicity and identity" (*Treatise of Human Nature*, Book I, *Of the Understanding*, ed. D. G. C. Macnabb [Cleveland: World, 1962], p. 302 (4.6).

36. Georges Poulet, *Studies in Human Time*, trans. Elliott Coleman (Baltimore: Johns Hopkins Press, 1956), p. 21. Poulet says of Bayle's *Dictionary*, with its involved footnotes, compounded cross-references, and constantly shifting argument, that it exemplifies "a way of thinking which continually changed its character and was unceasingly absorbed by the interest of the present moment: *diurnal* thought, he called it. He who says *diurnal* says also *journalistic*. . . . From Bayle (and Fontenelle) onward, philosophy becomes anecdotal, discontinuous; it becomes also versatile, picaresque, supple to the suggestions of ideas" (p. 22). According to Thomas Tickle, Addison kept a copy of the *Dictionary* constantly beside him at his writing table, so it may be that *The Spectator*, through Bayle, is itself a product of this "way of thinking."

37. Geoffrey Bullough, *Mirror of Minds: Changing Psychological Beliefs in English Poetry* (Toronto: University of Toronto Press, 1962), p. 124.

38. *The Rambler*, ed. Walter Jackson Bate and Albrecht B. Strauss, vols. 3–5 of *The Yale Edition of the Works of Samuel Johnson* (New Haven, Conn.: Yale University Press, 1969), 5:291, 294; all references will be to this edition. For discussions of Johnson's concepts of time and imagination see Walter Jackson Bate, *The Achievement of Samuel Johnson* (New York: Oxford University Press, 1953), pp. 63–91; Paul Kent Alkon, *Samuel Johnson and Moral Discipline* (Evanston, Ill.: Northwestern University Press, 1967), pp. 146–79; and Arieh Sachs, *Passionate Intelligence: Imagination and Reason in the Work of Samuel Johnson* (Baltimore: Johns Hopkins University Press, 1967), pp. 3–19.

CHAPTER FOUR

1. See Lawrence Stone, *The Family, Sex and Marriage in England 1500–1800* (New York: Harper and Row, 1977); Stone, "The Rise of the Nuclear Family in Early Modern England: The Patriarchal Stage," in *The Family in History,* ed. Charles E. Rosenberg (Philadelphia: University of Pennsylvania Press, 1975), pp. 13–57; Randolph Trumbach, *The Rise of the Egalitarian Family: Aristocratic and Domestic Relations in Eighteenth-Century England* (New York: Academic Press, 1978). Jean H. Hagstrum has identified a similar shift in attitudes in literary descriptions of love in *Sex and Sensibility: Ideal and Erotic Love from Milton to Mozart* (Chicago: University of Chicago Press, 1980); see esp. pp. 160–85. Philippe Ariès, *Centuries of Childhood,* trans. Robert Baldick (London: J. Cape, 1962) has been a very influential study of attitudes toward children and toward family structures, although his methodology has been seriously criticized; see for example, Lawrence Stone, "The Massacre of the Innocents," *New York Review of Books,* November 14, 1974, pp. 25–31. Jean-Louis Flandrin, *Families in Former Times: Kinship, Household, and Sexuality,* trans. Richard Southern (Cambridge: Cambridge University Press, 1979) deals mostly with family patterns in France, but includes comments on England on pp. 50–111 and 166–69; Peter Gay gives a concise overview of attitudes toward women, children, and the family in *The Enlightenment: An Interpretation* (New York: Alfred A. Knopf, 1966), 2:31–36, 201–4.

There is a notable controversy in studies of the family, since demographic and economic studies indicate that family structures remained essentially unchanged over several centuries, while studies of affective attitudes, such as Stone's and Hagstrum's, show significant changes in peoples' perceptions of family life. For demographic, economic, or anthropologically based studies of family structure see Peter Laslett, *The World We Have Lost,* 2d ed. (New York: Scribners, 1973), esp. pp. 84–112, "Mean Household Size in England Since the Sixteenth Century," in *Household and Family in Past Time,* ed. P. Laslett (Cambridge: Cambridge University Press, 1972), pp. 125–88, and "Characteristics of the Western Family Considered over Time," in *Family Life and Illicit Love in Earlier Generations: Essays in Historical Sociology* (Cambridge: Cambridge University Press, 1977), pp. 12–49; Barbara Laslett, "The Family as a Public and Private Institution: An Historical Perspective," *Journal of Marriage and the Family* 35 (1973): 480–92; John Hajnal, "European Marriage Patterns in Perspective," in *Population in History,* ed. D. V. Glass and D. E. C. Eversley (Chicago: Aldine, 1965), pp. 101–43; and Alan Macfarlane, *The Origins of English Individualism: The Family, Property, and Social Transition* (Oxford: Blackwell, 1978). Macfarlane includes a criticism of Stone and other historians of the family in *The Origins of English Individualism*, pp. 59–60.

Earlier surveys of the history of the family provide informative overviews, especially of legal and religious definitions of family relationships. See, for example, Willystine Goodsell, *A History of the Family as a Social and Economic Institution* (New York: Macmillan, 1923); and Carle C. Zimmerman, *Family and Civilization* (New York: Harper, 1947). A major study of legal and economic considerations in marriage is H. J. Habakkuk, "Marriage Settlements in the Eighteenth Century," *Transactions of the Royal Historical Society*, 4th ser., 32 (1950): 15–30. Studies of life in particular families in the seventeenth century include Gladys Scott Thomson, *Life in a Noble Household, 1641–1700* (Ann Arbor: University of Michigan Press, 1959), and Alan Macfarlane, *Family Life of Ralph Josselin* (Cambridge: Cambridge University Press, 1970). On attitudes toward woman in the early eighteenth century see Rae Blanchard, "Richard Steele and the Status of Women," *Studies in Philology* 26 (1929): 325–55; Janelle Greenberg, "The Legal Status of the English Woman in Early Eighteenth-Century Common Law and Equity," in *Studies in Eighteenth-Century Culture*, vol. 4, ed. Harold E. Pagliaro (Madison: University of Wisconsin Press, 1975), pp. 171–85; Katharine Rogers, "The Feminism of Daniel Defoe," in *Woman in the Eighteenth Century and Other Essays*, ed. Paul Fritz and Richard Morton (Toronto: Hakkert, 1976), pp. 3–24; Ian Watt, *The Rise of the Novel: Studies in Defoe, Richardson, and Fielding* (Berkeley and Los Angeles: University of California Press, 1957), pp. 138–64; and Robert Palfrey Utter and Gwendolyn Bridges Needham, *Pamela's Daughters* (New York: Macmillan, 1936), pp. 19–42. A less systematic and sometimes misleading sampling of statements about sex and marriage is included in Bernard I. Murstein, *Love, Sex, and Marriage Through the Ages* (New York: Springer, 1974).

2. William Gouge, *Of Domesticall Duties* (1622; rpt. ed., Norwood, N.J.: Johnson Reprints, 1976); Thomas Fuller, *The Holy State and the Profane State*, ed. Maximillian Graff Walten (New York: Columbia University Press, 1938), book 1; Jeremy Taylor, "The Marriage Ring; or, The Mysteriousness and Duties of Marriage," in *The Whole Works of the Right Rev. Jeremy Taylor, D. D.* (London, 1822), 5:248–79; William Fleetwood, *Relative Duties of Parents and Children, Husbands and Wives, Masters and Servants* (London, 1716).

3. Halifax, "Advice to a Daughter," in *Complete Works*, especially the section on "House, Family, and Children," pp. 20–27.

4. Frances Parthenope and Margaret M. Verney, comps., *Memoirs of the Verney Family During the Seventeenth Century*, 3d ed. (London: Longmans, Green, 1925), 1:500–501.

5. Clarissa Harlowe finds herself trapped in a family of this type, and Steele calls such negotiated marriages a *"Smithfield Bargain"* (*Spectator* 304).

But the Verney papers suggest that such arrangements had been an accepted mode of courtship; see, for example, information on marriages of the Verney daughters (1:416–17), on negotiations for marriages for Edmund and John Verney (2:48–68, 175–77, 271–81), and Sir Ralph Verney's recommended match, as patron, for a family chaplain (2:39). Similarly, Samuel Pepys and his uncles attempted to negotiate a marriage for Pepys's younger brother, and the Evelyn family negotiated so long for an acceptable contract for John Evelyn's daughter Mary that the negotiations fell through, even though Mary was deeply in love with her prospective husband; see *The Diary of Samuel Pepys*, ed. Robert Latham and William Matthews (Berkeley and Los Angeles: University of California Press, 1970–82), 3:176, 227–33, and W. G. Hiscock, *John Evelyn and His Family Circle* (London: Routledge and Kegan Paul, 1955), p. 132. For a background on these attitudes see Habakkuk, "Marriage Settlements," Blanchard, "Steele and the Status of Women," and Christopher Hill, "Clarissa Harlowe and Her Times," *Essays in Criticism* 5 (1955): 315–40. Hill points out that a libertine view of marriage, as a mirror opposite of the patriarchal view, saw marriage as no more than a contract, which placed no emotional obligations on the husband and wife so that their social and sexual lives could be independent of the family or of marriage.

6. Charles Lillie, ed., *Original and Genuine Letters Sent to the "Tatler" and "Spectator," During the Time those Works were Publishing* (London, 1725), 1:21, 111.

7. The marriages of Ralph Verney's five daughters include a range of emotional reactions to marriage; see, for example, Parthenope and Verney, comps., *Memoirs of the Verney Family*, 1:422–30. See, too, the closeness between husband and wife in the marriages of Dame Margaret Verney, Mary Verney, and Elizabeth Palmer (1:218–22, 379–82, and 2:371).

8. See especially Evelyn's letters to his brother George in *The Diary of John Evelyn, Esq., FRS, to Which Are Added a Selection from His Familiar Letters*, ed. William Bray, 3d ed. (London: Bickers and Son, 1906), 3:219–21, and to Lady Sunderland, 3:460.

9. See *The Diary of John Evelyn*, ed. E. S. de Beer (London: Oxford University Press, 1959), pp. 384–87 (January 27, 1658), and Hiscock, *John Evelyn and His Family Circle*, pp. 72–73, 76, and 82.

10. *The Life and Errors of John Dunton, Citizen of London* . . . (1818; rpt. ed., New York: Burt Franklin, 1969), 1:46, 70–71, 77–79, 101, and 286. Dunton also discusses the happy marriage of a friend in Boston and presents advice on marriage in 1:102–6, and 296–302.

11. *The Correspondence of Richard Steele*, ed. Rae Blanchard (Oxford: Oxford University Press, 1941), p. 332.

12. On childhood, see Ariès, *Centuries of Childhood*, p. 404, for a summary of his argument that the family was increasingly seen to be a source of senti-

mental affection, and see the discussions of childhood in Stone, *The Family, Sex, and Marriage,* pp. 405–82, and Trombach, *The Rise of the Egalitarian Family,* pp. 187–285; other works on childhood include J. H. Plumb, "The New World of Children in Eighteenth-Century England," *Past and Present* 67 (1975):64–95; Ivy Pinchbeck and Margaret Hewitt, *Children in English Society* (London: Routledge and Kegan Paul, 1969, 1973); and Joseph E. Illick, "Child-Raising in Seventeenth-Century England and America," in *The History of Childhood,* ed. Lloyd deMause (New York: Psychohistory Press, 1974), pp. 303–50. On marriage see Levin L. Schucking, *The Puritan Family: A Social Study from the Literary Sources* (1929), trans. Brian Battershaw (New York: Schocken Books, 1969), esp. pp. xii–xiii, 34, 91; for related studies see W. Haller and M. Haller, "The Puritan Art of Love," *Huntington Library Quarterly* 5 (1941–42): 235–72, and John Halkett, *Milton and the Idea of Matrimony: A Study of the Divorce Tracts* (New Haven, Conn.: Yale University Press, 1970). Schucking emphasizes that the moral commonplaces he outlines are not limited to Puritan attitudes but are part of a general emphasis on practical piety.

13. See *Amelia,* in *The Complete Works of Henry Fielding, Esq.,* ed. William Ernest Henley (1903; rpt. ed., New York: Barnes and Noble, 1967), 7:65 (7.1).

14. Locke, *Educational Writings,* pp. 115–16, 152–53, 162–71, 237–39 (secs. 4, 56, 67–70, 130).

15. Samuel Richardson, *Pamela; or, Virtue Rewarded, Part the Second,* vols. 2–4 of *The Novels of Samuel Richardson* (1902; rpt. ed., AMS Press, 1970), 4:219–70 (Letters 90–97).

16. See Gouge, *Of Domesticall Duties,* pp. 224–32, for example; Dunton, *Life and Errors,* p. 297; Philogamous, *The Present State of Matrimony; or, The Real Cause of Conjugal Infidelity and Unhappy Marriages* (London, 1739), pp. 37, 15.

17. Haller and Haller, "The Puritan Art of Love," p. 239.

18. This is the emphasis that Schucking (*The Puritan Family*) and Halkett (*Milton and Matrimony*) find in these works. Gouge's *Of Domesticall Duties,* for one instance, is a seven-hundred-page exposition of Ephesians 5:21–6:9, a passage that Edmund Verney also alludes to in his letter to his children, in Parthenope and Verney, comps., *Memoirs of the Verney Family,* 2:422.

19. For Defoe see *Conjugal Lewdness; or, Matrimonial Whoredom: A Treatise on the Use and Abuse of the Marriage Bed* (1727; rpt. ed., Gainesville, Fla.: Scholars' Facsimiles and Reprints, 1967), pp. 95–106.

20. See Dunton, *Life and Errors,* pp. 40–41.

21. Samuel Clarke, "A Discourse of Natural Religion," in *British Moralists, 1650–1800,* ed. D. D. Raphael (Oxford: Clarendon Press, 1969), 1:210.

22. *The History of Tom Jones, a Foundling,* ed. Fredson Bowers, with an

introduction and commentary by Martin C. Battestin (Middletown, Conn.:
Wesleyan University Press, 1975), pp. 981–82. See Murial Brittain Williams,
Marriage: Fielding's Mirror of Morality (University: University of Alabama
Press, 1973), esp. pp. 89–91, on marriage in *Tom Jones*; and see Augustus R.
Towers, *"Amelia* and the State of Matrimony," *Review of English Studies*, n.s.,
5 (1954): 144–57.

23. Arthur L. Cooke, "Addison's Aristocratic Wife," *PMLA* 72 (1957):
373–89, uses Lady Warwick's household records to reconstruct her character as a prudent and literate woman, and then draws conclusions about her
marriage to Addison. See Peter Smithers, *The Life of Joseph Addison*, 2d ed.
(Oxford: Oxford University Press, 1968), pp. 364–72, on Addison's marriage.

24. See Calhoun Winton, *Captain Steele: The Early Career of Richard Steele*
(Baltimore: Johns Hopkins University Press, 1964), pp. 86–90 and 185, and
Sir Richard Steele, M. P.: The Later Career (Baltimore: Johns Hopkins Univer-
sity Press, 1970), pp. 88–98.

It is difficult to assess Pope's suggestion to Spence that Steele and Addison
were homosexuals (Joseph Spence, *Observations, Anecdotes, and Characters of
Books and Men . . .* , ed. James M. Osborn [Oxford: Oxford University Press,
1966], 1:80). There is no other evidence to support Pope's suggestion apart
from the possibility that any close and prolonged friendship may have a ho-
mosexual element. Steele's and Addison's biographers do not examine the
issue. Winton devotes only one paragraph to the question in an appendix to
acknowledge Pope's comment without evaluating it (*Sir Richard Steele, M. P.*,
p. 253); Smithers does not discuss the issue at all. Whatever the facts may be
regarding their emotional lives, their writings are generally consistent. Both
in his letters and published writings, Steele is sympathetic and solicitous
toward women and has an affinity for domestic life, even though his own
temperament made him hard to live with. Addison is more distant with regard to women, but this is probably a reflection of a general emotional coldness. It may be most accurate to describe Addison as donnish, which may
imply homosexuality or, more likely, emotional reserve.

25. See especially his letters of March 1717, in Steele, *Correspondence*, pp.
331–34.

26. See Nos. 149, 176, 199, 236, 479, 490, 500, 520, 522, and 524, by
Steele, No. 261, by Addison, and No. 525, by Hughes, on courtship and
marriage; Nos. 192, 263, and 533, by Steele, Nos. 181 and 189, by Addison,
and No. 150, by Budgell, on parents and children; Nos. 80, 96, 107, and
137, by Steele, on masters and servants.

27. *"Pamphilio* has the happiest Houshold of any Man I know, and that
proceeds from the Human Regard he has to them in their private Persons, as
well as in respect that they are his Servants. If there be any Occasion,

wherein they may in themselves be supposed to be unfit to attend their Master's Concerns, by reason of an Attention to their own, he is so good as to place himself in their Condition. I thought it very becoming in him, when at Dinner the other Day he made an Apology for want of more Attendants. He said, *One of my Footmen is gone to the Wedding of his Sister, and the other I don't expect to Wait, because his Father died but two Days ago.*"

28. Maren-Sophie Røstvig, *The Happy Man: Studies in the Metamorphoses of a Classical Ideal* (Oslo: Oslo University Press, 1958), 2:18.

29. Joseph Hall, "The Happy Man," in *Works of Joseph Hall, D.D.* (Oxford, 1837), 6:102; see also Hall's "Heaven upon Earth; or, Of True Peace and Tranquillity of Mind," in *Works*, 6:4–43.

30. See the definition of a conversation piece that Ronald Paulson quotes from *The Conversation Piece in Georgian England* (catalogue of the 1965 Kenwood exhibition): "'a portrait group of a family or friends in some degree of rapport seen in their home surroundings or engaged in some favourite occupation', usually painted on a small scale" (*Emblem and Expression*, p. 121). Paulson expands the definition: "Ceremonies that teeter between public and private are in fact the essence of the English conversation piece. . . . The three elements of greatest importance are the surroundings or native habitat, the relationships between the people and between them and their milieu, and the function of these elements to define" (p. 121).

31. Jean Hagstrum similarly discusses variations in family descriptions in *The Tatler*, in *Sex and Sensibility*, pp. 169–70.

32. "I have thrown my self at his Feet, and besought him with Tears to pardon me, but he always pushes me away, spurns me from him; . . . About two Years ago I sent my little Boy to him, dressed in a new Apparel, but the Child returned to me crying, because he said his Grandfather would not see him, and had ordered him out of his House."

CHAPTER FIVE

1. Cowley, *Essays*, p. 186.

2. Kinsley, "Meaning and Format."

3. See D. F. Bond's introduction to *The Spectator*, 1:xxxvi–xliii, for a discussion of the extent to which Steele and Addison rewrote letters.

4. The original letter is printed in D. F. Bond, ed., *The Spectator*, 5:236–37.

5. I am following the distinction made by Stephen Ullman in *Language and Style* (Oxford: Basil Blackwell, 1964), pp. 23–28.

6. Compare *The Tatler* 49: "The Imposition of honest Names and Words upon improper Subjects, has made so regular a Confusion amongst us, that

we are apt to sit down with our Errors, well enough satisfied with the Methods we are fallen into, without attempting to deliver our selves from the Tyranny under which we are reduc'd by such Innovations. Of all the laudable Motives of human life, none has suffer'd so much in this Kind as Love; under which rever'd Name, a brutal Desire call'd Lust is frequently concealed and admitted."

7. Ullman, *Language and Style*, p. 221.

8. Eighteenth-century theories of language have been studied from various points of view. See for example: Hans Aarsleff, *The Study of Language in England, 1780–1860* (Princeton, N.J.: Princeton University Press, 1967); Stephen K. Land, *From Signs to Propositions: The Concept of Form in Eighteenth-Century Semantic Theory* (London: Longmans, 1974); Murray Cohen, *Sensible Words: Linguistic Practice in England, 1640–1785* (Baltimore: Johns Hopkins University Press, 1977). Theories about the relationships between cultural forms and the meanings of words were not formally developed until later in the century. Land emphasizes the role of Dugald Stewart, although he sees elements of a contextual theory of meaning in Berkeley's writings (pp. 111–22, 142–43); Cohen emphasizes the role of the elocution movement and philology (pp. 122–27). Studies of the meanings of literary texts based on cultural backgrounds had begun in the late seventeenth century; see E. R. Marks, *Relativist and Absolutist: The Early Neoclassical Debate in England* (New Brunswick, N.J.: Rutgers University Press, 1955).

9. *The True Patriot*, in Fielding, *Complete Works*, 14:51. See also *The Champion*, in Fielding, *Complete Works*, 15:157–61, 256–60; *The Covent-Garden Journal*, ed. Gerard Edward Jensen (New Haven, Conn.: Yale University Press, 1915), 1:153–57. And see Samuel Johnson's discussion of the role of "accident and custom" whereby "Words become low by the occasions to which they are applied, or the general character of them who use them," in *Rambler* 168, in *The Rambler*, ed. Bate and Strauss, 5:126.

10. *Hobbes's Thucydides*, ed. Richard Schlatter (New Brunswick, N.J.: Rutgers University Press, 1975), p. 222 (3.82).

11. John Locke, *An Essay Concerning Human Understanding*, ed. Alexander Campbell Fraser (Oxford, 1894), 2:54–55 (3.5.16).

12. See John W. Yolton, *Locke and the Compass of Human Understanding: A Selective Commentary on the "Essay"* (Cambridge: Cambridge University Press, 1970), pp. 196–223 (chap. 9, "Signs and Signification").

13. See also 2.22.5–7 (Locke, *An Essay Concerning Human Understanding*, ed. Fraser, 1:383–84):

> 5. If we should inquire a little further, to see what it is that occasions men to make several combinations of simple ideas into distinct, and, as it were, settled modes, and neglect others, which in the nature of things themselves, have as much an aptness to be combined and make distinct ideas, we shall find the reason of it to be the end of language; which being to mark, or communicate

men's thoughts to one another with all the dispatch that may be, they usually make *such* collections of ideas into complex modes, and affix names to them, as they have frequent use of in their way of living and conversation. . . .

6. This shows us how it comes to pass that there are in every language many particular words which cannot be rendered by any one single word of another. For the several fashions, customs, and manners of one nation, making several combinations of ideas familiar and necessary in one, which another people have had never an occasion to make, or perhaps so much as take notice of, names come of course to be annexed to them. . . .

7. Hence also we may see the reason, why languages constantly change, take up new and lay by old terms. Because change of customs and opinions bringing with it new combinations of ideas, . . . new names . . . are annexed to them.

And see Locke's comments on interpretations of ancient texts in 3.9.22 (2:120).

14. Stephen Land is right that Locke never fully explains how words become part of a shared vocabulary (*From Signs to Propositions*, pp. 18–19), but Aarsleff points out passages in Locke's *Essay* that become a foundation for Condillac's speculations about language originating in gesture. One important passage is in 3.1.5 (ed. Fraser, 2:4–5): "It may also lead us a little towards the original of all our notions and knowledge, if we remark how great a dependence our words have on common sensible ideas; and how those which are made use of to stand for actions and notions quite removed from sense, have their rise from thence, and from obvious sensible ideas are transferred to more abstruse significations, and made to stand for ideas that come not under the cognizance of our senses."

15. Ludwig Wittgenstein, *Philosophical Investigations*, trans. G. E. M. Anscombe (New York: Macmillan, 1953), p. 20e (sec. 43).

16. Ullman, *Language and Style*, p. 25. See also Karl-Otto Apel, *Analytic Philosophy of Language and the Geisteswissenschaften*, trans. Harald Holstelilie (Dordrecht, Holland: D. Reidel, 1967), pp. 35–57; and R. Rhees, "Can There Be a Private Language?" *Proceedings of the Aristotelian Society*, suppl. vol. 28 (1954): 77–94, reprinted in *Wittgenstein, The Philosophical Investigations: A Collection of Critical Essays*, ed. George Pitcher (Garden City, N.Y.: Doubleday-Anchor, 1966), pp. 267–85). See for example Rhees, "Private Language," p. 267: "Our words refer to things by the way they enter in discourse; by their connexions with what people are saying and doing, for instance, and by the way they affect what is said and done"; or see W. V. Quine's characterization of Dewey's view of language in *Ontological Relativity and Other Essays* (New York: Columbia University Press, 1969), p. 26: "Language is a social art which we all acquire on the evidence solely of other people's overt behavior under publicly recognizable circumstances." Wittgenstein's arguments have been applied to philosophical and sociological issues in Stephen Toulmin, *Human Understanding*, vol. 1 (Prince-

ton, N.J.: Princeton University Press, 1972), esp. pp. 37, 67–68; and Jeff Coulter, *The Social Construction of Mind: Studies in Ethnomethodology and Linguistic Philosophy* (Totowa, N.J.: Rowman and Littlefield, 1979).

17. Ludwig Wittgenstein, *Lectures and Conversations on Aesthetics, Psychology and Religious Belief*, comp. from notes taken by Yorick Smythies, Rush Rhees, and James Taylor, ed. Cyril Barrett (Berkeley and Los Angeles: University of California Press, 1967), p. 11 and note.

18. The phrase is from George Herbert Mead's analysis of linguistic behavior in *Mind, Self, and Society*, p. 147. Language for Mead arises from social interactions that are founded on gesture: "We want to approach language not from the standpoint of inner meanings to be expressed, but in its larger context of cooperation in the group taking place by means of signals and gestures" (p. 6).

19. Samuel Johnson, "Life of Addison," in *The Works of Samuel Johnson* (Oxford, 1825), 7:472.

20. Lannering, *Prose Style of Addison*; subsequent page references are in the text.

21. Blair, *Lectures*, 1:227; subsequent page references are in the text. Blair expands on the importance of stylistic rhythms in traditional rhetoric: "Wherever they treat of the Structure of Sentences, it is always the music of them that makes the principal object. Cicero and Quinctilian are full of this. The other qualities of Precision, Unity, and Strength, which we consider as of chief importance, they handle slightly; but when they come to the '*junctura et numerus*,' the modulation and harmony, there they are copious" (1:251). "The close or cadence of the whole Sentence . . . ," in particular, "demands the greatest care. . . . As an example of this, the following sentence of Mr. Addison's may be given: 'It fills the mind (speaking of sight) with the largest variety of ideas; converses with its objects at the greatest distance; and continues the longest in action, without being tired or satiated with its proper enjoyments'" (1:259).

22. See Lannering, *Prose Style of Addison*, pp. 40–41.

23. Paulson, *Fictions of Satire*, p. 215.

24. Adolph, *The Rise of Modern Prose Style*, pp. 258–61.

25. Humphreys, *Steele, Addison*, p. 24; Bloom and Bloom, "Addison on 'Moral Habits,'" p. 411.

26. Kenneth Burke, *A Rhetoric of Motives* (New York: Prentice-Hall, 1950), p. 21; Burke calls this "a way of life," "an *acting together*." See also Umberto Eco's analysis of rhetoric as a system of equivalences in *A Theory of Semiotics* (Bloomington: Indiana University Press, 1976), pp. 283–98.

27. Burke, *Language as Symbolic Action: Essays on Life, Literature, and Method* (Berkeley and Los Angeles: University of California Press, 1966), p. 46.

28. Coulter (*The Social Construction of Mind*) emphasizes how the meaning of an utterance depends on the context of social actions rather than on "internal contents" of mind; see esp. pp. 35–62.

29. L. M. O'Toole, "Analytic and Synthetic Approaches to Narrative Structure: Sherlock Holmes and 'The Sussex Vampire,' " in *Style and Structure in Literature: Essays in the New Stylistics*, ed. Roger Fowler (Ithaca, N.Y.: Cornell University Press, 1975), pp. 148–49.

CHAPTER SIX

1. See Paulson, *The Fictions of Satire*, pp. 210–20, and Thomas Lockwood, "The Augustan Author-Audience Relationship," *ELH* 36 (1969): 648–58, for discussions of the rhetoric of *The Spectator*'s type of Horatian satire.

2. James Boswell, *London Journal, 1762–1763*, ed. Frederick A. Pottle (New York: McGraw-Hill, 1950), pp. 68 and 39; and Horace Walpole, *A Selection of the Letters of Horace Walpole*, ed. W. S. Lewis (New York: Harper and Brothers, 1924), p. 265 (To John Crawford, September 26, 1774).

3. Michel Foucault, *The Order of Things: An Archeology of the Human Sciences, a Translation of "Les Mots et les Choses"* (New York: Random House, 1971), p. xi. The significance of "epistemes" (Foucault's term), or conceptual models or paradigms has been discussed by several writers. The importance of paradigms in scientific investigations has been discussed by Thomas Kuhn, in *The Structure of Scientific Revolutions* (Chicago: University of Chicago Press, 1962). John Pocock has modified Kuhn's notion of paradigms as a basis for discussing the language of political discourse, in *Politics, Language and Time: Essays on Political Thought and History* (New York: Atheneum, 1971). Edmundo O'Gormann has discussed the importance of conceptual models in giving meaning to historical events, in *The Invention of America: An Inquiry into the Historical Nature of the New World and the Meaning of Its History* (Bloomington: Indiana University Press, 1961). Stephen Toulmin discusses the adequacy of such theories of conceptual models and their relationship to the sociological and institutional elements of thought in *Human Understanding*, 1:65–130.

4. *The Diary of John Evelyn, Esq., FRS, to Which Are Added a Selection from His Familiar Letters*, ed. William Bray, 3d ed. (London: Bickers and Son, 1906), 3:349 (To Abraham Cowley, March 12, 1666/67).

5. Ibid., 3:352 (From Abraham Cowley, May 13, 1667).

6. Francis Bacon, "Of Marriage and Single Life," in *The Essayes or Counsels, Civill and Morall, of Francis Lo. Verulam, Viscount St. Alban* (1625; rpt. ed.,

Mentson, Yorkshire: Scolar Press, 1971), p. 36. Quinones describes this as a traditional humanist view of the family; see *The Renaissance Discovery of Time,* pp. 121–23.

7. Halifax, "The Lady's New-Year's-Gift," pp. 21–22.

8. Richard Sennett, in *The Fall of Public Man* (New York: A. A. Knopf, 1977), and Hannah Arendt, in *The Human Condition* (1958; rpt. ed., Garden City, N.Y.: Doubleday-Anchor, 1959), have analyzed the social experience of the eighteenth century in terms of the difference between public and private realms, although their terminologies and their lines of analysis differ from mine and from each other's. Arendt writes specifically about changes in social perceptions whereby those activities necessary for biological sustenance, which had been relegated to the household, become matters of political concern: "The emergence of society—the rise of housekeeping, its activities, problems, and organizational devices—from the shadowy interior of the household into the light of the public sphere, has not only blurred the old border line between private and political, it has also changed almost beyond recognition the meaning of the two terms and their significance for the life of the individual and the citizen" (p. 35).

9. Thomas Hobbes, *Leviathan,* ed. Herbert W. Schneider (New York: Liberal Arts Press, 1958), p. 165; John Locke, *Two Treatises of Government,* ed. Peter Laslett (Cambridge: Cambridge University Press, 1960), pp. 337 and 341.

10. Samuél Richardson, *Clarissa; or, The History of a Young Lady,* 7th ed. (London, 1774), 2:247, 248–49 (Miss Clarissa Harlowe to Miss Howe, April 6), and *Pamela, Part the Second,* 2:287, 3:300, 308, 309.

11. See Hagstrum, *Sex and Sensibility,* pp. 183–85. From one point of view, the history of the eighteenth-century novel can be seen as a progressive transformation of images of the family; see for example Ronald Paulson, "The Pilgrimage and the Family: Structures in the Novels of Fielding and Smollett," in *Tobias Smollett: Bicentennial Essays Presented to Lewis M. Knapp,* ed. G. S. Rousseau and P.-G. Bouce (Oxford: Oxford University Press, 1971), pp. 57–78. Julia Prewitt Brown in *Jane Austen's Novels* (Cambridge, Mass.: Harvard University Press, 1979) sees Austen as dealing with the achievement of order in the family and with its accommodation to the outside world; see esp. pp. 6–24.

12. John Pocock, *Politics, Language, and Time,* pp. 90–96, and *The Machiavellian Moment: Florentine Political Thought and the Atlantic Republican Tradition* (Princeton, N.J.: Princeton University Press, 1975), pp. 423–505.

13. Another consequence of these changes in the British economy is the growth of a professional bureaucracy (see Pocock, *Politics, Language, and Time,* p. 93, and J. H. Plumb, *The Growth of Political Stability in England, 1675–1725* [New York: Macmillan, 1967], pp. 105–32)—and it is among

this group that *The Spectator* found its greatest number of readers. Through a study of subscription lists for *The Spectator*, D. F. Bond has found that "the largest single group of subscribers . . . includes the great body of secretaries, commissioners, clerks, and agents in the various branches of government, civil and military, required to carry on the war abroad and manage affairs at home" (introduction to *The Spectator*, 1:xcii).

14. The phrase is Arendt's, *The Human Condition*, p. 35.

15. See J. Lee Ustick, "Changing Ideals of Aristocratic Character in Conduct in Seventeenth Century England," *Modern Philology* 30 (1932–33): 147–66; and Gertrude E. Noyes, *Bibliography of Courtesy and Conduct Books in Seventeenth-Century England* (New Haven, Conn.: Tuttle, Morehouse and Taylor, 1937), pp. 1–12.

16. J. Trotti de la Chetardie, *Instructions for a Young Nobleman; or, The Idea of a Person of Honor*, trans. F.S. (London, 1683), p. 3.

17. *The Works of the Most Reverend Dr. John Tillotson . . . Containing Fifty Four Sermons and Discourses on Several Occasions . . .* , 7th ed. (London, 1714), p. 387 (Sermon 23, "Of Forgiveness of Injuries, and Against Revenge").

18. Clarke, "A Discourse of Natural Religion," 1:209–10.

19. Pocock, *The Machiavellian Moment*, p. 464.

20. R. V. Routh, "Steele and Addison," in *From Steele and Addison to Pope and Swift*, vol. 9 of *The Cambridge History of English Literature* (Cambridge: Cambridge University Press, 1913), p. 35.

21. I am indebted for this idea of discovery to O'Gormann, *The Invention of America*, esp. pp. 40–47.

22. Johnson, "Life of Addison," in *Works*, 7:452.

23. Bonamy Dobrée, "Addison," in *English Literature in the Early Eighteenth Century, 1700–1740*, vol. 7 of *The Oxford History of English Literature* (Oxford: Clarendon Press, 1959), pp. 102–20; Elioseff, "Joseph Addison's Political Animal," p. 372. J. H. Plumb, "The *Spectator*," in *In the Light of History* (Boston: Houghton Mifflin, 1973), pp. 52–56, similarly condemns Addison's work for its intellectual shallowness. In its own time, Swift gave up reading *The Spectator* after a few months, saying that Steele could "fair-sex it to the world's end" (*Journal to Stella*, ed. Williams, 2:483 [Letter 40, February 8, 1711/12]).

24. See Thomas Lockwood, "Matter and Reflection in *Tom Jones*," *ELH* 45 (1978): 226–35. Martin Price in *To the Palace of Wisdom: Studies in Order and Energy from Dryden to Blake* (New York: Doubleday, 1964) speaks of Fielding's pairing of characters or scenes with commentary to combine "discursive effects" with narrative. As a result, "Fielding is neither essayist nor realistic novelist, nor both in turn. He is rather both at once and therefore something different from either" (p. 298). The preface to *Joseph Andrews*, in

particular, comes out of *The Spectator*'s world, with its speculations on affec-
tation and Fielding's description of himself as "a Comic History-Painter"
(*Joseph Andrews*, ed. Martin C. Battestin [Middletown, Conn.: Wesleyan
University Press, 1967], pp. 6–7).

25. *Pamela, Part the Second*, 4:107; *Clarissa*, 1:7 (Letter 2, January 13).

26. A. D. McKillop, *The Early Masters of English Fiction* (Lawrence: University of Kansas Press, 1956), p. 85.

27. Frances Burney, *Evelina; or, The History of a Young Lady's Entrance into
the World*, ed. Edward A. Bloom (London: Oxford University Press, 1970), p.
38 (Letter 12). Evelina's letters often resolve themselves into public versions
of Richardson's heroines' more private fears, as in *Evelina*, p. 85 (Letter 21):

> . . . we were engaged in a very lively conversation, when the servant announced
> Madame Duval, who instantly followed him into the room.
>
> Her face was the colour of scarlet, and her eyes sparkled with fury. She came
> up to me with a hasty step, saying, 'So, Miss, you refuses to come to me, do you?
> And pray who are you, to dare to disobey me?'
>
> I was quite frightened;—I made no answer;—I even attempted to rise, and
> could not, but sat still, mute and motionless.

28. Henry Mackenzie, *The Man of Feeling*, with an introduction by Kenneth C. Slagle (New York: Norton, 1958), p. 74 ("A Fragment").

29. McKillop, *Early Masters*, p. 187.

30. Lawrence Sterne, *The Journal to Eliza*, ed. Wilbur L. Cross, vol. 8 of
The Works of Lawrence Sterne (New York: J. F. Taylor, 1904), p. 55.

Index